"Dave Wilkerson was a man of prayer and dedication. The way he used to pray for me in the beginning days of my conversion set the stage for my life. This book is a beautiful reminder of his devotional life and a valuable tool for each of us to use in our daily walk."

Nicky Cruz

"The life and witness of David Wilkerson is a testimony to the power of Holy Spirit ministry and the wisdom and sanity of a life lived in alignment with God's Word and ways. This devotional guide will doubtless assist many on the pathway to such a Christ-honoring lifestyle."

Dr. Jack W. Hayford, chancellor/founder, The King's University; founding pastor, The Church On The Way, Van Nuys, California

"My friend Dave Wilkerson's voice continues to speak words of encouragement to people of faith. You will be blessed daily as you meditate on his devotional thoughts from the Word of God."

Pastor Jim Cymbala, The Brooklyn Tabernacle, Brooklyn, New York

"I knew David Wilkerson for the last seventeen years of his life. We have, within the pages of these devotionals he wrote, the privilege of understanding the things he embraced that allowed Christ to use his life so mightily. Although he saw in the Spirit what would cause many of us to tremble, he never lost his confidence in the all-sustaining power of God. In the pages of this book you will discover why."

Carter Conlon, senior pastor, Times Square Church, New York City

GOD
IS
FAITHFUL

GOD IS FAITHFUL

A Daily Invitation into *the* Father Heart *of* God

DAVID WILKERSON

Chosen
a division of Baker Publishing Group
Minneapolis, Minnesota

Published by Chosen Books
11400 Hampshire Avenue South
Bloomington, Minnesota 55438
www.chosenbooks.com

Chosen Books is a division of
Baker Publishing Group, Grand Rapids, Michigan

Printed in the United States of America

Library of Congress Cataloging-in-Publication Data
Wilkerson, David, 1931–2011.
God is faithful : a daily invitation into the father heart of God / David Wilkerson.
p. cm.
ISBN 978-0-8007-9535-1 (pbk. : alk. paper)
1. Devotional calendars. 2. God (Christianity)—Fatherhood—Meditations. 3. God (Christianity)—Faithfulness—Meditations. 4. God (Christianity)—Love—Meditations. I. Title.
BV4811.W59243 2012
242′.2—dc23 2012001937

Cover design by Studio Gearbox

12 13 14 15 16 17 18 7 6 5 4 3 2 1

From the family of David Wilkerson

To Barbara Mackery

for her faithfulness and steadfastness to Brother Dave
as his executive assistant for 41 years;
Barb's contribution to the ministry and to our family
has been indescribable.

To Bettina Marayag

for her continual encouragement to Brother Dave
about these devotional readings, and her enthusiasm
for getting them before a readership.

And to David and Carol Patterson

whose vision for these devotionals began long ago,
knowing how deeply the messages
would minister to the body of Christ;
and whose faithful labors and energy
have brought them to your hands today.

Contents

Introduction

My father, David Wilkerson, was an evangelist, pastor and writer, and oftentimes was used by God as a prophet. He was called by God at times to "set a trumpet to his mouth" and sound a warning call to America.

In one of my last conversations with him before he went to be with Christ, my father told me we are no longer in the time of warning about difficulties to come—but that we are presently in those times of difficulty. During these times of difficulty, he said, our mission now is to encourage the faint, to strengthen those who have become weak and to lift high the name of Jesus—as lover of our souls, provider of our needs and great advocate fighting on our behalf against the evil one.

Are you finding trials and tribulations pressing in on you? Are the perilous times tempting you to grow weary? Are you ready for a word "in season" that will build up your most holy faith? Then these daily devotions are for you. The writings contained here reflect the mission of my father's last days: to lift up the hands of the saints. I know you will be encouraged.

Gary Wilkerson

PART 1

The Father Heart of God

He Delights in Us, His Children

God's Delight

God not only loves His children, He takes great pleasure in us.

I see this kind of parental pleasure in my wife, Gwen, whenever one of our grandchildren calls. Gwen lights up like a Christmas tree when she has one of our dear little ones on the line. Nothing can get her off the phone. Even if I told her the President was at our door, she would shoo me away and keep talking.

How could I ever accuse my heavenly Father of delighting in me less than I do in my own offspring? At times my children have failed me, doing things contrary to what I taught them. But never once have I stopped loving them or delighting in them. If I possess that kind of enduring love as an imperfect father, how much more does our heavenly Father care for us, His children?

Joshua and Caleb stood up in the midst of Israel and cried, "If the Lord delights in us, then He will bring us into this land and give it to us" (Numbers 14:8). What a simple yet powerful declaration. They were saying, "Because our Lord delights in us, He will vanquish every giant. Therefore, we must not look at our obstacles, but keep our eyes on our Lord's great love for us."

All through Scripture we read that God delights in us: "But the blameless in their ways are His delight" (Proverbs 11:20). "The prayer of the upright is His delight" (15:8). "My strong enemy [was] . . . too strong for me. . . . But the Lord . . . delivered me because He delighted in me" (Psalm 18:17–19).

It is absolutely imperative that we believe God delights in us. Then we will be able to accept that every circumstance in our lives will eventually prove to be our Father's loving will for us. And He will bring joy out of our struggle.

YOU ARE GOD'S TREASURE

The Word says, "And an adulteress will prey upon his precious life" (Proverbs 6:26). The adulteress spoken of in this verse is Satan—and he hunts down those who are precious to God.

The Bible gives us a vivid illustration of this in Numbers 13 and 14. Israel had sent twelve spies to search out the Promised Land. When the spies returned after forty days, ten of them planted three lies in the hearts of God's people:

1. "There are too many people in the land. They are too strong for us."
2. "The cities are walled too high. The strongholds are impregnable."
3. "There are giants in the land, and we are no match for them. We're helpless, finished!"

These lies took the heart right out of Israel. Scripture says the people endured a night of despair. "So all the congregation lifted up their voices and cried, and the people wept that night" (Numbers 14:1). More than 2 million people were weeping, wailing, moaning—focused completely on their weaknesses and inabilities.

Beloved, the devil still lies to God's people today. He whispers, "Your trials and temptations are too overwhelming. You are too weak to resist the power coming against you."

The word that God spoke to Israel is for us today: "You shall be a special treasure to Me above all people: for all the earth is Mine" (Exodus 19:5). "For you are a holy people to the LORD your God, and the LORD has chosen you to be a people for Himself, a special treasure" (Deuteronomy 14:2).

Joshua and Caleb had a revelation of their preciousness in God's eyes. They said, "Because He delights in us, the land is as good as ours" (see Numbers 14:8).

David had the same revelation: "He delivered me because He delighted in me" (Psalm 18:19). Likewise, every victorious Christian today has this same revelation: "We cannot fail—because we are precious to the Lord!"

Called from Before Creation

The apostle Paul says of God, "Who has saved us and called us with a holy calling, not according to our works, but according to His own purpose and grace which was given to us in Christ Jesus before time began" (2 Timothy 1:9).

Every person who is "in Christ" is called by the Lord. And we all have the same mandate: to hear God's voice, to proclaim His Word, never to fear man and to trust the Lord in the face of every conceivable trial.

Indeed, God made this promise to His prophet Jeremiah when He called him (see Jeremiah 1:1–10). Just as it was with Jeremiah, we do not need a message prepared to speak before the world. He has pledged to fill our mouths with His Word at the exact moment it is needed—if we will trust Him.

Scripture shows us that Paul was tested as few ministers ever have been. Satan tried to kill him time after time. The so-called religious crowd rejected and ridiculed him. At times even those who supported Paul left him abused and forsaken.

But Paul was never confounded or perplexed before men. He was never dismayed or put to shame before the world. And Paul never burned out. On every occasion, he had an anointed word to speak from God, just when it was needed.

The fact is, Paul simply would not be shaken. He never did lose his trust in the Lord. Instead, he testified, "I know whom I have believed and am persuaded that He is able to keep that which I have committed to Him until that Day" (2 Timothy 1:12). He is saying, "I have committed my life fully to the Lord's faithfulness. Live or die, I am His." And he urged his young charge Timothy to do likewise: "Hold fast the pattern of sound words which you have heard from me, in faith and love which are in Christ Jesus" (verse 13).

Take Hold of Your Trial by Faith

If we didn't have conflict, pressure, trials and wars within, we would become passive and lukewarm. Decay would set in and our temple would lie in ruins. We would not be able to handle the territory we have gained. That is why the enemy's plan against us is clear: He wants to remove all the fight from us.

The simple truth is we find all our resources—strength to go on, power over the enemy—in our spiritual battles. On that day when we stand before the Lord, He will remind us: "Do you remember what you went through on that occasion? in that awful battle? in the midst of that awful trial? Look at what you accomplished through it all."

The fact is God put His treasure in human bodies. He has made you a temple, a house for His Spirit to dwell in. If you become lazy and careless, neglecting the maintenance work needed—regular prayer, feeding on God's Word, fellowshiping with the saints—decay will set in and you will end up in absolute ruin.

As I look back on my own years of ministry, I recall many times when it would have been easy for me to quit. I would pray, "Lord, I don't understand this attack. Where did it come from? When will it end? I don't see any purpose in it at all." But over time I began to see fruit from those trials. That fruit—resources, strength, spiritual power—supplied me in a way I could not have attained through any other means.

I urge you: Take hold of your trial and believe that God has allowed it. Know that He is using it to make you stronger—to help you take spoils from Satan, to make you a blessing to others and to sanctify it all to His glory.

"For our light affliction, which is but for a moment, is working for us a far more exceeding and eternal weight of glory" (2 Corinthians 4:17).

A Revelation of Love

Joseph's brothers did not know how much they were truly loved until God used a crisis to reveal it to them. "The famine was over all the face of the earth, and Joseph opened all the storehouses" (Genesis 41:56).

"When Jacob saw that there was grain in Egypt, Jacob said to his sons . . . 'Go down to that place, and buy for us there.' . . . So Joseph's ten brothers went down to buy grain" (42:1–3).

Twenty years had passed since these brothers' crime of selling Joseph into slavery. In that time he became Prime Minister of Egypt. For seven years Joseph had stored grain in preparation for famine. Now Jacob's sons went to Egypt intent on getting corn—but God was sending them to get a revelation of love! They were about to experience mercy, pardon and restoration—and they would learn what the grace of God was all about. Deserving nothing but judgment, they were going to receive pure grace.

Sin had kept the brothers out of touch with Joseph. In fact, they probably assumed he was dead. When they arrived at Pharaoh's court and came before Joseph, they did not recognize him, but he knew them immediately (see 42:8). His heart was filled with compassion at the sight of the brothers he loved so dearly.

These proud men were not yet ready for a revelation of grace and mercy, however. First they needed to see the exceeding ugliness of their sins and face their guilt and shame. The message of the cross of Christ is unconditional love—and God showed this truth to Joseph.

Joseph put his brothers in prison for three days—not to punish them, but to give them a chance to face the truth about their sin. It is impossible to understand God's grace until we come to the end of our own resources and experience His mercy. That grace delivers us from all shame and guilt.

WHO DREAMED UP THIS PLAN FOR SURVIVAL?

Then the word of the Lord came to him [Elijah], saying, 'Get away from here and turn eastward, and hide by the Brook Cherith, which flows into the Jordan'" (I Kings 17:2–3).

As Elijah looked ahead to the coming crisis, things looked absolutely hopeless to him. But God had a specific survival plan in mind for His faithful servant. "Go east to the Jordan River, and there you will find Cherith, a little tributary. You can get all the drinking water you need from that brook. In addition, I've arranged for food to be delivered to you daily, by My courier ravens."

How could any person ever dream up this kind of plan for survival? How could Elijah ever have imagined he'd be sent to a hidden brook to find water to drink, when there was nothing but drought everywhere in the land? How could he have envisioned a daily supply of bread being brought to him by ravenous birds that ate everything they sank their beaks into?

Later, times got hard for Elijah, because the brook finally dried up. But God stepped in again, giving the prophet another fresh word of direction. He said, "Arise, go to Zarephath, which belongs to Sidon, and dwell there. See, I have commanded a widow there to provide for you" (verse 9).

Again, I have to ask—how could anyone ever think a poor widow woman, in the midst of a depression, could feed a man for days, weeks, months? The fact is, God uses the most insignificant things of the world for His glory. He told Elijah, "If you will go to her and do what I tell you, you will survive. Listen to Me and you will make it through!"

The evidence is overwhelming: God—our adviser, counselor and survival expert—has a detailed plan for every one of His children, to help us face the worst of times.

It Began with Repentance

The Church as we know it today began with repentance. When Peter preached the cross at Pentecost, thousands came to Christ. This new Church was made up of one body, consisting of all races, filled with love for one another. Its corporate life was marked by evangelism, a spirit of sacrifice, even martyrdom.

This wonderful beginning reflects God's word to Jeremiah: "Yet I had planted you a noble vine, a seed of highest quality" (Jeremiah 2:21). The Lord's next words, however, describe what often happens to such works: "How then have you turned before Me into the degenerate plant of an alien vine?" (same verse). God was saying, "I planted you right. You were Mine, bearing My name and nature. Now you have turned degenerate."

What caused this degeneration in the Church? It always has been, and will continue to be, idolatry. God is speaking of idolatry when He says to Jeremiah, "But My people have changed their Glory for what does not profit" (verse 11).

The number-one idol among God's people is not adultery, pornography or alcohol. It is a much more powerful lust. What is this idol? It is a driving ambition for success. And it even has a doctrine to justify it.

The idolatry of being successful describes many in God's house today. These people are upright, morally clean, full of good works—but they have set up an idol of ambition in their hearts, and they cannot be shaken from it.

God loves to bless His people. He wants His people to succeed in all they undertake honestly. But there is now a raging spirit in the land that is overtaking multitudes. It is a spirit of love for recognition and acquiring of things.

A man of the world said, "He who dies with the most toys wins." Tragically, Christians, too, are caught up in this pursuit. How far we have strayed from the Gospel of dying to self, ego and worldly ambition!

GOD DELIGHTS IN YOU!

The Holy Spirit gave David a revelation that is the key to all deliverance. David could say, "The reason God delivered me from all my enemies and all my sorrows is because I am precious to Him. My God delights in me!" "He delivered me because He delighted in me" (Psalm 18:19).

Do you need deliverance from temptation or trial? From a problem that is far too big for you? The key to your victory is in this verse. God delights in you—for you are precious to Him!

These thoughts are found throughout the Psalms: "The LORD takes pleasure in those who fear Him, in those who hope in His mercy" (147:11). "For the LORD takes pleasure in His people" (149:4).

I can tell you of God's delight in you: "You are precious to the Lord." You may think, "That is sweet, but it is only a lovely thought." No, this truth is much more than a lovely thought. It is the key to your deliverance from every battle that rages in your soul and the secret to entering into the rest God has promised you.

Isaiah had a revelation of God's great delight in us. He prophesied, "Fear not . . . you are Mine. . . . When you walk through the fire, you shall not be burned" (Isaiah 43:1–2).

Isaiah was talking about what people go through spiritually and mentally. Israel was in captivity at the time, and God sent them a brokenhearted prophet. That prophet told them, "God wants you to know that you belong to Him."

Right now, you may feel overwhelmed by trials that threaten to consume you. God does not always keep them from coming, but He does promise this: "I will walk with you through it all. This trial or circumstance will not destroy you. It will not consume you. I take pleasure in you, My child. So, walk on. You will come out on the other side with Me beside you."

Turtledoves

God has kept me through all my struggles by showing me King David's secret hope. At one point in his life, David, lamenting and complaining, wondered why God was angry with him. He called on God to "Take [Your hand] out of Your bosom and destroy them" (see Psalm 74:11).

It seemed to David that the enemies of God were taking control. In his despair, he prayed, "Oh, do not deliver the life of Your *turtledove* to the wild beast!" (verse 19).

Like David, in my most trying times I was encouraged to see myself as His lovebird, resting on His promise to keep me out of the snares of the wicked. Like a turtledove, we long for the presence of our beloved Savior.

I picture Christ coming to me in the form of a dove—His Holy Spirit—revealing to me His constant love and continual care. How unspeakable that such a great and majestic God would condescend to relate to my needs as a turtledove. Did He not Himself descend as a dove upon Christ at the baptismal waters?

Child of God, are you going through difficult times? Is there suffering in your home? Do you hurt? Are you confused at times because of the severity of it all? Remember, you are the Lord's little turtledove—and He will never turn you over to the wicked one. He will deliver you from every snare of the enemy and show you how devoted He is to you in your hour of need. He is there beside you, at all times, as a dove, whispering and sharing His love with you.

The sparrow falls to the ground, but not the turtledove. He is kept in the hollow of God's hand, safe and secure in the Father's love. Best of all, the Lord will deliver us out of our troubles and prove His everlasting faithfulness to us. We shall come through it all, in full rest and trust in His power and love.

God's Gift to His Son

I can scarcely take it in when I read these words: "And the glory which You gave Me I have given them, that they may be one just as We are one" (John 17:22).

In a true sense, it may be said that God so loved His Son that He gave Him the world. Think of it. We have our Lord's word, confessed before His own Father, that He has given Himself to us as fully as His Father gave Himself to Him. He has given us the same intimate love His Father gave Him—and that is His glory manifested in us.

We have been brought into the same kind of special love relationship that Jesus shares with the Father. Even more, Christ opens up the circle of love between the two of them and brings us into it. We are made partakers of a glory beyond comprehension. How incredible that Jesus should bring us to the Father and plead, "that they may be one with Us!" We share completely in the fullness of God's love for His Son by being in Christ.

Did you not know we are God's gift to His Son—a gift of love? "They were Yours; You gave them all to Me." Christ is so in oneness with the Father, He brings the gift back to Him and says, "All Mine are Yours, and Yours are Mine" (verse 10). This kind of love can take nothing to itself—but gives its all.

What an honor—to have Christ place us in the palm of His great, loving hand and present us to the Father, saying, "Behold, Father—they are Ours! I will love them, Father, and You will love them." How can our minds grasp it all?

God Wants to Plant Us on the Mount of His Presence

"Many people shall come and say, 'Come, and let us go up to the mountain of the LORD, to the house of the God of Jacob; He will teach us His ways'" (Isaiah 2:3).

"Even them I will bring to My holy mountain, and make them joyful in My house of prayer" (56:7).

The message of the Holy Spirit today to all of God's people is, "Get back to the mount—get back into His holy presence." Many are now hearing that call and making time for prayer and seeking God. Others, however, go about their way, too busy with "Kingdom details" to climb the holy hill.

Isaiah saw both the glory of an awakened ministry and the tragedy of blind watchmen who were asleep. While some watchmen shake themselves and go back to the mount of God to hear a fresh word from heaven, others are lost in endless activities and self-advancement.

"His watchmen are blind, they are all ignorant. . . . Sleeping, lying down, loving to slumber. . . . They all look to their own way, every one for his gain, from his own territory" (56:10–11).

Isaiah said they got this way—self-centered, preoccupied, spiritually dead—because they are "those who forsake the Lord, who forget My holy mountain" (65:11).

The Spirit is raising up an army of "mountain men" who will spend time alone with God—shut up in His presence, hearing His voice, getting new vision, and returning with joy to deliver "those who wail for grief of spirit" (see 65:13–14). They shall return—with the power and dominion needed to save the Church from chaos.

Get to Know the Voice of God

God wants us to know that no matter how difficult things may get for us, He will sustain all who trust in Him. How does He do this? By the power of His still, small voice speaking to our inner man.

This is confirmed by the prophet Isaiah: "Your ears shall hear a word behind you, saying, 'This is the way, walk in it,' whenever you turn to the right hand or whenever you turn to the left" (Isaiah 30:21).

Isaiah delivered this word to Israel in the very worst of times. The nation was under judgment, in absolute ruin, with everything breaking down. Isaiah told Israel's leaders, "Turn to the Lord now! He wants to give you a word of direction—to go this way, go that way, here is the way."

But they would not listen. They decided to turn to Egypt to find help in being delivered. They thought they could rely on the Egyptians' chariots, horses and supplies to see them through.

God did not send judgment on Israel at that point. Rather, He decided to wait patiently until the bottom fell out of every plan. He said, "While they're running around scheming how to survive, I will wait. I want to show them My mercy, in spite of their wickedness!" (see verse 18).

Sure enough, things only got worse for the nation. Finally, when all their schemes had fallen through, God told the people, "Now, let Me take over. I know the way out, and I will direct you and deliver you. I will lead you by My voice—speaking to you, telling you what to do down to the last detail."

It is vitally important that you know the voice of God. He made it clear, "My sheep know My voice." There are many voices in the world today—loud, demanding voices. But there is that still, small voice of the Lord that can be known and heard only by those who trust what Jesus said.

His Name Is Forgiveness

"Who is a God like You, pardoning iniquity and passing over the transgression of the remnant of His heritage? He does not retain His anger forever, because He delights in mercy. He will again have compassion on us, and will subdue our iniquities. You will cast all our sins into the depths of the sea" (Micah 7:18–19).

How is our Lord distinguished from all the other gods worshiped throughout the world? Of course, we know our God is above all others, set apart in every way. But one clear way we know the Lord to be distinguished from others is by His name: "the God who pardons."

Scripture reveals our Lord as the God who forgives, the only God who has the power to pardon sin. "Who is a God like You, pardoning iniquity?"

We see this name of God confirmed throughout the Scriptures.

- Nehemiah declared, "But You are God, ready to pardon, gracious and merciful, slow to anger, abundant in kindness, and did not forsake them" (Nehemiah 9:17). The proper translation of the phrase "a God ready to pardon" is "a God of propitiation" or "a God of forgiveness."
- Moses asked the Lord for a revelation of His glory. He was not allowed to see God's face, but the Lord did reveal His glory to Moses through a revelation of His name. What name of God was revealed to Moses? "The Lord God, merciful and gracious, longsuffering, and abounding in goodness and truth, keeping mercy for thousands, forgiving iniquity and transgression and sin" (Exodus 34:6–7).
- David gives us the same Hebrew description of God. He writes, "For You, Lord, are good, and ready to forgive, and abundant in mercy to all those who call upon You" (Psalm 86:5). David penned these words out of his own personal failure and difficult experience. Truly he had found Him to be the God who pardons, just as He promised.

All of these tell us the name of our God: Forgiveness!

GETTING TO KNOW THE FATHER

I believe our natural children get to know our nature and character most during their times of crisis. When they are in the midst of pain and need, they recognize our deep care and provision for them.

When my children were growing up, I did not have to lecture them about what I am like. I never had to say, "I'm your father—I am patient and kind, full of mercy toward you. I am tenderhearted, ready to forgive you at all times." It would have been ludicrous for me to make this kind of proclamation. Why? Because my children learned about my love during their crisis experiences.

Now that they are grown and married with children, my sons and daughters are getting to know me through a whole new set of experiences. They are learning even more about me by my attitudes and actions toward them in this new time of need in their lives.

So it is with us in getting to know our heavenly Father. From the time of Adam down through the cross of Christ, the Lord gave His people an ever-increasing revelation of His character. Yet He did not do this by simply proclaiming who He was. He did not try to reveal Himself by merely announcing, "The following names describe My nature. Now, go and learn these, and you will discover who I am."

God revealed these aspects of His nature to His people by actually *doing* for them what He proclaimed Himself to be. He saw His children's needs, foresaw the enemy's strategy against them and intervened supernaturally on their behalf.

Get to know your heavenly Father—slowly, purposefully, on a heart level. Ask the Holy Spirit to recall to you the heavenly provision God has given you during your times of need. Then ask the Spirit to build into you a true heart knowledge of I AM—the God who is everything you need, at all times.

Learn to Stand Up and Fight on Your Own

You have to learn to fight your own battles. You cannot depend on someone else for your deliverance.

Perhaps you have a prayer warrior friend you can call and say, "I have a fierce battle before me. Will you pray for me? I know you have power with God!" That is scriptural—but it is not God's complete will for you. God wants *you* to become a warrior. He wants you to be able to stand up against the devil.

God promised Gideon, "Surely I will be with you, and you shall defeat the Midianites as one man" (Judges 6:16). God assured him, "I have sent you—therefore, I will be with you."

Then the people of the city came looking for the godly man who tore down their idols (see verses 28–30). Where was Gideon? He was hiding, still unsure of God's promises, still wondering if God was with him. Gideon cried, "If the Lord is with us, why then has all this happened to us? And where are all His miracles which our fathers told us about?" (verse 13).

So it is with many of us. Jesus has promised us, "I am with you always" (Matthew 28:20). Yet we have not learned to stand on His Word and fight!

Things will begin to change the moment you are fully persuaded that God is with you—that He speaks to you and will show you all you need to know. You are stronger than you think. Like Gideon, you may wonder, "How can I fight? I am so weak, so inexperienced." God answered Gideon, "Go in this might of yours" (Judges 6:14).

"What might?" Gideon must have wondered. In truth, his might was bound up in God's word to him: "Surely I will be with you."

Beloved, that same word—"I am with you"—is your strength to fight. You will receive that strength believing this word—and by acting on it. God is faithful!

GOD'S LOVE IS CONVEYED TO US ONLY THROUGH JESUS CHRIST

According to John, all of God's love dwells in Jesus. He writes, "And of His fullness we have all received" (John 1:16). How have we received the Father's love? We have obtained it by being in Christ.

You may ask, "What is so important about knowing God's love is conveyed to us through Christ? How does that impact our lives?"

We have to look to Christ as our example. Jesus has already told us the Father loves us in the same way He loves the Son. So, what impact did the Father's love have on Jesus?

"By this we know love, because He laid down His life for us" (1 John 3:16). Here was the fruit of God's love in Jesus: He gave of Himself as a sacrifice for others. The second half of this verse tells us the purpose of God's love in our own lives. It reads, "And we also ought to lay down our lives for the brethren." God's love leads us to present our bodies as living sacrifices, as Jesus did.

Have you ever thought about what it means to truly lay down your life for your brothers and sisters? John is not talking about becoming martyrs on foreign soil or registering as an organ donor. Nor does he mean we are to take the place of some condemned criminal on death row.

No, the only kind of Christian who can bring life and hope to his brethren is a "dead" one. Such a servant has died to this world—to all self, pride and ambition.

This "dead" Christian has allowed the Holy Spirit to take a spiritual inventory of his soul. He sees through the ungodliness in his heart and willingly goes to God's altar, crying, "Lord, consume me. Take it all." He knows that only through being cleansed by Christ's blood can he give his life in love for his brethren.

Wilderness Journey

Dietrich Bonhoeffer, the German theologian, likened the Christian to someone trying to cross a sea of floating ice pieces. The Christian cannot rest anywhere while crossing—except in his faith that God will see him through. He cannot stand anywhere too long, otherwise he sinks. After taking a step, he must watch for the next. Beneath him is the abyss and before him is uncertainty, but always ahead is the Lord—firm and sure. This traveler does not see the land yet, but it is there as a promise in his heart. Likewise the Christian traveler keeps his eyes fixed on his final place.

I prefer to think of life as a wilderness journey—like that of the children of Israel. The battle of King Jehoshaphat, along with all the children of Judah, is also our battle (see 2 Chronicles 20). Sure, it is a wilderness; yes, there are snakes, dry water holes, valleys of tears, enemy armies, droughts, impassable mountains. Yet when the children of the Lord stood still to see His salvation, He spread a table in that wilderness—raining manna from above, destroying enemy armies by His power, bringing water out of rocks, taking poison out of snakebites, leading the people by pillar and cloud, giving them milk and honey, and bringing them into the Promised Land with a high and mighty hand.

God instructed them to tell every following generation: "'Not by might nor by power, but by My Spirit,' says the Lord of hosts" (Zechariah 4:6).

It is time for you to stop looking in the wrong direction for help. Get alone with Jesus in a secret place and tell Him all about your confusion. You will wonder if God is working at all, but there is nothing to lose. Peter summed it all up: "Lord, to whom shall we go? You have the words of eternal life" (John 6:68).

"Look to Me, and be saved . . . for I am God, and there is no other" (Isaiah 45:22).

THE UNRELENTING LOVE OF GOD

The word *unrelenting* means "undiminished in intensity or effort—unyielding, uncompromising, incapable of being changed or persuaded by arguments." To be unrelenting is to stick to a determined course.

What a marvelous description of the love of God. Nothing can hinder or diminish His loving pursuit of both sinners and saints. David, the psalmist, expressed it this way: "Where can I go from Your Spirit? Or where can I flee from Your presence? If I ascend into heaven, You are there; if I make my bed in hell, behold, You are there" (Psalm 139:7–8).

In speaking of the great highs and lows of life, David is saying, "There are times when I'm so blessed I feel lifted with joy. At other times I feel like I am living in hell, condemned and unworthy. But no matter where I am, Lord—no matter how blessed I feel or how low my condition is—You are there. I cannot get away from Your unrelenting love!"

Paul was bent on destroying God's Church. He hated Christians and breathed out threats of slaughter against all who followed Jesus. After his conversion, Paul testified that even during those hate-filled years—while he was full of prejudice, blindly slaughtering Christ's disciples—God loved him.

The apostle wrote, "But God demonstrates His own love toward us, in that while we were still sinners, Christ died for us" (Romans 5:8). He was saying, "Even though I wasn't conscious of it, God was pursuing me with unrelenting love."

Through the years, Paul became increasingly convinced that God would love him fervently to the end, through everything. May his declaration be ours as well: "For I am persuaded that neither death nor life, nor angels nor principalities nor powers, nor things present nor things to come, nor height nor depth, nor any other created thing, shall be able to separate us from the love of God which is in Christ Jesus our Lord" (Romans 8:38–39).

He Brought Us Out to Bring Us In

Before the cross, there was no general access to God. Only the high priest could enter the holy of holies. Jesus' cross made a path for us into the Father's presence. By His grace alone, God tore down the wall that blocked us from His presence.

Consider Israel's miraculous deliverance. As God's people crossed over on dry land they saw the waves crash down on their enemy behind them. It was a glorious moment, and they held a mighty praise meeting: "We're free! God has delivered us from the hand of oppression."

Israel's story represents our own deliverance from the guilt of sin. We know that Satan was defeated at the cross, and we were immediately set free from his iron grip. Yet there is more to God's purpose in saving and delivering us. You see, the Lord never meant for Israel to settle on the victory side of the Red Sea. His greater purpose in bringing them *out of Egypt* was to take them *into Canaan,* His land of fullness. In short, He brought them *out* in order to bring them *in*—into His heart, into His love. The same is true today.

Israel's first test came just a few days later, and they ended up murmuring and complaining, totally dissatisfied. Why? They had experienced God's deliverance, but they had not learned His great love for them.

Here is the key to this teaching: You cannot come into joy and peace—indeed, you cannot know how to serve the Lord—until you see His delight in your deliverance; until you see the joy of His heart over His communion with you; until you see that every wall has been removed at the cross; until you know that everything of your past has been judged and wiped away.

God says, "I want you to move on into the fullness that awaits you in My presence!" Do not miss God's greater purpose.

Into Arabia

If I seek to please man, I cannot be a servant of Christ. If my heart is motivated by the approval of others—if that mindset influences the way I live—my loyalties will be divided. I always will be striving to please someone other than Jesus.

A few years after the apostle Paul was converted, he went to the church in Jerusalem to try to join the disciples there. "But they were all afraid of him, and did not believe that he was a disciple" (Acts 9:26).

The apostles knew Paul's reputation as a persecutor. "And I was unknown by face to the churches of Judea which were in Christ. But they were hearing only, 'He who formerly persecuted us now preaches the faith which he once tried to destroy'" (Galatians 1:22–23).

Barnabas helped the apostles get over their fear of Paul and they offered him fellowship. But Paul decided to itinerate among the Gentiles. Indeed, Paul is careful to describe his calling very clearly: "I make known to you, brethren, that the gospel which was preached by me is not according to man. For I neither received it from man, nor was I taught it, but it came through the revelation of Jesus Christ" (verses 11–12).

In Galatians 1:17, Paul points out that "I went to Arabia." He is saying, in essence, "I did not get my revelation of Christ from the saints in Jerusalem. Instead, I went into Arabia—to the desert—to have Christ revealed to me. I spent precious time there, hearing and being taught by the Holy Spirit."

What Paul is saying here applies to all who desire to have the mind of Christ: "I received my anointing on my knees—from the Lord Himself." Paul had emptied himself of selfish ambition and found total satisfaction in Christ and His faithfulness. When your mind is set on pleasing Christ, you will never need the applause and approval of men.

The Crown of Victory

Because of God's promise, we are able to claim victory and dominion even before the battle begins. David sang, "The king shall have joy in Your strength, O Lord; and in Your salvation how greatly shall he rejoice! You have given him his heart's desire, and have not withheld the request of his lips" (Psalm 21:1–2).

You may wonder, "How could David rejoice? He faced the most intense attack he had ever known. How could he have joy when he might have been wounded or killed?"

David answers, "For You meet him with the blessings of goodness; You set a crown of pure gold upon his head" (verse 3). What David says here is life-changing: "I face a powerful enemy who is bent on destroying me, but my soul is at peace. The Lord has foreseen my struggle, and He has showered me with assurances of His love. My enemy may cause me to stumble or fall, and at times it might seem I am finished. But God has told me that if I will just get up, I will receive His strength and win the battle."

David then made this statement of faith just before going to war: "You set a crown of pure gold upon [my] head" (verse 3). The crown of gold David mentions here is a symbol of victory and dominion. He was saying, "I am going to war riding on God's promise to me. He said I would walk out of the battle wearing the crown of victory."

The doctrine of God's goodness is this: He has anticipated all our struggles—all our battles with sin, flesh and the devil—and in His mercy He has paid our debt before it can even come due. Our victory is a done deal.

The Lord assures us that even if we are cast down temporarily, we will emerge from the battle standing upright—all because Jesus has paid our debt.

GOD OF OUR MONSTERS

God said to Job, "Look now at the behemoth [hippopotamus], which I made along with you" (Job 40:15). "Can you draw out Leviathan [crocodile] with a hook, or snare his tongue with a line which you lower?" (41:1).

Why would God have Job look into the faces of these two massive monsters—a hippopotamus and a crocodile?

First, the Lord posed this problem: "Look, Job, the hippopotamus is coming for you. What are you going to do? Can you wrestle him down in your physical strength? No? Maybe you can try to sweet-talk him." Then the Lord said, "Now, behold the crocodile that is threatening. How will you handle him? This creature has a heart of stone, no concept of mercy."

This was more than a simple lecture about the animal kingdom. God was telling Job something about life's "monsters." He was showing His servant that these two ferocious, overpowering creatures represented the monstrous problems raging in his life.

"Consider this hippo that tramples down everything in sight. He is simply too big a problem for you to handle, Job. Nothing can tame him. Only I know how to stop such a monstrous creature.

"What about the crocodile, Job? No human in his own strength can strip this creature of his thick armor. The same is true of your spiritual enemy, the devil. Only I can win the battle with him."

God is speaking not just to Job but to all believers, declaring, "Face the truth about the monsters in your life. You cannot handle them. I am the only One who can."

Job answered rightly, saying, in effect, "My God is all-powerful. He can do all things, and no purpose of His can ever be thwarted. I know I cannot stand up against the hippo or the crocodile, but that does not matter. I know God can! My part is to stand still and see the salvation of my faithful Lord" (see 42:1–2).

He Pleased God

Enoch enjoyed close fellowship with the Lord. His communion with God was so intimate that the Lord translated him to glory long before his life on earth might have ended. "By faith Enoch was translated so that he did not see death, 'and was not found because God had taken him'; for before he was taken he had this testimony, that he pleased God" (Hebrews 11:5).

Why did the Lord choose to take Enoch up to heaven? The opening words of this verse tell us very plainly: It was because of his faith. Moreover, the closing phrase tells us Enoch's faith pleased God. The Greek root word for *please* here means "fully united, wholly agreeable, in total oneness." In short, Enoch had the closest possible communion with the Lord that any human being could enjoy. And this intimate fellowship was pleasing to God.

The Bible tells us Enoch began walking with the Lord after his son, Methuselah, was born. Enoch was 65 years old at the time and spent the next 300 years fellowshiping with God intimately. Hebrews makes it clear that Enoch was so in touch with the Father, so close to Him in hourly communion, that God chose to bring him home to Himself. The Lord said to Enoch, in essence, "I cannot take you any further in the flesh. To increase my intimacy with you, I have to bring you to My side." So He whisked Enoch away to glory.

According to Hebrews 11:5, it was Enoch's intimacy that pleased God. To our knowledge, this man never performed a miracle, never developed a profound theology, never did any great works worthy of mention in Scripture. Instead, we read this simple description of that faithful man's life: "Enoch walked with God."

Enoch had intimate communion with the Father. His life is a testimony of what it means to truly walk in faith.

Chasing Away the Vultures

In Genesis 15, God made a glorious agreement with Abraham. He instructed the patriarch to take a female heifer and a female goat and cut them in two. Then Abraham was to take a turtledove and a pigeon and lay them on the ground, head to head. Again, Abraham did as he was instructed, faithful to obey.

As these creatures lay bleeding, vultures began to descend on the carcasses. Suddenly, Abraham felt a terrible darkness surrounding him. It was Satan in a panic—symbolized by the circling vultures.

How do you think Satan reacts when he sees all the promises of God becoming yours, as you give your life to Jesus? He goes into a jealous rage. Then, when he sees your firm resolve to go all the way with the Lord, all of hell goes into a panic.

What did Abraham do when the vultures came? Scripture says he chased them away. Likewise, the Lord has shown us a way to deal with menacing vultures. We do not have to be afraid of the devil's attacks, because we have been given mighty weapons of warfare.

Whenever any voice of doubt or questioning of God comes to your mind, line it up against what you know about your loving Lord. Do not accept as true any thoughts based on feelings. Measure all questions against Jesus' promises about the victory He has won for us.

Simply put, if thoughts come to you that are accusing—if they cause doubt and fear, or are condemning, or bring a sense of rejection—you can know they are not of God. We all have to be prepared for such horrible thoughts. Even the Lord Jesus was subject to these kinds of mental assaults from the enemy during His wilderness temptation.

When vultures come at you, bringing thoughts of unworthiness and insecurity, chase them away with God's Word. The sacrifice that the Lord has led you to make is pleasing to Him, and He will honor it.

Filled with the Spirit

His divine power has given to us all things that pertain to life and godliness, through the knowledge of Him who called us to glory and virtue" (2 Peter 1:3).

For years I have claimed to be filled with the Spirit. I have prayed in the Spirit, talked to the Spirit, walked in the Spirit and heard His voice. I truly believe the Holy Spirit is the power of God.

I can take you to the exact location where I was filled with the Spirit, at eight years of age. I have read everything that Scripture says about the Holy Spirit. I have preached that the Holy Spirit empowers me to witness and that He sanctifies me. Yet at times I have found myself praying, "Do I really know this incredible power that lives in me? Or is the Spirit just a doctrine to me?"

The fact is, you can have something very valuable and not know it. You will not enjoy what you have, because you do not understand how valuable it is.

There is a story about a poor farmer who faithfully worked his small acreage, tilling the rocky soil for decades. At the farmer's death, the farm was passed down to his son. One day while plowing, the son found a gold-streaked nugget. He had it appraised and was told it was pure gold. The young man soon discovered that the farm was full of gold. Instantly he became a wealthy man. Yet that wealth was lost on his father, even though it was on his land for the entirety of his life.

So it is with the Holy Spirit. Many of us live in ignorance of what we have, of the power that resides in us. Some Christians live their entire lives thinking they have all the Holy Spirit brings, yet they truly have not received Him in His fullness and power. He is not accomplishing in them the eternal work He was sent to do.

Let God's Spirit fill and empower you. He is there to accomplish all of God's purposes in you!

IN TIME OF NEED

Consider one of the most powerful promises in all of God's Word:

> God is our refuge and strength, a very present help in trouble. Therefore we will not fear, even though the earth be removed, and though the mountains be carried into the midst of the sea. . . . Though the mountains shake with its swelling. There is a river whose streams shall make glad the city of God, the holy place of the tabernacle of the Most High. God is in the midst of her, she shall not be moved; God shall help her, just at the break of dawn. The nations raged, the kingdoms were moved; He uttered His voice, the earth melted. The Lord of hosts is with us; the God of Jacob is our refuge. . . . He makes wars cease.
>
> Psalm 46:1–7, 9

God's Word to us here is so powerful, so immovable. He tells us, "Never again do you need to fear. The earth may quake, the oceans may swell, the mountains may crumble into the sea. Things may be in complete chaos, causing a total uproar all around you. Yet because of My Word, you will have peace like a river."

Right now, the whole world is in a fearful time. Nations are trembling over terrorism, economic disaster, personal troubles and mounting sufferings. In the midst of it all, Psalm 46 echoes to God's people throughout the world: "I am in your midst. I am with you through it all. My people will not be destroyed or moved."

God knows we all encounter turmoil, temptations and times of confusion that cause our souls to quake. His message for us in Psalm 46 is meant for just such times. If we give in to fear, becoming downcast and full of despair, we are living contrary to His reality in our lives. The Bible tells us that Christ Himself is in us and we are in Him—and that is cause for rejoicing, no matter how the world shakes!

When the Holy Spirit Comes

The prophet Isaiah describes what happens when the Holy Spirit falls upon a people. He prophesies, "Until the Spirit is poured upon us from on high, and the wilderness becomes a fruitful field, and the fruitful field is counted as a forest" (Isaiah 32:15).

Isaiah is saying, "When the Holy Spirit comes, what was once a barren wilderness becomes a harvest field—and that field of fruit grows into a forest. You will be able to take cuttings from the forest year after year and build on your fruitfulness continually."

The prophet adds, "Then justice will dwell in the wilderness, and righteousness remain in the fruitful field" (verse 16). According to Isaiah, the Holy Spirit also brings with Him a message of judgment against sin, which produces righteousness in the people.

Isaiah is not speaking of a one-time outpouring of the Spirit, what some people think of as "revival." Rather, he is describing something that lasts. Studies by Christian sociologists show that most present-day revivals last for an average of five years and leave in their wake much confusion and dissension.

Isaiah continues: "The work of righteousness will be peace, and the effect of righteousness, quietness and assurance forever. My people will dwell in a peaceful habitation, in secure dwellings, and in quiet resting places" (verses 17–18).

Peace comes because righteousness is at work. The Holy Spirit is busy sweeping out all unrest, disturbances and condemnation. What follows is peace of mind, peace in the home and peace in God's house. When God's people have the peace of Christ, they are not easily moved from it.

Every generation needs an outpouring of the Holy Spirit. The Church today has not seen anything compared to what the Holy Spirit wants to accomplish.

A Cloud of Witnesses

Hebrews 12:1 tells us that the world is encircled by a "cloud of witnesses." Who are these witnesses? They are those with Christ in glory.

Our generation lives in a world far more wicked than Noah's. What does this great cloud of heavenly witnesses have to say to the present world? What can they say to a human race whose sins exceed even those of Sodom?

Our society has become so immoral, violent and anti-God that even secularists bemoan how far we have fallen. Christians everywhere wonder why God has delayed His judgments on such a wicked society.

We who love Christ may not understand why such gross evil is allowed to continue. But the cloud of heavenly witnesses understands.

The apostle Paul is among that cloud of witnesses, and he bears witness to God's unlimited love for even "the chiefest of sinners." Before his conversion, Paul cursed the name of Christ and helped kill Christians. Paul would say that God is being patient with this present generation because there are multitudes who sin in ignorance, just as he did.

The apostle Peter is also among the cloud of witnesses, and he too understands why God is so patient. Peter cursed Jesus, swearing he never knew Him. Multitudes still curse and deny Christ, and the Lord will not give up on them, just as He never gave up on Peter.

As I consider these witnesses, I see the faces of former drug addicts and alcoholics, prostitutes and pushers, murderers and wife-beaters, infidels and pornography addicts. They all repented and died in the arms of Jesus, and now they are witnesses to the mercy and patience of a loving Father.

I believe all of these would say with one unified voice that Jesus did not judge them before they received His mercy. God still loves this mad, immoral world. May we love the lost as He does.

God Has Set His Heart on You

What do the witnesses from Hebrews 12:1 have to say to you and me? What is their message to fellow overcomers in the Body of Christ? Simply this: "For the eyes of the Lord are on the righteous, and His ears are open to their prayers" (1 Peter 3:12).

I do not believe this great crowd of heavenly witnesses would speak to us about holding to complicated theologies or doctrines. I believe they would speak to us in the simplicity of truth:

- We are to look unto Jesus, the author and finisher of our faith. We are to keep preaching the victory of the cross, enduring the accusations of sinners, and laying aside our besetting sin, running with patience the race set before us (see Hebrews 12:1–2).
- Peter sinned against the greatest light a man could ever have. This man walked in Jesus' presence. He touched the Lord and received his calling from Christ personally. Peter could have lived in condemnation, but God set His heart on him.
- Paul would tell us not to fear our afflictions. Jesus suffered every day of His ministry and He died in suffering. When Christ called Paul to preach the Gospel, He showed him how many great afflictions awaited him.

Throughout his years in ministry, Paul was indeed afflicted. Yet afflictions prove that God has set His heart on you. "That no one should be shaken by these afflictions; for you yourselves know that we are appointed to this" (1 Thessalonians 3:3).

When God sets His heart on you, you will be tried often. But the longer and harder your affliction, the more deeply God has set His heart on you, to show you His love and care.

That is the witness of Paul's life and of Jesus' life. The enemy may come against you, but our Lord has raised up a standard against him. We find absolute rest in Jesus, whose heart is set on us!

God Has Everything under Control

The whole world is trembling right now over the outbreak of terror and calamities throughout the earth. Every day we wake up to learn of another disaster.

Nonbelievers are becoming convinced there are no solutions left, that everything is spinning into chaos. But God's people know differently. We know there is no reason to fear, because the Bible repeatedly reminds us that the Lord has everything under control.

The psalmist writes, "For the kingdom is the LORD's, and He rules over the nations" (Psalm 22:28). Likewise, the prophet Isaiah declares to the world, "Come near, you nations, to hear; and heed, you people!" (Isaiah 34:1). He is saying, "Listen, nations, I want to tell you something important about the Creator of the world."

Isaiah states that when God's indignation is aroused against nations, it is the Lord Himself who delivers them to slaughter.

> Behold, the nations are as a drop in a bucket, and are counted as the small dust on the scales. . . . All nations before Him are as nothing, and they are counted by Him less than nothing and worthless. . . . It is He who sits above the circle of the earth. . . . To whom then will you liken Me?
>
> Isaiah 40:15, 17, 22, 25

Isaiah then speaks to God's people who are troubled by world events: "Look up to the glorious sky and behold the millions of stars. Your God created and named every one. Are you not more precious to Him than they? Therefore, fear not" (see verse 26).

Our Father knows the end from the beginning. Let us ask ourselves: "Where is the Lord's eye focused?" Certainly not on the world's tin-god dictators or their threats.

Scripture assures us these wild men's bombs, armies and powers are as nothing to the Lord. He laughs at them as mere specks of dust, and soon He will blow them all away (see verses 23–24).

The Father Knows

Jesus calls us to a way of living that gives no thought about tomorrow and puts our future wholly into His hands: "Therefore do not worry, saying, 'What shall we eat?' or 'What shall we drink?' or 'What shall we wear?' . . . For your heavenly Father knows that you need all these things. But seek first the kingdom of God and His righteousness, and all these things shall be added to you" (Matthew 6:31–33).

Jesus does not mean that we are not to plan ahead for our future. Yet we can be constantly harassed by two little words: *What if?* "What if the economy fails and I lose my job? What if I lose my health insurance? Or what if my faith fails me in trying times?" We all have a thousand "what if" anxieties.

Jesus interrupts our "what ifs" and tells us, "Your heavenly Father knows how to take care of you. You do not need to worry. He will not ever forsake you."

> Look at the birds of the air, for they neither sow nor reap nor gather into barns; yet your heavenly Father feeds them. . . . Consider the lilies of the field, how they grow: they neither toil nor spin. . . . Now if God so clothes the grass of the field, which today is, and tomorrow is thrown into the oven, will He not much more clothe you, O you of little faith?
>
> verses 26, 28–30

We gladly give all our yesterdays to the Lord, turning over to Him our past sins. We trust Him for forgiveness of all our past failures and fears. Why do we not do the same with our tomorrows? The truth is, most of us want to reserve the right to hold on to our dreams for the future. We make our plans and then later ask Him to bless and fulfill those hopes.

He asks us to put all those plans in His hand—to seek Him first—and He will be our source for all things.

THE DELIVERER

The apostle Peter tells us, "If God did not spare the . . . ancient world, but saved Noah . . . bringing in the flood on the world of the ungodly; and turning the cities of Sodom and Gomorrah into ashes . . . making them an example to those who afterward would live ungodly; and delivered righteous Lot . . . then the Lord knows how to deliver the godly out of temptations" (2 Peter 2:4–9).

Despite the severity of these examples, God is sending a clear message of comfort to His people: "I have just given you two of the greatest examples of my compassion. If, in the midst of a world-engulfing flood, I can deliver one righteous man and his family out of the havoc, then can I not deliver you also? Can I not provide a miraculous way of escape?

"If I can send down fire-and-brimstone judgment that consumes entire cities at one time, yet I manage to send angels into the chaos to deliver Lot and his daughters, then can I not also manage to send angels to deliver you out of your trials?"

The lesson here for the righteous is this: God will do whatever it takes to deliver His people out of fiery trials. He knows how to deliver you, and He will go to any extreme to accomplish it no matter what your circumstance.

Peter's phrase "the Lord knows how to deliver" means simply, "He has already made plans." The wonderful truth is that God already has plans for our deliverance even before we cry out to Him.

"For I know the thoughts that I think toward you, says the LORD, thoughts of peace and not of evil, to give you a future and a hope" (Jeremiah 29:11). The last phrase literally means "to give you what you long for." God wants us to keep praying so we will be ready for His deliverance.

He Promises to Hear

Often people write to our ministry saying, "I have no one to talk to, no one to share my burden with, no one who has time to hear my cry. I need someone I can pour my heart out to."

King David was constantly surrounded by people. He was married and had many companions at his side, yet he cried out for someone to listen to him. It is simply in our nature to want another human being, with a face, eyes and ears, to listen to us and advise us.

When Job became overwhelmed by his trials, he cried out with grief, "Oh, that I had one to hear me!" (Job 31:35). He uttered this cry while sitting with his so-called friends. Those friends had no sympathy for his troubles; in fact, they were messengers of despair.

Job turned only to the Lord: "Surely even now my witness is in heaven, and my evidence is on high. . . . My eyes pour out tears to God" (16:19–20).

David urged God's people to do likewise: "Trust in Him at all times, you people; pour out your heart before Him: God is a refuge for us" (Psalm 62:8).

Eventually, suffering comes to us all, and right now you may be asking, "Why is this happening to me? Is God mad at me? What did I do wrong? Why doesn't He answer my prayers?"

The Holy Spirit wants you to find a private place where you can pour out your soul to the Lord. Speak to Jesus about everything—your problems, your present trial, your finances, your health—and tell Him how overwhelmed and discouraged you are. He will hear you with love and sympathy.

God answered David. He answered Job. And for centuries He has answered the heart's cry of everyone who has trusted His promises. He has promised to hear you and guide you. Go to Him and come out renewed.

OUT OF THE PAW OF THE LION

It is for our benefit that God tells us to remember. The memory of our past deliverances helps to increase our faith for what we are going through right now.

Are you facing a crisis at home, at work, in your family? The only way to face a giant is to do as David did: Remember the lion and the bear. By remembering God's faithfulness to him in his past crises, David could go up against Goliath without fear.

When David volunteered to fight Goliath, "Saul said to David, 'You are not able to go against this Philistine to fight with him.' . . . But David said to Saul, 'Your servant used to keep his father's sheep, and when a lion or a bear came and took a lamb out of the flock, I went out after it and struck it, and delivered the lamb from its mouth. . . . Your servant has killed both lion and bear; and this uncircumcised Philistine will be like one of them'" (1 Samuel 17:33–36).

David knew the danger he was facing against Goliath. He was not some naïve kid full of bravado and looking for a fight. David was simply remembering his past deliverances. Now he looked his enemy squarely in the eye and stated, "The LORD, who delivered me from the paw of the lion and from the paw of the bear, He will deliver me from the hand of this Philistine" (verse 37).

Multitudes of God's people today face giants on all sides. Have you forgotten the time when you were close to death, but the Lord raised you up? Do you remember the financial disaster when the Lord saw you through? It is good to look back and remember His goodness.

Many things we will not understand until we are home with Jesus. Yet I am persuaded God has a way out of every situation.

Being in Christ

Blessed be the God and Father of our Lord Jesus Christ, who has blessed us with every spiritual blessing in the heavenly places *in Christ*" (Ephesians 1:3, my emphasis).

Paul tells us here, "All who follow Jesus are blessed in heavenly places, where Christ is." What an incredible promise to God's people. Yet it becomes mere words if we do not know what these spiritual blessings are.

Paul wrote this epistle to the "faithful in Christ Jesus" (verse 1), believers who were sure of their salvation. The Ephesians had been well trained in the Gospel of Jesus Christ and the hope of eternal life.

These "faithful ones" fully understood that "He [God] raised Him from the dead and seated Him at His right hand in the heavenly places" (verse 20). They knew they had been chosen by God from "before the foundation of the world, that we should be holy and without blame before Him in love" (verse 4) and adopted "by Jesus Christ to Himself" (verse 5). God had brought them into His family because when they heard the word of truth they believed and trusted it.

Many forgiven, redeemed people live in misery, continually going from peaks to valleys, from spiritual highs to depressing lows. How can this be? It is because many never get past the crucified Savior to the resurrected Lord who lives in glory.

Jesus said to the disciples, "Because I live, you will live also. At that day you will know that I am in My Father, and you in Me, and I in you" (John 14:19–20). We are now living in "that day" that Jesus spoke of.

What is meant by the expression, "our position in Christ"? Position is "where one is placed, where one is." God has placed us where we are, which is in Christ.

Jesus is in paradise, but He also abides in you and me. He has made us His temple on the earth, His dwelling place.

WHATEVER HAPPENED TO JOY?

The Holy Spirit yearns to bring God's people back to serving the Lord with joy and gladness. How grieved heaven must be to witness the wet blanket of despair and sadness that has fallen upon multitudes of believers.

The psalmist declared, "Happy are the people whose God is the Lord" (Psalm 144:15).

Isaiah said, "Therefore with joy you will draw water from the wells of salvation" (Isaiah 12:3).

When the Holy Spirit began to deal with me on the matter of serving Him with joy, I had a difficult time facing the seriousness of the subject. I did not fully understand God's attitude and joy's importance compared to all the heartbreaking problems present in the world today.

Few Christians have the knowledge of the truth about liberty and the life-freeing sacrifice at Calvary. They have never allowed the cross to set them free from all fear and bondage. We cannot rejoice and be exceedingly glad in our relationship with the Lord when we have a poor or limited knowledge of what happened at the cross.

It is not necessary to understand everything in order to live joyfully unto the Lord. But you do need to know this one foundational truth: *God was completely satisfied with Christ's sacrifice on the cross.* It was all that was needed! God now willingly, joyfully forgives all who repent.

Let the Spirit give you an understanding of the truth that we are called to liberty. God wants us to have an abundance of a full and complete joy—pressed down and running over!

God's Word makes it perfectly clear that He yearns to be enjoyed by His saints: "that they may have My joy fulfilled in themselves" (John 17:13). "And the ransomed of the LORD shall return, and come to Zion with singing, with everlasting joy on their heads. They shall obtain joy and gladness, and sorrow and sighing shall flee away" (Isaiah 35:10).

AS A LITTLE CHILD

Matthew tells us Christ called a little child to Him and took the youngster into His arms. The Lord wanted to give His disciples a profound illustrated sermon. He told them, "Assuredly, I say to you, unless you are converted and become as little children, you will by no means enter the kingdom of heaven. Therefore whoever humbles himself as this little child is the greatest in the kingdom of heaven. And whoever receives one little child like this in My name receives Me" (Matthew 18:3–5).

In these verses, Jesus lays out the kind of relationship He desires with His people. He is saying, "Look at this child. Here is My future Church. This young one represents every new believer who is going to come to Me in childlike faith, from every nation, race and tribe. I tell you, my Church must relate to Me as this child does."

Next Jesus called for His disciples to humble themselves. He commanded them, "Become as little children." He was saying, "I am building my Church upon you. If you want any part of it, you must become as humble as this little child in my arms."

I believe that by doing this Jesus is asking those who would serve Him for two simple things: repudiation of all self-dependency and an uncomplicated devotion.

He told His disciples very directly, "Whoever causes one of these little ones who believe in Me to sin, it would be better for him if a millstone were hung around his neck, and he were drowned in the depth of the sea" (verse 6).

Jesus was expressing His wrath toward those who teach that the cross is not sufficient to save. He was talking to the very foundation stones of His Church—His own disciples—warning them not to be offended by the cross. They had to accept the fact that He alone was full payment for our sins.

The same is true today. Let us come to Him in childlike faith, with uncomplicated belief, trusting in His work for us.

CHASTENING LOVE

Because God loves you, He will work to cleanse you with a *loving* chastening. You may feel God's arrows in your soul because of your past and present sins, but if you have a repentant heart and want to turn from error, you can call upon His chastening love. You will be corrected, but with His great mercy and compassion. You will not feel His wrath as the heathen do, but rather the rod of His discipline, applied by His loving hand.

Your present suffering may come from making wrong decisions. How many children are breaking their parents' hearts, bringing them to the end of their ropes? Many times this happens because of the parents' own past years of sin, neglect and compromise.

When you have arrived at your lowest point, it is time to seek the Lord in brokenness, repentance and faith. It is time to receive a new infusion of Holy Ghost power, renewed as His strength overflows you.

When you cry out to God, He pours strength into you: "In the day when I cried out, You answered me, and made me bold with strength in my soul" (Psalm 138:3).

There is an erroneous doctrine that says if you are in agreement with God you will never suffer; just call out to God and He will come running and solve everything immediately. This is not the Gospel! The heroes of faith listed in Hebrews 11 all walked in close relationship with God, and they suffered stonings, mockings, torture and violent deaths (see verses 36–38). Paul himself was shipwrecked, stoned, whipped, left for dead, robbed, jailed and persecuted. These were all testings, the proving of his faith to the glory of God.

God wants us to be able to say, "I believe You rule over the trials of my life even when I do not understand. Help me understand the lessons You want me to learn, Jesus. Whether I live or die, I am Yours!"

Facing the Rod of God

The psalmist writes about one of God's greatest promises: "If his sons forsake My law and do not walk in My judgments, if they break My statutes and do not keep My commandments, then I will punish their transgression with the rod, and their iniquity with stripes. Nevertheless My lovingkindness I will not utterly take from him" (Psalm 89:30–33).

God promises to never remove His love from us, no matter how badly we may fail. Yet many believers skip over the heavy warning in this verse: If we forsake God's law and refuse to keep His commands, He will visit our transgressions with His divine rod.

The Bible tells us that whomever the Lord loves, He chastens. We see this truth illustrated vividly in David's life, who sinned awfully, justifying it and keeping it hidden for months. Finally, God said, "Enough," and sent a prophet to expose David's sin. The prophet, Nathan, used an analogy to tear apart every excuse David had until finally the king admitted, "I have sinned. I am guilty."

David wrote, "My strength fails because of my iniquity, and my bones waste away" (31:10). Your peace, joy and strength will drip away until they are completely gone. David confessed, "Nor is there any health in my bones because of my sin" (38:3). He was saying, "I simply cannot rest because all my strength is gone due to my sin."

David had lost the peace of the Lord and was experiencing God's piercing arrows. As a result, he was being taught the fear of God.

No matter who you are, if you harbor a secret sin you will experience continual disturbances in your life, your home and family, your work. Confusion, worry and fears will replace your peace and strength.

God does not want to expose His servants. Rather, it is His heart to forgive and cover our sins. In love He will discipline us.

PART 2

God's Hand of Goodness

He Delights in Blessing Us

Forgiven

Jesus tells us, "Most assuredly, I say to you, he who hears My word and believes in Him who sent Me has everlasting life, and shall not come into judgment, but has passed from death into life" (John 5:24).

The Greek word that Jesus uses for *judgment* here means "condemnation." He is saying, "If you believe in Me, you will not come into condemnation but will pass from death over into life."

Indeed, Scripture tells us that once the Lord forgives our sins He wipes them from His memory.

- "I, even I, am He who blots out your transgressions for My own sake; and I will not remember your sins" (Isaiah 43:25).
- "For I will forgive their iniquity, and their sin I will remember no more" (Jeremiah 31:34).
- "For I will be merciful to their unrighteousness, and their sins . . . I will remember no more" (Hebrews 8:12).
- "He will again have compassion on us, and will subdue our iniquities. You will cast all our sins into the depths of the sea" (Micah 7:19).

This is good news for every Christian who has ever worked to mortify the deeds of his flesh in his own strength. How many promises have you made to God, only to break them? How many times have you tried to please the Lord by fighting off your lusts and habits, only to fail?

Isaiah tells us God takes our trespasses and flips them over His shoulder. "For You have cast all my sins behind Your back" (Isaiah 38:17). This means God will never look at our sins or acknowledge them again.

If God forgets our sins, why don't we? Why do we always allow the devil to dig up muck from our past and wave it in our face, when all our sin is already covered by Christ's blood?

The cleansing, forgiving power of Christ's blood is all-encompassing. This marvelous truth enables us to walk in victory!

Help Yourself

Help yourself! I am not speaking of the godless self, but the regenerated, Christ-possessed self.

One of the most important verses in God's Word is John 4:14: "But whoever drinks of the water that I shall give him will never thirst. But the water that I shall give him will become in him a fountain of water springing up into everlasting life." Jesus speaks of the life-giving water He has put in us that shall pour forth out of our innermost being.

Let me prove to you beyond any shadow of a doubt that everything you need in this life has already been given to you when Christ came in:

- "As His divine power has given to us all things that pertain to life and godliness, through the knowledge of Him who called us by glory and virtue" (2 Peter 1:3).
- "That the God of our Lord Jesus Christ, the Father of glory, may give to you a spirit of wisdom and of revelation in the knowledge of Him" (Ephesians 1:17, NASB).
- "Make you perfect in every good work to do His will, working in you what is well pleasing in His sight, through Jesus Christ" (Hebrews 13:21).
- "Now to Him who is able to do exceedingly abundantly above all that we ask or think, according to the power that works in us" (Ephesians 3:20).
- "But if the Spirit of Him who raised Jesus from the dead dwells in you, He who raised Christ from the dead will also give life to your mortal bodies through His Spirit who dwells in you" (Romans 8:11).

I know the Spirit knows and sees all and that He alone has all the answers I need. I know I do not need to go to man or to anyone outside of myself. Everyone who calls Christ Lord and trusts Him has the Holy Spirit in him to help make life abundant and glad.

KNOWING GOD BEGINS WITH KNOWING JESUS

You cannot know God in fullness until you see Christ as God wants you to see Him. Jesus said, "He who has seen Me has seen the Father" (John 14:9). We must see Jesus not as man teaches, but as the Spirit reveals Him to us, as God wants us to know and see Him.

There are many volumes in my library about Jesus, written by good men. Yet I believe many of these men have never seen Jesus as God would have us see Him. Here is how I believe God wants us to see His Son: "Every good gift and every perfect gift is from above, and comes down from the Father of lights, with whom there is no variation or shadow of turning" (James 1:17).

Jesus was a gift in whom God wrapped up all His resources: "He gave His only begotten Son" (John 3:16). Christ is God's good and perfect gift to us, come down from the Father.

In the Old Testament, God gave Israel many wonderful gifts in the wilderness: a cloud to shelter them from the desert sun; fire at night to assure and lead them; water out of a rock to drink; a branch to heal bitter waters; a brass serpent to heal the snakebitten. Yet all these good things were only shadows.

Who was the rock from which water came? Who was the fire? The manna? The brass serpent? Everything God did for Israel *was through Jesus*. That's right—Jesus was every one of those gifts. "Brethren, I do not want you to be unaware that all our fathers were under the cloud, all passed through the sea . . . and all drank the same spiritual drink. For they drank of that spiritual Rock that followed them, and that Rock was Christ" (1 Corinthians 10:1–4).

Today we have much more than the shadow. We have the actual substance—Christ Himself—and He lives in us!

WAKE UP AND LIVE—NOW!

Most of us are still looking to the future for fulfillment. We think some future event or change in our circumstance will bring us peace and joy. We say, "Just wait, my day is coming—somehow, sometime, somewhere. I don't know what is out there for me, but it is coming." We are like children waiting for Christmas and counting the days.

David once wrote during a mournful, introspective season in his life that he felt time was going too fast. He had accomplished so little, he thought. Everything at the time seemed to be in vain. "Surely every man walks about like a shadow; surely they busy themselves in vain; he heaps up riches, and does not know who will gather them. And now, Lord, what do I wait for?" (Psalm 39:6–7).

David was depressed and his situation appeared hopeless. Out of a perplexed heart he wrote, "Lord, what am I waiting for?"

Recently I was walking alone in the hills and God spoke to my heart in the same way: "David, what is it you're waiting for? Why isn't this the best day of your life? Why can't your *now* be full and joyous? There is nothing you don't already have in My Son, Jesus."

Now I ask you, dear reader: What are *you* waiting for?

"Oh, I am waiting for Mr. Right," you may answer. You are looking for that godly person you think will rescue you from loneliness and fill your soul with unspeakable joy. Some married people are bored with their mates, waiting for them to go to glory because they are looking for romance to come into their empty lives.

Nothing out there will save you from who you are. If you think someone else is going to solve your loneliness problem, you are badly mistaken. You must find deliverance, peace, hope and joy—*now*.

Jesus is the only one who can fill the void. Wake up to Him—and live!

God Wants to Teach Us to Know His Voice

Those who truly know God have learned to recognize His voice above all others. He wants you to be absolutely convinced that He desires to talk to you.

Not long ago the Lord showed me that I was still wavering about hearing His voice speak to my soul. Oh, I know He speaks and that the sheep need to know the Master's voice, but I doubted my ability to hear Him. I spent all my time "checking" the voice I heard. A multitude of voices come at us all the time, so how can we know God's voice?

I believe three things are required of those who would hear God's voice:

1. *An unshakable confidence that God wants to speak to you.* He wants you to know His voice so you can do His will. What God tells you will never go beyond the boundaries of Scripture.
2. *Quality time and quietness.* You need to be willing to shut yourself in with God and let all other voices hush away.
3. *Asking in faith.* We do not obtain anything from God (including hearing His voice) unless we truly believe He is able to convey His mind to us and enable us to understand His perfect will.

Jesus said, "If a son asks for bread from any father among you, will he give him a stone?" (Luke 11:11). If you ask your heavenly Father for a word, do you think for a moment He will instead let the devil come and trick you?

God is not a tease! He will not allow the devil to deceive you. When God speaks, peace follows—and Satan cannot counterfeit that peace. If you are in a place of quiet and rest, convinced God can speak to you, then you have an assurance that never changes. You can go back to God a thousand times and you will receive the same word—because it is truth.

STRENGTH FOR THE JOURNEY

No one on earth can place you in ministry. You may receive a diploma from a seminary, be ordained by a bishop or commissioned by a denomination, but the apostle Paul reveals the only true source of any call to ministry: "And I thank Christ Jesus our Lord who has enabled me, because He counted me faithful, putting me into the ministry" (1 Timothy 1:12).

What does Paul mean by this? Three days after Paul's conversion, Christ placed him in the ministry of suffering: "For I will show him how many things he must suffer for My name's sake" (Acts 9:16). Paul makes clear that we all have this ministry.

Christ pledged to remain faithful to Paul and enable him through all his trials. Paul declared, in essence, "Jesus promised to give me more than sufficient strength for the journey. Because of Him, I will not faint or give in but will emerge with a testimony."

I thank God for those who feed their minds and souls with spiritual things. They keep their gaze fixed on Christ, spending quality time worshiping Him and building themselves up in faith. The Holy Spirit is at work in these saints, changing their character to be like Christ, that they will be ready for all hard sufferings to come.

Here is Paul's final word on the matter: "We give no offense in anything, that our ministry may not be blamed. But in all things we commend ourselves as ministers of God. . . . As sorrowful, yet always rejoicing; as poor, yet making many rich" (2 Corinthians 6:3–4, 10).

How do we "make many rich"? By shining forth the hope of Christ in the midst of our sufferings. We offer true riches when we cause others to ask, "Where does this person find such peace?" They will know we have been given strength for the journey.

Giving Thanks in All Things

The apostle Paul wrote, "Giving thanks always for all things to God the Father in the name of our Lord Jesus Christ" (Ephesians 5:20). The root word for *thanksgiving* in Hebrew means "adoration." In short, worship is attached to thanksgiving.

"In everything give thanks; for this is the will of God in Christ Jesus for you" (1 Thessalonians 5:18). Is it true we are to give thanks "in *all* things—in *every*thing"? Yes, in sickness and in health; in good times and in bad; in storms and in sunshine. David said, "Let us come before His presence with thanksgiving" (Psalm 95:2).

All too often we do not come into the Lord's presence with thanksgiving. Instead, we come to Him burdened down with our problems and fail to give Him thanks for keeping us through all things. All true lovers of the Lord know that He has never failed, that He is faithful.

When was the last time you stopped everything to offer thanks to the Lord for what He has done? "Oh, give thanks to the Lord! Call upon His name; make known His deeds among the peoples. Sing to Him, sing psalms to Him; talk of all His wondrous works" (Psalm 105:1–2).

I give thanks to the Lord for all His wondrous works we have witnessed in our ministry and for what He is going to do in the future. We give God all glory for enabling us to build churches, houses and schools in some of the poorest nations on earth. We marvel at how He meets the needs of so many fatherless children and widows. We have been allowed by God to feed thousands of children and to supply the needs of suffering people worldwide.

Because of Him, we are able to give abundantly. Without asking or begging, we see funds come in to meet every need. The Lord has supplied every need—and for that I give God praise!

THE LOVE OF GOD NEVER FAILS

When David penned the words of Psalm 13, he asked, "How long, O Lord? Will You forget me forever? How long will You hide Your face from me? How long shall I take counsel in my soul, having sorrow in my heart daily? How long will my enemy be exalted over me?" (Psalm 13:1–2).

David must have felt that God had left him altogether. He woke up suffering each day with a black cloud hanging over him. For a season, David spoke out of his despair, crying, "God, will this feeling of isolation go on forever? When will my prayers ever be answered?"

When troubles assail us and deliverance seems impossible, we may sink under the pressure. Someone reading these words right now could be on the verge of total despair, facing an awful situation that seems to have no answer.

Because David felt hopeless he asked, "How long shall I take counsel in my soul?" He spoke of forming one plan after another, trying to find ways out of his trouble—but all his plans and arrangements failed. Now he had nothing else to think of, no workable solution. He was at the end of it all.

How did David arise from this pit of despair? Here is his testimony: "I have trusted in Your mercy. . . . I will sing" (Psalm 13:5–6).

We are given several reasons to keep trusting our way through our present trials: No matter how the storms may rage, our Lord will still be feeding the fowls of the air, dressing the lilies of the field, and supplying an ocean full of fish with their daily needs. "Your heavenly Father feeds them" (Matthew 6:26).

What kind of Father would feed all the creatures of the earth and neglect His own children? Truly the Lord loves you, and He will not turn a deaf ear to your cries. Hold on and wait patiently. He is faithful—He will never fail you!

Are We Putting Limits on God's Power and Promises?

We limit God with our doubts and unbelief. Scripture says of Israel, "Yes, again and again they tempted God, and limited the Holy One of Israel" (Psalm 78:41).

We trust God in most areas of our lives, but our faith always has limits. I limit God in the area of healing. I have prayed for physical healing for many and have seen God perform miracles—but when it comes to my own body, I limit God. I douse myself with medicine or run to a doctor before I ever pray for myself. It is not wrong to go to doctors, but sometimes I fit the description of those who "did not seek the Lord, but the physicians" (2 Chronicles 16:12).

Do you pray for God to bring down walls in China or Cuba—but when it comes to the salvation of your own family, you do not have faith? You think, "God must not want to do anything because He does not seem to be hearing me." If you think this, you are ignoring His ways. God's desire is to "do exceedingly abundantly above all that we ask or think, according to the power that works in us" (Ephesians 3:20).

Israel murmured continually, "Is God able? Sure, He made a way for us through the Red Sea, but can He give us bread?" God gave them bread. "But can He give us water?" God gave them water from a rock. "But can He give us meat?" God gave them meat from the sky. "But can He deliver us from our enemies?" Time after time God provided and delivered in every area. Yet the people spent forty years crying, "Can God . . . ? Can God . . . ?"

Beloved, we ought to be proclaiming, "God can! God can!" He did—and He will do all that we ask and believe Him for. Our God is faithful!

THE LOVE OF THE FATHER

I wonder how many of God's people sincerely cry out to Him, "Glorify me with Yourself! I yearn to be closer to You, Lord. More than signs or wonders, I must have Your presence."

Hear Jesus' exalted plea: "Father, I desire that they also whom You gave Me may be with Me where I am, that they may behold My glory which You have given Me" (John 17:24).

The glory Jesus is talking about has to do with an intimate kind of love—a love that permits no distance or separation from the object of its affection. It desires a complete oneness, an eternal union. The Lord eagerly longed for the day when all His children would behold it with their own eyes.

Actually, our Lord was praying, "Father, they must see this glorious love. I want them to know how greatly I am loved, from before the world was created."

Won't that be something when we, the redeemed, are brought into God's great banquet hall? We will be permitted to behold the love of the Father for His dear Son, our blessed Savior. Our Lord's prayer will be answered when He looks to His blood-purchased children and joyfully proclaims, "See, children, is it not so? Did I not tell you the truth? Does He not love Me so? Have you ever seen such great love? You see now My glory, My Father's love for Me and My love for Him."

What a joy to know we serve a Savior who is so loved. Is it not terrifying to contemplate that Satan cut himself off from such glory, such love? Surely the devil's greatest loss is to exist without a sense of the heavenly Father's love. In contrast, God's children are embraced in oneness with Jesus while still on earth. God loves us as He loves His own Son. This truth ought to bring us into His rest.

The Glory of God

"Glorify Me together with Yourself" (John 17:5).

No human can rightly define God's glory any more than a human can define Him. Glory is the fullness of God, and that is a subject too high for our finite minds. Yet, we do know in part.

When God gives His glory, He gives Himself. The one who receives His love also gets His mercy, His holiness and His strength. Those who seek the glory of God must learn that He truly desires to give Himself to us in His fullness—meaning He wants us to enjoy fullness of rest and confidence.

Before He left the earth to return to His heavenly Father, Jesus prayed, "And now, O Father, glorify Me together with Yourself, with the glory which I had with You before the world was" (verse 5).

Jesus was in the bosom of the Father, one with Him, before the world was, and that was glory. Union with the Father was the delight and glory of His being. He had *intimacy, union,* and *oneness.*

We know so little of His glory. We think only in terms of cosmic power and splendor, and thus are such strangers to the real meaning of God's glory. For example, we do not understand what Jesus meant when He said, "I am glorified in them" (verse 10).

Did you not know that Jesus Christ is glorified in us, His Church? He abides in us in all His divine fullness, and we are complete in Him. When He comes to abide, He comes in all His glory, might, majesty, holiness, grace and love. Simply put, we have received the glory of a full and complete Christ.

We have an open heaven before us—therefore, let us come boldly to the throne of His glory and make our petitions known. How wonderful to come away with assurance and hope that He loves us completely.

WHERE DO YOU TURN FOR ENCOURAGEMENT?

Where can you find wholly devoted Christians who have an easy, trouble-free life? Show me a Spirit-led, God-filled, anointed servant of the Lord, and I will show you one who is chased, chastened, often baffled and familiar with deep waters and fiery furnaces.

Those who seek to avoid difficulties seldom get the revelation of God's fullness. They attempt to use faith to exempt themselves from crises, not realizing they are robbing themselves of the great opportunity to find out what is really in them. The day comes when trouble can no longer be avoided, and they cave in, having no proven source of inner strength.

Paul wrote, "That He would grant you, according to the riches of His glory, to be strengthened with might through His Spirit in the inner man" (Ephesians 3:16).

The Lord needs servants who are not tossed about by every wind and wave of doctrine; who have discernment and are not being deceived; who need no special teacher with some new revelation; who do not need a human shepherd to guide their every step. They are not dependent on another for their happiness or spiritual strength. Instead, they have been tested and have proven that the very life of God is in them, providing grace and mercy to help in every need. Christ has been revealed not only *to* these servants but *in* them.

We can learn valuable lessons from King David's experience at Ziklag. "David strengthened himself in the Lord his God" (1 Samuel 30:6). It is imperative that we learn to encourage ourselves in the Lord because of the troubled times ahead.

I beseech you in the name of the Lord: Open your eyes to the mighty power of God at work in you. Appropriate the fullness and completeness of the Lord Jesus Christ. No matter what fiery furnace you may be cast into, your supreme Lord will walk you through it.

Precious in His Sight

I have told my children, "When you are hurting and in need, just call me. I will be there for you. I don't care where I am, I will come!" I am just an earthly father—but how much more our heavenly Father cares for us. Will He not respond when we call?

The Bible says, "He will deliver the needy when he cries; the poor also, and him who has no helper. He will spare the poor and needy, and will save the souls of the needy. He will redeem their life from oppression and violence; and precious shall be their blood in His sight" (Psalm 72:12–14).

God tells us, in effect, "All you who are poor, who are needy, who seem helpless—the enemy has been attacking you. Don't you know you are precious to Me? All you have to do is cry out and I will deliver you from the wiles of Satan."

David testified, "This poor man cried out, and the Lord heard him, and saved him" (34:6).

You do not have to know a lot of religious terms to cry out to Him. The one thing you must know is that no matter what failures or sins you have committed, His repentant ones will always be precious in His eyes. Christ said, "Behold, I stand at the door and knock. If anyone hears My voice and opens the door, I will come in and dine with him, and he with Me" (Revelation 3:20).

Why is He knocking? It is because your life is precious to Him—and He will not let you go. Time after time He will come and speak to your heart: "Call on Me now in your need."

You may have been in churches where people condemned you and put you down, but they were judging you from your outward appearance. God does not do that—He sees your potential. He will give you joy and beauty in place of dirt, filth and ashes. He will set you free.

Snake Handlers

You cannot work effectively for Christ unless you are willing to take the risks involved. Jesus warned about the risks of encountering serpents. What did He mean?

The Bible says the wicked are like poisonous serpents, and we must be like snake handlers. It is significant that Scripture calls Satan "that serpent of old" (Revelation 12:9). Christ promised us, "They will take up serpents" (Mark 16:18).

In Ecclesiastes we are warned: "Whoever breaks through a wall [hedge] will be bitten by a serpent" (10:8). The hedges are filled with serpents. Yet Jesus commands, "Go out into the highways and hedges, and compel them to come in" (Luke 14:23). This assumes God's protection in His calling.

Soul winners are promised, "If they drink anything deadly, it will by no means hurt them" (Mark 16:18). This refers to a believer's imbibing a poison by accident (or even by force, in countries where persecution takes place).

Yet there is another meaning embedded in this passage. Just as surely as Christians drink of the blood of Christ—the river of life—we are also subject to the poison of this world when we go out to preach the Gospel. We absorb so much of the spirit of this world that we can take in deadly things in our spiritual lives.

Unless we receive Holy Ghost protection, I do not see how Christian workers can go where sinners are. We cannot help drinking some of these unmentionable things into our spirit, but through the power of Christ the poison will not hurt us. He causes all poison to drain out, and we are able to stand cleansed and pure—unharmed.

The Lord, My Shepherd

Psalm 23 is a comforting message well known even among nonbelievers. Written by King David, its most famous passage is contained in the opening verse: "The Lord is my shepherd; I shall not want." David is saying, "I shall not lack anything, because the Lord leads, guides and nourishes me."

In this brief verse, David gives us yet another reflection of God's character and nature. The literal Hebrew translation of the first part of this verse is Jehovah Rohi, which means "the Lord my Shepherd."

Jehovah Rohi is not passive; He does not merely point us toward the grassy pasture and pools of water, and say, "There is what you need. Go and get it." Nor does He turn a blind eye to our needs. No, He knows every pain we endure, every tear we shed, every hurt we feel. He knows when we are too weary to go another step. He knows just how much we can take.

Most of all, our God knows how to rescue us and bring us to a place of healing. Time after time our Shepherd comes after us, fetches us and takes us to a place of rest. He continually makes us lie down for a time of healing and restoration.

The Lord says in Exodus 29:45, "I will dwell among the children of Israel and will be their God." The Hebrew word for *dwell* here is *shekinah,* meaning "to abide by, or to settle down beside." Jehovah Rohi—the Lord our Shepherd—is compelling us to follow Him into His rest, so that He might *shekinah* in our midst. This word signifies not just a passing presence, but a permanent one—a presence that never leaves. It is His very near and eternal presence.

Our Shepherd comes to us in the midst of our pain and depressed condition and binds up our wounds. With His presence He strengthens the parts of us that have become sick and diseased. That is a true Shepherd!

We Are Not without Hope

We who know Christ's righteousness are not to live as those who are without hope. We have been blessed with both the love and the fear of God. And His will for us in the darkest, most terrible times is to obtain His joy and gladness. Even as we see judgment falling around us, we are to sing, shout and rejoice—not because judgment has come but in spite of it.

In Isaiah 51:10, God reminds His people, "[I] made the depths of the sea a road for the redeemed to cross over." The next verse begins with the word *So*—meaning, "in light of what I have just said." God was telling His people, in effect, "I am still the Lord, the Ancient of Days, the worker of miracles—and My arm is still strong to deliver you."

What does God want to get across to us in light of this truth? He says it all in one verse, Isaiah 51:11:

- "*So* the ransomed of the LORD shall return, and come to Zion with singing." In other words, "I am going to have a people who return to Me with trust, faith and confidence. They will take their eyes off the conditions surrounding them and get back their song of joy."
- "With everlasting joy on their heads." The joy that God's people experience will not be just for a Sunday morning or a week or a month. It will last through the years, through hard times, even to the very end.
- "They shall obtain joy and gladness." God looked down through the ages and said, "I am going to have a people who will obtain joy."
- "Sorrow and sighing shall flee away." This does not mean all our suffering will end. It means our trust in our faithful Lord will put us above every pain and trial.

With these truths in mind, nothing should be able to rob us of our joy in Christ.

God Will Not Let You Break

Remind yourself today that God knows exactly how much you can take and that He will not permit you to reach a breaking point. Our loving Father said, "No temptation has overtaken you except such as is common to man; but God is faithful, who will not allow you to be tempted beyond what you are able, but with the temptation will also make a way of escape, that you may be able to bear it" (1 Corinthians 10:13).

The worst kind of blasphemy is to think that God is behind all your hurt and pain—that it is the heavenly Father disciplining you, thinking you need more heartbreaks before you are ready to receive His blessings. Not so!

It is true that the Lord chastens those He loves, but that chastening is only for a season and is not meant to hurt us. God is not the author of confusion in our lives, and neither are we. The enemy tries to hurt us through other humans, just as he tried to hurt Job through his unbelieving friends.

Your heavenly Father watches over you with an unwavering eye. Every move is monitored, every tear bottled. He feels your every hurt and knows when you have been exposed to harassment from the enemy. At some point He steps in and says, "Enough!"

When your pain no longer draws you close to the Lord and instead begins to downgrade your spiritual life, God moves in. He will not permit one of His trusting children to go under because of too much pain and agony of soul.

God will lift you out of the battle for a while, and He will do it right on time. He will never allow your hurt to destroy your mind. He promises to come and wipe away your tears and give you joy for mourning. His Word says, "Weeping may endure for a night, but joy comes in the morning" (Psalm 30:5).

WHEN SIFTING COMES

"And the Lord said, 'Simon, Simon! Indeed, Satan has asked for you, that he may sift you as wheat'" (Luke 22:31).

It is important to understand that Satan seeks to sift only those who threaten his work. He goes after the tree that has the most potential to bear fruit. That is exactly why the devil desired to sift Peter.

For three years Peter had been casting out devils and healing the sick. I believe that when Satan had heard Jesus promise the disciples another baptism—one of Holy Spirit power and fire—he trembled. Now the devil heard God's ultimate plan for Peter—and he realized that the works of the past three years would be nothing compared to the greater things Peter and the others would perform. The devil was looking for a measure of corruption in Peter to build on, to make Peter's faith fail.

Perhaps like Peter you are being shaken and sifted. Maybe you're asking, "Why me? Why now?" First of all, you ought to rejoice that you have such a reputation in hell. Satan is sifting you because you play an important part in God's Church in these last days.

God is doing a new thing in this last generation, and you have been set apart by Him to be a powerful witness to many. He has set you free and is preparing you for His eternal purposes. The greater your gifts and the greater your surrender to the will of God, then the greater your potential—and the more severe your sifting will be.

When someone is going through the fire of sifting, what should those around him do? What did Jesus do about Peter's imminent fall? He said to him, "I have prayed for you, that your faith should not fail" (verse 32). When you see brothers and sisters compromising or heading for trouble or disaster, love them enough to warn them as firmly as Jesus warned Peter. Most of all, tell them, "I am praying for you."

Rest in the Love of the Father

Have you ever had a friend or loved one say to you, out of the blue, "Are you mad at me? Did I do something wrong?"

The question startles you, because no such thing is true. You answer, "I'm not mad at you. You didn't do anything to hurt me."

But they press you: "Was it something I said?"

"No, no," you answer, "everything is fine."

Finally, to convince that person, you have to hug him and say, "Look, I love you—I'm not upset. But if you keep this up, you *are* going to upset me!"

Beloved, this is how we treat our heavenly Father. At the end of the day, we go to our secret closet of prayer thinking, "Let me see, how did I grieve Jesus today? What did I do wrong? What did I forget to do? I'm such a mess I don't know how He can love me."

We pray, "Lord, forgive me one more time. Someday I will be so obedient that You will find it easy to love me." God is there all the time, however, waiting to embrace us. He wants to show us how much He loves us—and He wants us to lie back and rest in His love.

When the Prodigal Son came home, he was welcomed back into his father's house. He received a new robe, ate at his father's table and had full forgiveness. The one thing this son knew above all else was that he was secure in his father's love. He knew his father would bear with him, work with him, love him.

That is how our heavenly Father is with us. No matter how far we may stray from Him we have continual access to return. Yet we must believe that God's Word says He has "made us accepted in the Beloved" (Ephesians 1:6).

Our Father waits with outstretched arms for us every day. He longs to embrace all who relish their access to Him and continually return to His love.

At the End of Your Rope?

Are you at the end of your rope? Weary, cast down, about to give up? I challenge you to answer the following questions with a simple yes or no:

- Does the Word of God promise to supply all your needs?
- Did Jesus say He would never leave you?
- Did He say He would keep you from falling and present you faultless before the Father's throne?
- Is He more willing to give than you are to receive? Is He greater than "he that is in the world"?
- Are His thoughts toward you good thoughts? Is He a rewarder of those who diligently seek Him?
- Is He preparing a place for you in glory? Is He coming in the clouds to gather His people home? Are you going with Him when He comes?

Your answer to all of these should be, "Absolutely, yes!"

Now ask yourself: "Do I really believe God is faithful to His Word, or do I waver in my trust?"

> My brethren, count it all joy when you fall into various trials, knowing that the testing of your faith produces patience. But let patience have its perfect work, that you may be perfect and complete, lacking nothing. If any of you lacks wisdom, let him ask of God, who gives to all liberally and without reproach, and it will be given to him. But let him ask in faith, with no doubting, for he who doubts is like a wave of the sea driven and tossed by the wind. For let not that man suppose that he will receive anything from the Lord.
>
> James 1:2–7

You can lay hold of God's wisdom—all the wisdom needed to solve life's problems—if you will truly believe with no wavering. Cast your very life and future on this promise!

He Has Already Made Provision

When God calls us to any specific work, He has already made provision for everything we need to accomplish it.

"God is able to make all grace abound toward you, that you, always having all sufficiency in all things, have an abundance for every good work" (2 Corinthians 9:8).

This verse is not just a hope—it is a promise. It begins with the words, "God is able!"

God is not interested in just meeting your need. He always wants to give you more than you need. That is what the word *abound* means—"an ever-increasing, super-abundant supply." "Now to Him who is able to do exceedingly abundantly above all that we ask or think, according to the power that works in us" (Ephesians 3:20).

Think of what is being promised here: When you are down and tired and think you can go no farther, God is able to so invigorate you that you will have all you need—at all times, in every possible situation.

It is as if the Lord is saying, "Listen, all you shepherds! Listen, all you who faithfully attend My house and labor in prayer, praise and intercession. I want to give you an abundance of strength, hope, joy, peace, rest, encouragement, wisdom. In fact, I want you to have an overabundance of all you need—at all times!"

God never intended for us to be spiritual paupers, poor in the things of the Lord. On the contrary, the bountiful servant is the one who enjoys a revelation of all the great provisions God has prepared for him. He goes after this revelation by faith.

"But as it is written, 'Eye has not seen, nor ear heard, nor have entered into the heart of man the things which God has prepared for those who love Him'" (1 Corinthians 2:9).

Ask the Lord to open your mind and spirit to the resources He has promised. They are freely given!

Walking in the Glory

One thing that can keep us going in hard times is an understanding of God's glory. This may sound like a high, lofty concept to you, but I am convinced the subject of God's glory has very practical value for every true believer. By grasping it, we unlock the door to an overcoming life.

The glory of God is a revelation of our Lord's nature and being. You may recall that Moses got a literal glimpse of God's glory. Before then, the Lord had sent out Moses with no explanation of Himself other than the words, "I AM." Moses wanted to know something more of God, so he pleaded with Him, "Please, show me Your glory" (Exodus 33:18).

God responded by taking Moses aside and putting him in the cleft of a rock. Then He revealed Himself to Moses in all His glory (see 34:6–7). The way God wants us to know His glory is through the revelation of His great love toward humankind. That is just what He revealed to Moses.

Often when we think about the glory of God, we think of His majesty and splendor, His power and dominion. This is not the glory He wants us to know Him by. The Lord is forever waiting to show us His love—to forgive us, show us mercy and restore us to Himself.

Up to this point, Moses had viewed the Lord as a God of law and wrath. Moses had trembled with terror in the Lord's presence as he pled with Him on behalf of Israel. Now, however, at the first sight of God's glory, Moses was no longer fearful of the Lord. Instead, he was moved to worship because he saw God's nature of love, kindness and mercy.

Once we receive a revelation of God's glory, our worship cannot help but change. Each new revelation of His love brings supernatural change.

The Revelation of God's Love

But you, beloved, building yourselves up on your most holy faith, praying in the Holy Spirit, keep yourselves in the love of God, looking for the mercy of our Lord Jesus Christ unto eternal life" (Jude 20–21).

As I read these verses, I hear the Spirit whisper to me: "David, you have never yet come into the fullness and joy of My love. You have the theology right—but you have not yet experienced the ecstasy and rest of keeping yourself in My love. You have only been in up to your ankles, while there is a whole ocean of My love for you to swim in."

The Bible is filled with the truth of God's love, yet we allow ourselves to wonder how the Lord could ever love us. The revelation of God's love comes in part when we are born again. If you were to ask most Christians what they know of God's love for them, they would answer, "I know God loves me because He gave His Son to die for me." Then they would quote John 3:16: "For God so loved the world that He gave His only begotten Son, that whoever believes in Him should not perish but have everlasting life."

It is a wonderful moment when you grasp this truth. You suddenly realize, "God loved me when I was lost, and He proved His love for me by sacrificing His own Son on my behalf."

Few Christians, however, learn how to be kept in God's love. We know something of our love toward the Lord, but we seldom seek the revelation of God's love for us. Understanding the love of God is the secret to an overcoming life.

How long has God loved you? He has loved you since He has existed—because God is love. It is His very nature. There was no beginning to His love for you, and there is no end to it.

A Little Taste of Heaven

A foretaste is an advance taste or realization. The Bible calls it a down payment or earnest—"the guarantee of our inheritance" (Ephesians 1:14). It means to enjoy a taste of the whole before we have the whole.

Our inheritance is Christ Himself—and the Holy Spirit brings us into His very presence as a foretaste of being received as His Bride, to enjoy everlasting love and communion with Him.

In Ephesians 1:13 Paul describes a people of God who are "sealed with the Holy Spirit," specially marked by a work of the Spirit. The Holy Spirit has produced in them a distinguishing mark, a glorious inner work—something supernatural that changed them forever.

What happened to them? What did the Holy Spirit do in these believers? What marked and sealed them forever as the Lord's possession? Simply this: The Holy Spirit gave them a foretaste of the glory of God's presence. He came to them, rolled back heaven, and they experienced a supernatural manifestation of His exceeding greatness. Likewise, He gives us "a little heaven" to go to heaven with—a whetting of our appetite.

If you truly love Jesus, He is present in your every waking moment. Some Christians think, "When I get to heaven, everything will change. I will become the special bride of the Lord then." No, dying does not sanctify anybody. This Holy Spirit is alive and working in you today—to produce in you a passionate love for Christ on this side of death.

The Christian who is truly walking in the Spirit has an insatiable appetite for Jesus. Such a person yearns for His presence. Like Paul, he is anxious to depart and be with the Lord!

How Big Is Your Jesus?

John 14 contains two magnificent promises. In the first, Jesus states, "Most assuredly, I say to you, he who believes in Me, the works that I do he will do also; and greater works than these he will do, because I go to My Father. And whatever you ask in My name, that I will do, that the Father may be glorified in the Son. If you shall ask anything in My name, I will do it" (John 14:12–14).

Two verses later, Jesus promises, "And I will pray the Father, and He will give you another Helper, that He may abide with you forever, the Spirit of truth, whom the world cannot receive, because it neither sees Him nor knows Him; but you know Him, for He dwells with you and will be in you. I will not leave you orphans; I will come to you" (verses 16–18). Christ is saying, "I will give you the Spirit of truth, and His power will abide in you."

These are two incredible promises from Jesus. Yet there is one verse sandwiched between them: "If you love Me, keep My commandments" (verse 15). Why does this statement appear here? Christ is telling us, "There is a matter of obedience connected to these promises." In short, both promises have to do with keeping and obeying God's Word. They were given to be fulfilled so that nothing would hinder us from claiming the power that is in Christ.

I am convinced that asking little or nothing in Jesus' name is a reproach to Him. Year after year, many Christians settle for less and less. Finally, they settle for salvation only.

Does your Christ end at just enough strength to make it through another day? Sadly, many believers make Christ look insignificant and powerless by their unbelief and the limited size of their requests. I want more out of my Christ. I want Him to be bigger than ever in my life!

All the Grace You Need to Overcome

We have often heard grace defined as the unmerited favor of God. Yet I believe grace is much more. In my opinion, grace is everything that Christ is to us in our times of suffering: power, kindness, mercy and love meant to see us through our afflictions.

As I look back over the years—years of great suffering, temptation and trials—I can testify that God's grace has been enough. I know what it is to question God as my wife endured cancer over and over, and then both our daughters were also stricken. Today they are all healthy and for that I thank the Lord. I also know what it is to be buffeted by a messenger of Satan. I have been grievously tempted and enticed, and enemies have stirred up against me on all sides. I have been slandered by rumors, falsely accused, rejected by friends. In those dark times, I fell on my knees and cried out to God.

His grace has always brought me through—and that is enough for today. Someday in glory, my Father will reveal to me the beautiful plan He had all along. He will show me how I obtained patience through all my trials; how I learned compassion for others; how His strength was made perfect in my weakness; how I learned His utter faithfulness toward me; how I longed to be more like Jesus.

Even though I may ask why, He continues to give an ever-increasing measure of Christ's strength. In fact, many great revelations of His glory have come during my hardest times. Likewise, in your lowest moments, Jesus will release in you the fullest measure of His strength.

We may never understand our pain, depression and discomfort. We may never know why some of our prayers are not answered—but we do not need to know. Our God has already answered us: "You have My grace. My beloved child, that is all you need."

The Measured Glory of God

And He said to them, 'Take heed what you hear. With the same measure you use, it will be measured to you; and to you who hear, more will be given. For whoever has, to him more will be given; but whoever does not have, even what he has will be taken away from him'" (Mark 4:24–25).

Jesus knew these words might sound strange to the natural ear, so He preceded His message by saying, "If anyone has ears to hear, let him hear" (verse 23). Jesus was telling us, "If your heart is open to God's Spirit, you will understand what I have to say."

What, exactly, is Jesus saying in this passage? He is speaking of the glory of God in our lives—Christ's manifest presence. In short, the Lord measures His glorious presence in various amounts, whether to churches or to individuals. Some do not receive any of His glory while others receive an ever-increasing measure, emanating from their lives and churches in greater and greater amounts.

God has promised to pour out His Spirit on His people in these last days. Scripture points to a triumphant, glory-filled Church at the close of time. Indeed, Jesus said the gates of hell will not prevail against His Church. We will not be limping into heaven—beaten down, depressed, whimpering, defeated, discouraged. No—our Lord is going to bring greater power to His Body! This power will not be manifested merely in signs and wonders but in the glorious transformation of hearts touched by God's Spirit.

How can we obtain a greater measure of Christ's glory? The Lord tells us very clearly: "With the same measure you use, it will be measured to you" (verse 24).

Jesus states plainly that He measures out different amounts of His glory to us, according to how we measure out our hearts to Him. Our part is simply to move ever closer to Him—in our worship, obedience and diligence.

When Questions Arise

And when He had fasted forty days and forty nights, afterward He was hungry. Now when the tempter came to Him, he said, 'If You are the Son of God, command that these stones become bread'" (Matthew 4:2–3).

At a moment when Jesus was physically vulnerable, the devil brought His first temptation.

There is no sin in being hungry. So, what is the issue here? Satan was challenging Jesus: "If You are fully God, then You have God's power in You. And right now You are in a very hard place. Why don't You use the power God gave You to deliver Yourself? He gave it to You to use properly, didn't He?"

Here is one of the most insidious temptations facing truly godly people. Like your example, Jesus, you have a passion for God. You have set your heart to be wholly surrendered to Him. Then the Lord leads you into a wilderness experience and after a while, questions arise in your mind. You begin to lose your bearings, wondering about God's eternal purposes in your life. While you try to pray and gain victory, Satan's temptations seem fiercer than ever.

The enemy wants you to act independently of the Father. The devil says, "Your suffering is not of God. You do not have to go through this. You have God's power in you, through the Holy Spirit. Just speak the word and free yourself. Satisfy your own hunger."

How did Jesus answer the devil's temptation? "It is written, 'Man shall not live by bread alone, but by every word that proceeds from the mouth of God'" (verse 4). Christ said, in essence, "My coming to earth is not about My needs, hurts or physical comfort. I came to give to humankind, not to save Myself."

Even at the height of His suffering, Jesus did not lose sight of His eternal purpose. And if our Lord learned dependence and compassion through a wilderness experience, so will we.

God's Riches in Us

When the Lord takes up residence in us, He brings with Him all His power and resources. Suddenly, our inner man has access to God's strength, wisdom, truth and peace—everything we need to live in victory. We do not have to cry out to Him to come down from heaven because He is already in us. Paul tells us just how powerful we are in Christ.

> For this reason I bow my knees to the Father of our Lord Jesus Christ . . . that He would grant you, according to the riches of His glory, to be strengthened with might through His Spirit in the inner man, that Christ may dwell in your hearts through faith; that you, being rooted and grounded in love, may be able to comprehend with all the saints what is the width and length and depth and height—to know the love of Christ which passes knowledge; that you may be filled with all the fullness of God. Now to Him who is able to do exceedingly abundantly above all that we ask or think, according to the power that works in us, to Him be glory in the church by Christ Jesus.
>
> Ephesians 3:14–21

What an amazing passage. Paul lists but a few of the incredible treasures the Lord has made available to us. Indeed, all of God's riches are available to us in Christ Jesus.

Some Christians have created an image of a self-centered God whose only pleasure is in receiving praise. May that never be said about our Lord! That is not at all why He has come to abide in us. The Lord wants us to know He is not just out in the dark expanse of the cosmos somewhere, but is very present in us.

Paul notes, "But now in Christ Jesus you who once were far off have been brought near by the blood of Christ" (2:13). He makes it absolutely clear that God is here, right now, abiding in us. That is true riches!

Where Does God Dwell?

After Jesus was taken up to heaven, the apostle John received a magnificent vision of glory. He said, "But I saw no temple in it, for the Lord God Almighty and the Lamb are its temple. . . . The Lamb is its light" (Revelation 21:22–23). In other words, the only temple in heaven is Jesus Himself.

Now that God's temple is in glory, sitting at His right hand, where does the Lord dwell on earth? God Himself asks, "What house will you build Me? Where is the place of My rest?" We know that no building can contain God—not St. Peter's Cathedral in the Vatican, not St. Patrick's Cathedral in New York City, nor any of the great European cathedrals. As Paul stated on Mars Hill in Athens, "God, who made the world and everything in it, since He is Lord of heaven and earth, does not dwell in temples made with hands" (Acts 17:24). Simply put, if we look for God's dwelling place in some building, we are not going to find it.

Jesus says, "If anyone loves Me, he will keep My word; and My Father will love him, and We will come to him and make Our home with him" (John 14:23). A home is a residence, a place to stay. And the Lord has found His habitation: "Do you not know that *you* are the temple of God and that the Spirit of God dwells in you?" (1 Corinthians 3:16, emphasis mine).

When the Holy Spirit fell on the disciples in the Upper Room, He filled them with Himself. Their bodies became God's temple, and the Spirit gave them power to live victoriously.

Paul says, "Therefore glorify God in your body and in your spirit, which are God's" (1 Corinthians 6:20). You belong to God, and He wants you to be His resting place. Now, open up your heart to the truth and give Him glory by receiving it.

God's Promised Rest

"There remains therefore a rest for the people of God. For he who has entered His rest has himself also ceased from his works as God did from His" (Hebrews 4:9–10).

You may wonder, "What does it mean to enter this promised rest? What should it look like in my life?" I pray that God will remove the scales from our eyes and allow us to grasp this. Simply put, entering into His promised rest means fully trusting that Christ has done all the work of salvation for us. We are to rest in His saving grace, by faith alone.

This is what Jesus means when He urges, "Come to Me, all you who labor and are heavy laden, and I will give you rest" (Matthew 11:28). It means the end of all fleshly striving, all human efforts to obtain peace. And it means relying totally on Jesus' work for us.

Our battle is not against flesh and blood. The Old Testament makes it clear that the battle takes place in the spiritual realm.

Time after time Israel made empty, futile promises to God: "We want to serve You, Lord. We will do whatever You command us." But history proves they had neither the heart nor the ability to follow through on their word. God had to strip them of all faith in themselves.

Everything we need is to come from our precious Lord's presence. Paul states, "For in Him we live, and move and have our being" (Acts 17:28). This speaks of uninterrupted fellowship. Through the victory of the cross, our Lord has made Himself available to us every hour of the day or night.

We all have to make a decision: "I want Christ's rest. I want to be set free from all flesh. So I am going to move forward into His presence and claim my possession. I want Jesus to be my all, my only source of satisfaction—my soul's rest."

THE TRUE MEANING OF THE PROMISED LAND

God gave our forefather Abraham the land of Canaan "as an everlasting possession" (Genesis 17:8). You might think, "Abraham had to rejoice over this. God promised His descendants a permanent homeland, as far as they could see, and it would last into eternity."

Yet the New Testament tells us the world will be destroyed by fire. It will be burned completely out of existence, after which the Lord will bring about a new heaven and earth.

How could God's "everlasting possession" to Abraham be a mere piece of real estate? How could land be eternal?

The fact is, this land of promise was symbolic of a place beyond the earth. I believe Abraham knew this in his spirit. The Bible says that as Abraham moved about in Canaan, he always felt alien: "By faith he dwelt in the land of promise as in a foreign country" (Hebrews 11:9). Clearly, Abraham's heart longed for something beyond the land itself.

"For he waited for the city which has foundations, whose builder and maker is God" (verse 10). Abraham could see the true significance of the land-blessing and realized, "This place is not the real possession. It is just an illustrated sermon of the great blessing to come."

Abraham grasped the true meaning of the Promised Land. He knew Canaan represented *the coming Messiah*. Jesus Himself tells us, "Your father Abraham rejoiced to see My day, and he saw it and was glad" (John 8:56).

The Holy Spirit enabled this patriarch to see down through the years to the day of Christ. He knew that the meaning of his Promised Land meant a place of total peace and rest. Of course, this place of rest is Jesus Christ Himself. Yes, the Lord Jesus is our promised possession. We are His, but He is ours as well. God invites us to obtain our everlasting possession by simple faith.

Confessing Christ

"Therefore whoever confesses Me before men, him I will also confess before My Father who is in heaven. But whoever denies Me before men, him I will also deny before My Father who is in heaven" (Matthew 10:32–33).

Jesus is speaking of an agreement we have with Him. Our part is to confess Him, or represent Him, in our daily lives. We are to live by His promises of protection and personal care for us—and we are to testify of His marvelous blessings by how we live.

Confessing Christ means more than believing in His divinity. It is more than stating He is the Son of God—crucified, buried, resurrected and seated at the Father's right hand. The Bible says even demons believe this and tremble at the knowledge. So, what does Jesus mean when He says we are to confess Him before men?

"*Therefore* whoever confesses Me" (verse 32). By using the word *therefore,* Jesus is saying, "In light of what I have just said." What had Christ just told His listeners? He had said, "Are not two sparrows sold for a copper coin? And not one of them falls to the ground apart from your Father's will" (verse 29). Jesus was telling them, "Think of the millions of birds throughout the earth. Now think of all the birds that have existed since Creation. To this day, not one bird has died or been snared without your heavenly Father's knowledge."

He then pointed out, "But the very hairs of your head are all numbered" (verse 30). Christ was emphasizing, "God is so great, He is beyond your ability to comprehend."

Jesus concluded by saying, "Do not fear therefore; you are of more value than many sparrows" (verse 31). He is saying, "Think about what I have just revealed to you. You are to confess this truth to the whole world so that they know of My love for them."

THROUGH EVERY BATTLE A VICTOR

God promised that you would come out of every battle a victor, crowned by His strength. "Be exalted, O LORD, in Your own strength! We will sing and praise Your power" (Psalm 21:13).

The Holy Spirit drives out all fear from us—fear of falling, of being cut off from God, of losing the presence of the Holy Spirit—by implanting in us His joy. We are to go forth rejoicing, as David did, because God has assured us we will prevail.

So few Christians, however, have this joy and exceeding gladness. Multitudes never know rest of soul or the peace of Christ's presence. They walk around as if in mourning, picturing themselves under the thumb of God's wrath rather than under His protective wings. They see God as a harsh taskmaster, always ready to bring a whip down on their backs. So they live unhappily, with no hope, more dead than alive.

In God's eyes, our problem is not sin, it is trust. Jesus settled our sin problem once and for all at Calvary. He does not harp on us, "This time you have crossed the line." No, His attitude toward us is just the opposite. His Spirit is constantly wooing us, reminding us of the Father's loving-kindness even in the midst of our failures.

When we become focused on our sin, we lose all sight of what God wants most: "Without faith it is impossible to please Him. . . . He is a rewarder of those who diligently seek Him" (Hebrews 11:6). This verse says it all. Our God is a rewarder, and He is so anxious to shower us with His loving-kindness that He blesses us way ahead of schedule.

This is the concept our heavenly Father longs for us to have of Him. He is saying, "I want to assure My child that I have forgiven him through My Son's cleansing blood." He makes a way for us to emerge from every battle a victor.

God's Fire Still Burns

Sadly, much of Christ's Body today resembles a modern-day Valley of Dry Bones, a wilderness filled with the bleached-out skeletons of fallen Christians. Ministers and other devoted believers have flamed out because of besetting sin, and they are filled with shame, hiding out in caves of their own making. Like Jeremiah, they have convinced themselves, "I will not make mention of Him [the Lord], nor speak anymore in His name" (Jeremiah 20:9).

God is still asking the same question he asked Ezekiel: "Can these dead bones live again?" (see Ezekiel 37:3). The answer to this question is an absolute, "Yes!" How can dead bones be made alive? By the renewing of our faith in God's Word.

The Word of the Lord is itself a consuming fire, the only true light we have during our dark nights of despair. It is our only defense against the enemy's lies when he whispers, "It is all over for you."

The only thing that will bring us out of our darkness is faith in God's Word. The Lord has promised, "I will not let you go down; therefore, you have no reason to despair. Rest in my Word" (see 1 Kings 8:56).

You may think, "This dark night is worse than anything I have ever known. I have heard a thousand sermons on God's Word, but none of it seems of any value to me now." Do not fret—God's fire still burns in you. Exercise your faith, trust the Lord, and you will see all your doubts and temptations consumed.

God's Spirit is breathing life again into every set of dry bones—and they are being revived. They are crying as Jeremiah did, "God's fire has been shut up in me for too long. I simply cannot hold it any longer. I can feel the Lord's power putting life into me. And I am going to speak the Word He gave me. I am going to proclaim His mercy and healing power" (see Jeremiah 20:9).

Why Is "Greenness" Important?

They were commanded not to harm the grass of the earth, or any green thing, or any tree, but only those men who do not have the seal of God on their foreheads" (Revelation 9:4).

Why is "greenness" important to our faith? In this Scripture passage, the locusts are commanded not to touch anything green. Simply put, they could not hurt anyone who was walking in faith.

What does this tell us? Even at the height of attacks from the enemy, those who place their trust in God will stand tall, like solid green trees. They will not be harmed by locusts of any kind. The best defense against every kind of hellish attack, every scorpion-like sting, is spiritual health. This kind of health comes only as we turn to the Lord and trust in His promises.

Let me ask you: Do you fully trust in God's forgiveness? Do you depend on His blood to cleanse you of every iniquity? If you feel condemned and are constantly striving to please God, you are not green and healthy. God's foremost desire is that you accept His gift of forgiveness and rest in it. You have accepted God's forgiveness—but do you trust in His unconditional love for you?

Our Lord does not cut us off every time we fail. He is not constantly looking over our shoulder, demanding we get it right. He simply asks that we come to Him, confessing, "I believe Your Word, Lord. Forgive me, wash me, and hold me in Your arms."

God's desire for us is that we live all our days without fear. If we have repented of our past, we are covered by Christ's cleansing blood.

Here is God's promise to all who place their trust in Him: "Some trust in chariots, and some in horses; but we will remember the name of the Lord our God. They have bowed down and fallen; but we have risen and stand upright" (Psalm 20:7–8). Because of Him, we stand tall like green trees!

The Power of Staying Green

As I studied Revelation 9, the chapter on the locusts, I was struck by verse 4, about God's command to the locusts not to destroy anything green. It became clear to me that the key to remaining safe in time of terror is to "stay green."

David wrote, "I am like a green olive tree in the house of God . . . forever and ever" (Psalm 52:8). The "green" that David refers to here signifies spiritual health. It means to flourish, grow, be fruitful. David is telling us, "My health comes from trusting God. I flourish because I turn to Him, and my trust in Him produces spiritual life in me."

Here is a glorious truth about the power of staying green. "Cursed is the man who trusts in man and makes flesh his strength, whose heart departs from the Lord. For he shall be like a shrub in the desert, and shall not see when good comes, but shall inhabit the parched places in the wilderness, in a salt land which is not inhabited" (Jeremiah 17:5–6).

The Lord is cautioning, "If you put your faith in human power rather than in Me, you will be cursed." On the other hand, here is what trusting in the Lord will produce: "Blessed is the man who trusts in the Lord, and whose hope is the Lord. For he shall be like a tree planted by the waters, which spreads out its roots by the river, and will not fear when heat comes; but its leaf will be green, and will not be anxious in the year of drought, nor will cease from yielding fruit" (verses 7–8).

As we trust wholly in the Father, with our roots in His river of health, His divine strength—luscious, green, spiritual health—flows through us. We will flourish as green trees, healthy and strong, and when the hour of trial comes we will not languish or wilt. Instead, our faith will be growing.

My Life Is Preserved

The Bible tells us Jacob received an incredible revelation through a face-to-face encounter with God: "So Jacob called the name of the place Peniel: 'For I have seen God face to face, and my life is preserved'" (Genesis 32:30).

What was the circumstance surrounding this revelation? It came at the lowest point in Jacob's life. He was caught between two powerful forces: his angry father-in-law, Laban, and his hostile, embittered brother, Esau.

Jacob had labored over twenty years for Laban, who had cheated him time after time. Finally, Jacob had had enough, so without telling Laban he took his family and fled.

Laban gave chase from the east with a small army, ready to kill Jacob. Only when God warned Laban in a dream not to harm Jacob did this man let his son-in-law go. No sooner was Laban out of the picture, however, than Esau came from the west. He too led a small army and was ready to kill his brother for stealing his birthright.

Jacob faced total calamity. Things looked hopeless and he was convinced he was about to lose everything. In that dark hour, however, Jacob had an encounter with God as never before. He wrestled with an angel that scholars believe was the Lord Himself.

Likewise, God appeared to Job in a whirlwind when Job was in his darkest hour. The Lord took him up into the cosmos and down into the depths of the sea, showing him things no person had ever seen. Job emerged from that experience praising God, saying, "You can do anything, Lord. I repent for questioning Your judgment. I see that everything is under Your control. You have had a plan all along" (see Job 42:2–5).

Something marvelous happens when we simply trust our faithful God. A peace comes over us, enabling us to say, "It does not matter what comes out of this ordeal. My God has everything under control. He preserves my life. I have nothing to fear."

Delight Yourself in the Lord

Our peace always depends on our resignation into God's hands, no matter what our circumstance. The psalmist writes, "Delight yourself also in the Lord, and He shall give you the desires of your heart" (Psalm 37:4).

If you have fully resigned yourself into God's hands, then you are able to endure any and all hardships. Your Father's desire is for you to be able to go about your daily business without fear or anxiety, totally trusting in His care. The more resigned you are to God's care, the more indifferent you will be to the conditions around you.

If you are resigned to Him, you will not constantly be trying to figure out the next step. You will not be scared by the frightful news swirling around you or overwhelmed about the days ahead—because you have entrusted your life, family and future into the Lord's safe and loving hands.

Sheep are not worried as they follow their shepherd because they are totally resigned to his leading them. Likewise, we are the sheep of Christ, who is our great Shepherd. Why should we ever be concerned, disquieted or worried about our lives and futures? Our Shepherd knows perfectly how to protect and preserve His flock—because He leads us in love.

In my own life, I have had to learn to trust God one problem at a time. Think about it: How can I say I trust God with everything if I have not proven I can trust Him with just one thing? Merely saying the words, "I trust the Lord completely," is not sufficient. I have to prove it over and over in my life.

Many people today have said, "I resign, I commit, I trust," only after they saw there was no other way out of their situation. But true resignation, the kind that pleases God, is done freely, prior to our coming to our wits' end. So "delight yourself in Him."

The Lord's Mercies Never Fail

The Bible tells us that the Lord is no respecter of persons. Because He does not show favoritism—because His promises never change from generation to generation—we can ask Him to show us the same mercies He has shown His people throughout history.

The Lord's mercies never fail, and every believer has examples of His past mercies. So, when you fear you may have sinned too often against the Lord's mercy—when you think you have crossed a line and God has given up on you; when you are discouraged, cast down by failure; when you wonder if God is putting you on a shelf or withholding His love from you because of past sins—lay hold of this truth with a truly repentant heart: *God changes not.*

Bind God to His Word. Write down every remembrance you have of what He has done for you in past years. Then go to Scripture and find other instances of His "mercy precedents" with His people. Bring these lists before the Lord and remind Him: "God, You cannot deny Your own Word. You are the same yesterday, today and forever."

Often we rush into God's presence unprepared, making our requests passionately, but we wilt because we approach Him with only emotion. We must be prepared with our grasp of His Word to us. We know the Son, so we can stand before the Judge and bind Him to His own arguments: "Father, I have nothing to bring You but Your own Word. You promised that I would be complete in Christ, that You would keep me from falling and that Jesus would be my intercessor. Oh, Lord, have mercy and grace on me now, in my hour of need. Amen!"

I truly believe that God is wonderfully blessed when we approach His throne with this kind of boldness, binding Him to His own Word. It is as if He is saying to us, "Finally, you got it. You see what I want you to have. You bless Me!"

ACCESS TO GOD

As I sought the Lord in prayer I asked Him: "What is the most important aspect of Your making us Your temple?" Here is what came to me: *access with boldness and confidence.* Paul says of Christ, "In whom we have boldness and access with confidence through faith in Him" (Ephesians 3:12).

In the Jewish Temple there was very little access to God. In fact, such access was available only to the high priest, and that was only once a year. When the time came, the priest entered God's presence in the Temple with fear and trembling; he knew he could be struck down for approaching the mercy seat with unforgiveness sin in his heart.

Today God has emerged from that small, restricted room and come directly to us in all our corruption. He tells us, "You do not have to hide your filth and despair from Me. I have chosen to live in you, and I am about to turn your body into My home."

Going even further, God says, "I will send my Holy Spirit to sanctify you and prepare your heart as My bride. I want you to come boldly to My throne and ask Me for power, grace, strength, everything you need. I have brought heaven down into your soul so you can have access to it all."

The sole reason your body is holy is because the Holy Spirit lives there. Indeed, you are kept holy only by His continual presence. You cannot do it. You would become a nervous wreck just trying to guard all the entrances! You would get discouraged when you failed to keep out all the dust and filth that blows in. You would get weary just running from room to room, sweeping and polishing, trying to make things look good.

Every Christian ought to rejoice in this fact: God is in you! He is with you always—so who can be against you?

THE PEACE OF CHRIST

Jesus knew the disciples needed the kind of peace that would see them through any and all situations. He told them, "Peace I leave with you, My peace I give to you" (John 14:27).

Surely this word amazed the disciples. In their eyes, it was almost an unbelievable promise: Christ's peace was to become their peace!

These twelve men had marveled at the peace they had witnessed in Jesus for the previous three years. Their Master was always calm, never ruffled, never afraid.

We know that Christ was capable of spiritual anger and that He also wept. But He led His life on earth at peace—peace with the Father, peace in the face of temptation, peace in times of rejection and mockery. He even had peace during storms at sea, sleeping on the deck of the boat while others trembled with terror.

The disciples had witnessed Jesus being dragged to a high ridge by an angry mob determined to kill Him. Amidst the abuse and insults, He calmly walked away from that scene, untouched and full of peace.

Now Jesus was promising these men the very same peace. When they heard this, the disciples must have looked at each other in wonder: "You mean we are going to have the same peace He has? This is incredible!"

Jesus added, "Not as the world gives do I give to you" (same verse). This was not going to be the so-called peace of a numb, zoned-out society. Nor would it be the temporary peace of the rich, who try to purchase peace of mind with material things. No, this was the very peace of Christ Himself, a peace that surpasses all human understanding.

When Christ promised the disciples His peace, it was as if He was saying to them and to us today: "I know you do not understand the times you face. But I will give you peace to face whatever is coming." Amen!

Amazing Peace

Jesus gives us more than one reason why we need His peace. He had just told the twelve, "I will no longer talk much with you" (John 14:30). Then He explained why: "For the ruler of this world [Satan] is coming."

What was the context of His statement? Jesus knew Satan was at work in that hour. The devil had already enlisted Judas to betray Him, and Christ knew that the religious hierarchy in Jerusalem was being empowered by the principalities of hell. He was also aware that a devil-inspired mob was coming shortly to take Him prisoner. That is when Jesus said to the disciples, "Satan, the wicked one, is coming. I will not be talking to you much more."

Jesus knew He needed time with the Father to prepare for the coming conflict, and He knew that Satan was doing all he could to shake His peace. The devil would harass and attempt to discourage Him, all in an effort to break Christ's faith in the Father—anything to get Him to avoid the crucifixion.

You may be in turmoil, thinking, "It is over for me. I am not going to make it." But Jesus says, "I know what you are going through. Come and drink of My peace."

It does not matter what you are going through. Your life may look like it was struck by a tornado. You may endure trials that cause others to look at you as a modern-day Job. But in the midst of your troubles, when you call on the Holy Spirit to baptize you in the peace of Christ, He will do it.

People will point to you and say, "That person's world has come apart, yet he is determined to trust God's Word. How does he do it? He should have quit long ago, but he hasn't given up. Through it all, he has not compromised anything he believes. What amazing peace!"

Peace and the Holy Spirit

On whom does Jesus bestow His peace? You may think, "I am not worthy of living in Christ's peace. I have too many struggles in my life. My faith is so weak."

You would do well to consider the men to whom Jesus first gave His peace. None of them was worthy, and none had a right to it.

Think about Peter. Jesus was about to bestow His peace on a minister of the Gospel who would soon be spewing out cursings. Peter was zealous in his love for Christ, but he was also going to deny Him.

Then there was James and his brother John, men with competitive spirits, always seeking to be recognized. They asked to sit at Jesus' right and left when He ascended to His throne in glory.

The other disciples were no more righteous. They simmered with anger at James and John for trying to upstage them. There was Thomas, a man of God who was given to doubt. All the disciples were so lacking in faith it amazed and stressed Jesus. Indeed, in Christ's most troubling hour, they would all forsake Him and flee. Even after the resurrection, when word spread that "Jesus is risen," the disciples were slow to believe.

What a picture: These men were full of fear, unbelief, disunity, sorrow, confusion, competitiveness, pride. Yet it was to these same troubled servants that Jesus said, "I am going to give you My peace."

The disciples were not chosen because they were good or righteous or had talent. They were fishermen and day laborers, meek and lowly. Christ called and chose the disciples because He saw something in their hearts. He knew each one would submit to the Holy Spirit.

Ask the Lord for His peace. He is faithful to give it to you, through His Spirit.

Run Your Fingers through Your Hair

Christ described the last days as a troubling and frightful time: "On the earth distress of nations, with perplexity . . . men's hearts failing them from fear and the expectation of those things which are coming on the earth" (Luke 21:25–26). What was Jesus' antidote to the fear that was to come?

He gave us the illustration of our Father watching the sparrow and of God numbering the very hairs on our heads. He told these illustrations to His twelve disciples as He sent them out to evangelize the cities and towns of Israel. He had just anointed them with power to cast out demons and heal all manner of sickness. Think of what an exciting moment that had to be for the disciples. They were given power to work wonders!

But then came these fearful warnings from their Master: "You won't have any money in your pocket. You won't have even a roof to sleep under. Instead, you will be called heretics and devils. You will be beaten in synagogues, dragged before judges, thrown into prison. You will be hated, betrayed and persecuted, and you will have to flee from city to city to avoid being stoned."

I picture these men now wide-eyed as they listened to Jesus. They must have been gripped with fear, wondering, "What kind of ministry is this? This is the bleakest outlook on life I have ever heard."

In the very same scene, however, Jesus told these beloved friends three times: "Do not fear!" (Matthew 10:26, 28, 31). Then He gave them the antidote to all fear: "The Father's eye is always on the sparrow. How much more will it always be on you, His beloved ones?"

In our hard times, we need only to look at the little birds and run our fingers through our hair. That will remind us of how our Father cares for us through all things.

THE LORD'S MERCIES

In ancient Israel, the Ark of the Covenant represented the mercy of the Lord, a powerful truth that came to be embodied in Christ. We are to receive His mercy, trusting in His saving blood, and be saved eternally. You can ridicule the law, mock holiness, tear down everything that speaks of God, but when you mock or ridicule God's mercy, judgment comes—and swiftly. If you trample on His blood of mercy, you face His awful wrath.

That is what happened to the Philistines when they stole the ark. Deadly destruction came on them until they had to admit, "This isn't just chance. God's hand is clearly against us." Consider what happened when the ark was taken into the heathen temple of Dagon, to mock and challenge Israel's God. In the middle of the night, the mercy seat on the ark became a rod of judgment. The next day, the idol Dagon was found fallen on its face before the ark, its head and hands cut off (see 1 Samuel 5:2–5).

All who want to bring Christ's Church under the power of secularism or agnosticism will be judged. Jeremiah says, "Through the LORD's mercies we are not consumed, because His compassions fail not" (Lamentations 3:22). When men make a mockery of that great mercy which is Christ, judgment is sure.

Only the mercy of the Lord delays judgment—and right now our society is benefiting from that mercy. Incredibly, our country is in a race to remove God and Christ from society. The Lord will not be mocked, but He has shown mercy on this nation. I believe that is why He is still pouring out blessings on us.

We are not to despair over the present conditions in America. We may grieve over the awful corruption, mockery and sin, but we have hope, knowing God is in full control—and He is merciful.

A Weapon against Fear

We have to remind ourselves of how great God is—of what He has done in the past to deliver all who trusted Him—and claim that majestic power for our present trial. Fear cannot get a stranglehold on the heart of anyone whose eyes are full of a vision of God's greatness and majesty.

Nehemiah understood this principle well. He paced back and forth on the walls of Jerusalem while below him a weary remnant tried to rebuild the city. The Israelites were surrounded by fierce adversaries and fear was beginning to set in. The city walls were not finished, and the worn-out workers were forced to toil with a hammer in one hand and a sword in the other.

What was the answer to their fears? Nehemiah brought to their memory how awesome their God is: "And I looked, and arose and said to the nobles, to the leaders, and to the rest of the people, 'Do not be afraid of them. Remember the Lord, great and awesome, and fight'" (Nehemiah 4:14).

Dearly beloved, are you afraid? Has your problem shaken your confidence in the Lord? If so, remember how great your God is. Moses said to Israel: "If you should say in your heart, 'These nations are greater than I; how can I dispossess them?'—You shall not be afraid of them, but you shall remember well what the Lord your God did to Pharaoh and to all Egypt. . . . You shall not be terrified of them: for the Lord your God, the great and awesome God, is among you" (Deuteronomy 7:17–18, 21).

"He is your praise, and He is your God, who has done for you these great and awesome things which your eyes have seen" (Deuteronomy 10:21).

God declares to us, "I am the Lord, I do not change" (Malachi 3:6). Today, He is still seeking to show His greatness to all who appropriate His power.

THE SAME GLORY

"And he who loves Me will be loved by My Father, and I will love him, and manifest Myself to him" (John 14:21). "That they all may be one, as You, Father, are in Me, and I in You; that they also may be one in Us . . . *and the glory which You gave Me I have given them,* that they may be one just as We are one: I in them, and You in Me, that they may be made perfect in one" (17:21–23, emphasis mine).

Jesus says, in essence, "The glory that You gave Me, Father, I have given to them." Christ is saying that we have been given the same glory that the Father gave to Jesus. Amazing! Yet, what is this glory and how do our lives reveal it?

The glory Jesus refers to is unimpeded access to the heavenly Father. Jesus made it easy for us to access the Father continually, opening the door for us by the cross: "For through Him [Christ] we both [we and those afar off] have access by one Spirit to the Father" (Ephesians 2:18). The word *access* means "the right to enter." It signifies free passage, as well as ease of approach: "In whom we have boldness and access with confidence through faith in Him" (3:12).

Christ said, "I can do nothing on My own. I do only what the Father tells Me and shows Me" (see John 5:19). Today we have been given the very same degree of access to the Father that Christ had. And we are invited to make any request of Him: "Let us therefore come boldly to the throne of grace, that we may obtain mercy and find grace to help in time of need" (Hebrews 4:16).

Like Jesus, let us pray often and fervently, accessing God our Father!

Learning to Forgive Ourselves

To me, learning to forgive ourselves is the most difficult part of forgiveness. As Christians, we are quick to offer the grace of our Lord to the world, but we often parcel it out meagerly to ourselves.

Consider King David, who committed adultery and then murdered the husband to cover up his offense. When his sin was exposed, David repented, and the Lord sent the prophet Nathan to tell him, "Your sin has been pardoned." Yet even though David knew he was forgiven, he had lost his joy. He prayed, "Make me to hear joy and gladness, that the bones You have broken may rejoice. . . . Restore to me the joy of Your salvation, and uphold me by Your generous Spirit" (Psalm 51:8, 12).

Why was David so disturbed? After all, he had been justified before the Lord. The fact is, it is possible to have your sins blotted out of God's Book but not out of your conscience. David wrote this psalm because he wanted his conscience to stop condemning him for his sins. David could not forgive himself, and now he was enduring the penalty: a loss of joy. The joy of the Lord comes as a fruit of accepting His forgiveness.

I have been greatly impacted by the biography of Hudson Taylor, one of the most effective missionaries in history. A godly man of prayer who established churches throughout China's vast interior, Taylor ministered for years without joy. He was downcast over his struggles and thoughts of unbelief.

In 1869 Taylor experienced a revolutionary change within. He saw that Christ had all he needed and that there was only one way to Christ's fullness: through faith. Taylor determined to stir up his faith, yet even that effort proved vain. Finally, in his darkest hour, the Holy Spirit gave him a revelation: Faith comes not by striving, but by resting on the promises of God. Taylor obeyed and became a joyful servant.

May you experience the forgiveness the Lord has already given you—and see your joy return.

The Power of Forgiving

Forgiving is not just a one-time act, but a way of life. It is meant to bring us into every blessing in Christ: "But I say to you, love your enemies, bless those who curse you, do good to those who hate you, and pray for those who spitefully use you, and persecute you, that you may be sons of your Father in heaven" (Matthew 5:44–45).

According to Jesus, forgiving is not a matter of choosing whom we would forgive. We cannot say, "You have hurt me too much, so I am not forgiving you." Christ tells us, "For if you love those who love you, what reward have you? Do not even the tax collectors do the same?" (verse 46).

It does not matter who our grudge might be against. If we hold on to it, it will lead to bitterness that poisons every aspect of our lives. Spiritual famine, weakness and a loss of faith are the result, afflicting not just us but everyone in our circle.

Over decades of my ministry I have seen terrible devastation in the lives of those who withheld forgiveness. Yet I also have seen the glorious power of a forgiving spirit. Forgiveness transforms lives and fills our cup of spiritual blessing to the brim with abundant peace, joy and rest in the Holy Spirit.

"For if you forgive men their trespasses, your heavenly Father will also forgive you. But if you do not forgive men their trespasses, neither will your Father forgive your trespasses" (6:14–15). Make no mistake: God is not making a bargain with us here. We can never earn God's forgiveness. Only the shed blood of Christ merits forgiveness of sin.

Rather, Christ is saying, "Full confession of sin requires that you forgive others. True repentance means confessing and forsaking every grudge, crucifying every trace of bitterness toward others. Anything less is not repentance."

Forgive others—for when you forgive, you reveal the Father's nature to the world.

Do Not Be Afraid of Failure

When Adam sinned, he tried to hide from God. When Jonah refused to preach to Nineveh, his fear drove him into the ocean. When Peter denied Christ, he was afraid to face his Master.

Something worse than failure is the fear that goes with it. Adam, Jonah and Peter ran away from God not because they lost their love for Him, but because they were afraid He was too angry with them to understand.

The accuser of the brethren waits like a vulture for you to fail. Then he uses every lie in hell to make you give up on faith, or to convince you that you are too sinful to come back.

It took forty years to get the fear out of Moses and make him usable in God's program. If Moses, Jacob and David had become resigned to failure, we might never have heard of them. Yet Moses rose up again to become one of God's greatest heroes.

Jacob faced his sins, was reunited with the brother he had cheated, and reached new heights of victory. David ran to God, found forgiveness and peace, and returned to his finest hour. Jonah retraced his steps, did what he had refused to do at first, and brought a whole city to repentance. Peter rose out of the ashes of denial to lead the Church to Pentecost.

In 1958, I sat in my little car weeping; I thought I was a terrible failure. I had been unceremoniously dumped from a New York City courtroom after I thought I was led by God to witness to seven teenage murderers. My attempt to obey God and to help those young hoodlums seemed to be ending in horrible failure.

I shudder to think of how much blessing I would have missed had I given up in that dark hour. How glad I am today that God taught me to face my failure and go on to His next step for me!

The Lord Our Peace

God's character is revealed in His names—and knowing these names and believing His nature provides great protection against enemy attack. God declared through Hosea, "My people are destroyed for lack of knowledge" (Hosea 4:6).

The implication here is powerful. God is telling us that having an intimate knowledge of His nature and character, as revealed through His names, is a powerful shield against Satan's lies.

This brings us to one of our Lord's names: Jehovah Shalom. We find this name mentioned in the book of Judges, where the Lord revealed Himself to Gideon in the form of an angel (see Judges 6:22–24). What does this name, Jehovah Shalom, mean exactly?

As a noun, the Hebrew word *shalom* means "completeness, health, welfare." It implies being whole, in harmony with God and man, having wholesome relationships. It also indicates a state of being at ease—not restless, but having peace both inwardly and outwardly, being at rest spiritually and emotionally. In short, *shalom* signifies wholeness in a life or work. As a verb, *shalom* means to be completed or finished, or to make peace.

Once more, I am driven to ask, "What does this particular name of God have to do with me and with the Church today?" Simply this: *Shalom* cannot be earned. We will never receive the Lord's *shalom* until we realize, "This is very serious business. This is God Almighty I am dealing with, the Creator and sustainer of the universe. How can I continue taking Him for granted? Why do I still test His grace, living as if He is deaf and blind to my secret acts and doubts?"

Do you tremble at God's Word? Are you ready to obey everything it says? If so, you will receive the revelation of Jehovah Shalom. He will come to you personally as "the Lord, your peace," filling your spirit with supernatural strength against every enemy. You cannot earn this kind of peace—it is a gift from God, to be sought from Him.

The Secrets of the Lord

Matthew tells us Jesus spoke to the crowds in parables: "All these things Jesus spoke to the multitude in parables . . . that it might be fulfilled which was spoken by the prophet, saying, 'I will open My mouth in parables; I will utter things which have been kept secret from the foundation of the world'" (Matthew 13:34–35).

Many believers skim over the parables quickly, thinking they see the obvious lesson. Or they may dismiss a parable's meaning as not applying to them. Yet, according to Christ, each parable holds an incredible secret.

The Bible states there are secrets of the Lord: "His secret counsel is with the upright" (Proverbs 3:32). These hidden truths have power to truly set Christians free.

Consider one of the Lord's parables: "Again, the kingdom of heaven is like a merchant seeking beautiful pearls, who, when he had found one pearl of great price, went and sold all that he had and bought it" (Matthew 13:45–46).

Who is the merchant in this parable? He was a traveling wholesale trader and also an assayer, or tester. In other words, he made his living by evaluating costly pearls for their quality and worth.

We know that Jesus is the pearl of great price that the merchant finds. He is very costly, of incalculable value, because the merchant sells all his other possessions to gain him. Obviously, the pearl belonged to the Father, and Jesus is the Father's most valued and treasured possession.

Christ is the treasure, and in Him we have found all we will ever need. No more trying to find purpose in ministry or fulfillment in family or friends. No more needing to build something for God, or be a success, or feel useful. No more keeping up with the crowd, or trying to prove something.

In Him I have found all I am looking for. My treasure, my pearl, is Christ. He brings joy, peace, purpose, holiness.

Promises

Our great need for patience is repeated throughout the book of Hebrews:

- "For when God made a promise to Abraham, because He could swear by no greater, He swore by Himself . . . *and so, after he had patiently endured, he obtained the promise*" (Hebrews 6:13–15).
- "Do not become sluggish, but imitate those who through faith and patience inherit the promises" (verse 12).
- "For you have need of endurance [patience], so that after you have done the will of God, you may receive the promise" (10:36).

God has given us many wonderful promises—to break every bondage of sin, to cleanse and sanctify us, to conform us to the very image of Christ. His Word assures us, "Now to Him who is able to keep you from stumbling, and to present you faultless before the presence of His glory with exceeding joy" (Jude 24).

Yet God does all of these things for us only in His time. He ignores all demands for an instant cure-all. In short, true faith on our part demands that we patiently wait on our Lord. Our response to Him should be, "Lord, I believe You are true to Your Word. By the power of Your Spirit within me, I am going to wait patiently until You bring these things to pass in my life."

You may endure awful trials and hear Satan's horrendous lies, and at times you may fail. In fact, you may wonder if you will ever reach the goal. Yet as you endure all these afflictions, hold on to faith with patience, trusting God is at work. He has said, "By faith, you will receive the promise."

Romans 4:20–22: "[Abraham] did not waver at the promise of God through unbelief, but was strengthened in faith . . . therefore it was accounted to him for righteousness."

The Bible could not make this any clearer. Righteousness is believing the promises of God!

PART 3

A Believing Heart

He Delights in Our Faith

I AM

I once asked the Holy Spirit to give me a one-paragraph description of faith so that the men in our Teen Challenge drug center could understand it. I had in my library a book that used over three hundred pages to define faith, but I never understood it. (I don't think the man who wrote it understood it, either.)

Moses once asked the same question: "Who are You, God? Who shall I tell the people You are?" God answered Moses in two words when He described Himself: "Moses, tell the people, 'I AM' sent you" (see Exodus 3:14).

According to modern thinking, God highly oversimplified Himself. Can you imagine Moses telling people when they ask, "Who sent you?" that "I AM sent me"? I AM *who*, exactly?

God asks, "What do you need? Deliverance? Then I AM *deliverance.* I AM whatever you need."

Faith for us is hearing God say, "I AM," and answering in our own lives, "HE IS." Faith simply accepts God's description of Himself. God says, "I am delivering you from the storm." I say, "He is delivering me from the storm." Faith is taking God at what He says he is—because God is faithful!

What is the storm, the diversity, in your life? How do you face it? Ask Him to give you faith to believe. Ask Him for faith that no matter what happens—no matter what conditions you face, no matter what storm you face—belief in Him is the only way out.

Paul said, "I have learned in whatever state I am, to be content" (Philippians 4:11). I believe that the moment faith gripped Paul, he was content. He was in the center of God's will and he had the promise of God. He had prayed through. It did not matter what happened from that moment on. God had taken the sting out of the storm.

He can take the fear out of the storm for you, too. Will you let Him? Ride out your storm—God is not about to let you go under.

The Last Outpouring

I do not believe we have yet seen the glory and fullness of the outpouring of the Holy Spirit as prophesied by Joel. What we have seen are just a few sprinkles! Yes, we have had a worldwide charismatic renewal, and love has brought many together in the Body of Christ—yet it is all just a foretaste.

God will permit nothing to hinder what He plans to do. The enemy is in for a surprise. Just as it appears the Church will be inundated by a satanic flood, the Spirit will raise up a standard. If you understand what that standard is, you will understand what God is about to do.

The standard Scripture speaks of is a holy people—pure, undefiled, delivered from the corruption in the world. The standard is a new breed of sanctified Christians who will shine forth as lights in the midst of a wicked and perverse generation. It will not be just a renewal of love and praise, but a restoration of holiness unto the Lord.

There will still be shouting and praise, but it will be the shout of victory over sin and compromise, fulfilling the purpose of the last outpouring: "That whoever calls on the name of the Lord shall be saved" (Joel 2:32). Saved from what? From sin! From the spirit of the world!

We will not have had the fullness of the Spirit's outpouring, however, until baptized people separate themselves completely from the world. We must emphasize separation and purity of heart. The purpose of the Spirit's coming is to sanctify and prepare a people without spot or wrinkle for the Lord's return.

When the fullness of the Spirit's outpouring comes upon all flesh, conviction for sin will be everywhere. "He will convict the world of sin, and of righteousness, and of judgment" (John 16:8). That is the outpouring of the Holy Spirit.

Ever-Increasing Faith

"The apostles said to the Lord, 'Increase our faith'" (Luke 17:5). The men who comprised Christ's close circle were asking something important of their Master here. They wanted a greater understanding of the meaning and workings of faith. They were saying, "Lord, what sort of faith do You desire from us? Give us a revelation of the kind that pleases You so we can grasp faith in its fullest meaning."

On the surface, their request seems commendable. Yet I believe the disciples asked this of Jesus because they were confused. In the previous chapter, Christ had baffled them, saying, "He who is faithful in what is least is faithful also in much. . . . Therefore if you have not been faithful in the unrighteous mammon, who will commit to your trust the true riches?" (16:10–11).

Jesus knew these men wanted to avoid what they considered to be lesser matters of faith. So He told them, "If you are faithful in the little things, the foundational matters of faith, you will be faithful in the greater things too. So, prove yourself trustworthy in the basic requirements of faith. Otherwise, how can you be trusted with a deeper measure?"

If we are honest, we will admit we are much like Jesus' disciples. We also want to proceed straight to the larger matters of faith, to obtain the kind of faith that moves mountains. Also like the disciples we often judge faith by visible results.

True faith, in God's eyes, has nothing to do with the size or amount of a work you aim to accomplish. Rather, it has to do with the focus and direction of your life. God is not as concerned with your grand vision as He is with who you are becoming. He is more interested in winning all of me than in my winning all the world for Him.

Our Only Food

It is true—we are what we eat. Jesus said His flesh is our "meat" or food. "Unless you eat the flesh of the Son of Man and drink His blood, you have no life in you" (John 6:53).

"[They] said, 'This is a hard saying; who can understand it?'" (verse 60). The Jews could not comprehend such a thought, and "many of His disciples went back and walked with Him no more" (verse 66).

If we relegate this eating of the Lord to the Communion table alone, we do not understand what Jesus meant. The Lord's Supper is not just symbolic—rather, it reminds us that He became our source of life through death.

We are to come daily to eat and drink of Him. The more we eat of Him, the more spiritual life will be demonstrated in us. We have an open invitation to come to His table to eat and become strong. Partaking of Christ is to feed on God's Word and commune with Him in the prayer of faith.

When sheep are not fed, they grow skeletal and weak, becoming easy prey for the enemy. But God has provided a way to make every child of His strong to resist the enemy. This strength comes from eating the Bread of God sent down from heaven. Our spiritual health and strength depend on this.

I see in these days a remnant ministry made up of servants and handmaidens anointed to come into the fullness of Christ. They have no other source of life but Him. They are bursting forth with life because they have been in the presence of the Lord so often.

Jesus was in such close union with the Father, so committed to doing only His will, that the Father's words became His very food and drink. He was daily sustained by hearing and seeing what the Father wanted, which was the result of spending much time alone with Him. We are to do the same.

After the Sifting

When Peter was sifted he failed miserably—*but not in his faith.* You may be thinking, "How could that be? This man denied knowing Jesus three different times."

I know Peter's faith did not fail because just as he swore, Peter looked into the eyes of Jesus—and melted. He remembered how the Lord had said, "You will deny Me three times"—and "Peter went out and wept bitterly" (Luke 22:61–62). *Wept bitterly* in the Greek actually means "he cried a piercing, violent cry." I picture Peter walking toward the Judean hills, falling on his face with hands outstretched, crying, "O Father, He was right. I did not listen. Forgive me, O Lord—I love Him."

I can see Peter standing up with the Spirit of God flowing through him, his hands raised to the sky, shouting, "Satan, be gone! I failed Him, but I still love Him. He promised—in fact, He prophesied—that I would come back and be a strength to others, a rock."

Indeed, Peter was the first to reach the tomb when the disciples were told Jesus had risen. He was there worshiping when Jesus was translated to glory, and he stood as God's spokesman on the day of Pentecost.

A flood of new converts is coming back to the Lord today, Jews and Gentiles alike. Where will they find strength in the troubled times ahead? From the returning, *sifted saints,* who can say with authority, "Do not trust yourself, lest you fall" (see 1 Corinthians 10:12). Even if you have failed, you can look into the face of Jesus as Peter did and remember He is praying for you.

Does some kind of deep trouble brew in your heart? Hear the words of Jesus and realize that Satan may have been given permission to sift you. Do not take it lightly—keep your eyes on Him.

An Ever-Increasing Revelation of Jesus Christ

Ever since the cross, all spiritual giants have had one thing in common: an unusually close communion with the Lord. They became lost in the glorious vastness of Christ and died lamenting they still knew so little of Him. So it was with Paul, with all the disciples, and with many early Church fathers; with Luther, Zwingli, and the Puritans; with the pious English preachers and with many godly leaders today.

Every one of these giants shared the same ruling passion: an ever-increasing revelation of Jesus Christ. They cared nothing for the spectacular, the earthly, the things of this world, success, ambition or worldly fame. They prayed only for a fuller revelation of the glory and vastness of their Lord.

Satan is displaying great power, and hell is unleashing all its fury on this generation. The enemy's strongholds are much more fortified, powerful and entrenched than in any past generation. Without a doubt, Satan is becoming better known, less feared and more accepted.

A basic Bible school knowledge of Christ will not be enough in this final war. Knowing *about* Him is not enough—we need to seek for a greater revelation of Him from the Holy Spirit. That requires one to spend much time at His table sitting in His presence, hearing His voice, waiting on Him for divine wisdom.

Paul was committed to an ever-increasing revelation of Jesus. All he had of Christ came by revelation: "By revelation He made known to me the mystery" (Ephesians 3:3). The Holy Spirit knew the deep and hidden secrets of God, and Paul prayed constantly for the gift of grace to understand and preach "the unsearchable riches of Christ" (verse 8).

God is looking for believers who will seek a revelation of Him that is all their own—a very deep personal intimacy that unlocks "the unsearchable riches of Christ."

The Greatest Test of All

"Then Moses stretched out his hand over the sea; and the Lord caused the sea to go back by a strong east wind all that night, and made the sea into dry land, and the waters were divided" (Exodus 14:21).

Before the Israelites was a path that would lead them to safety. In this crucial moment, God wanted His people to look at those walls and believe He would hold back the water until they arrived safely on the other side. Simply put, God wanted His people to have a faith that declared, "He who began this miracle for us will finish it. He has already proven to us He is faithful."

There was a reason God wanted this kind of faith for Israel at this point. They were about to face a journey through the wilderness where they would endure deprivation, danger and suffering. Now He said, "I want My people to know I will do them only good. I want them to have no fear because they know I am trustworthy in all things."

A true worshiper is not someone who dances *after* the victory or sings God's praises *after* the enemy has been vanquished. That is what the Israelites did. When God parted the Red Sea and they arrived on the other side, they sang and danced, praised God and extolled His greatness. Yet just three days later at Marah these same people murmured bitterly against God. These were not worshipers—they were shallow shouters!

A true worshiper is one who has learned to trust God in the storm. He is not afraid of the future, because he is no longer afraid to die.

I pray that all who read this message can say in the midst of their storm: "Yes, the economy may collapse. Yes, I may still be facing a dark, stormy night. But God has proven Himself faithful to me. No matter what comes, I will rest in His love."

SHARING IN GOD'S GREAT GOODNESS

If you ask anything in My name, I will do it" (John 14:14). We are told to ask largely and expect great things. We show forth the greatness of Christ by the greatness of our supplications. We are to make our needs known, but if we ask only for food, shelter and success we diminish our testimony of His greatness.

Scripture says the Kingdom of God is "joy, peace in the Holy Ghost." We serve a triumphant Christ and we are called to share in His triumph. So, do you ask for more of Christ's likeness? Do you ask in faith, in Jesus' name, for the rest He has promised?

God is waiting for and desiring greater requests from His children. Asking "in Jesus' name" is an invitation to share in the great goodness He has laid up for those who believe and who ask largely. God has a preconceived plan for every situation in your life, no matter what you face. You may be able to think of ways God could solve your crisis—but God's Word tells us that the human mind cannot conceive the ways of God.

God will not tell us what His plan is. He will not even give us a hint. He insists on our having faith in His promises, His majesty, His past miracles on our behalf. His word to us is: "Believe!" Your Lord has a way prepared—and He has the power to fulfill His plan. He would love to pull back the curtain and show us a passing view of His invisible ways but He will not.

Faith is evidence that cannot be seen. There can be no rest for us in our fiery trials until we fully believe He stands ready to do the unthinkable, the impossible. Our part is to simply trust that He will perform what He promised. Ask today for an ever-increasing spirit of rejoicing, even in your most trying time.

Do You Still Believe?

Recently I had an unusual experience while in meditation with the Lord. His still, small voice asked of me, "Do you still believe?"

"Do you still believe I love you unconditionally? That you are right now being led by the Holy Spirit—that every tear you shed I bottle—that at this very hour, in this place, you are in the perfect will of God?

"Do you believe that all things still work together for good to them that love Me? That I hear your prayers, even when you have no audible words to express them, when all seems dark and you are overwhelmed—when it seems I have shut the heavens to you?

"Do you still believe I feed all living things: the fish, the cattle, the fowls, all creeping things? Do you still believe I count every hair on your head—that I take note of every fallen bird on the face of the earth?

"Do you still believe when death comes to your loved ones? Do you still believe that I give comfort and strength to face even the grave?

"Do you still believe I love you? That I forgive all your sins past and present, and will forgive all future sins, if you rest and trust in Me? Do you believe I understand when Satan sends his messengers against you to implant lies, doubts, blasphemies, fears, despair?

"Do you still believe you are in the palm of My hand? That you are more precious than gold to your Savior? That eternal life is your future? That there is no power that can pluck you out of My hand? That I still am touched by every infirmity and affliction you endure? Do you still believe these things are true?"

My answer is emphatically, "YES! I still believe it all and more—much more!"

Read Psalm 103 and ask yourself, "Do I still believe it? All of it?"

Faith Is an Invitation More than a Command

Faith is a command. It is written, "The just *shall* live by faith." Without faith it is impossible to please God. Scripture adds, "If anyone draws back, My soul has no pleasure in him" (Hebrews 10:38).

I shudder when I think of the terror and dangers of unbelief. Unbelief is a bottomless pit of fear, anguish and discouragement, and the consequences are horrendous. Unbelief begins with fearing what we cannot see. One fear today leads to two fears tomorrow, then three, until fear becomes a ball of uncontrollable anguish and confusion.

More and more I see that fear and unbelief end up as hopelessness, leading into a wilderness of despair and emptiness. This is not a small issue with God—it is a matter of life and death. Fear is torment.

God's children are enduring afflictions and troubles of various kinds today. Some face overwhelming and frightful sufferings, both physical and spiritual, and are losing heart. If you are going through the refining fires, I have a word for you: *Faith is an invitation to partake of the great goodness of the Lord.*

I refer you to one of the most encouraging promises in all of God's Word.

> Oh, how great is Your goodness, which You have laid up for those who fear You, which You have prepared for those who trust in You in the presence of the sons of men! You shall hide them in the secret place of Your presence from the plots of man; you shall keep them secretly in a pavilion from the strife of tongues.
>
> Psalm 31:19–20

This is a bold, glorious promise! God says, "As you trust Me before men, I will open My storehouse of great goodness and pour it on you. I will hide you in the secret of My presence. I will not allow strife to overwhelm you."

Do not give up. We are too close to the end of the race, and our Lord awaits us!

A Bold Step of Faith

The disciples were on a stormy sea, frightened and far from shore, when Jesus came toward them on the water. It is one thing to have the Lord come to us in our trials and circumstances to calm our troubled souls. It is something else altogether for us to step out in the midst of turmoil and go after Him.

The disciples who stayed in the boat no doubt were thinking, "It is enough to have Him nearby, to know He cares for us in this storm. Let's just sit still and wait until He reaches us."

But Peter left the ship, a very bold step of faith. One glimpse of His Savior was enough for him. He cried out, "Lord, if it is You, command me to come to You on the water" (Matthew 14:28).

Jesus said, "Come." So, keeping his eyes firmly fixed on the Lord, Peter took that great step of faith—and for a while he walked on the water. Peter was not showing off his faith or trying to belittle those who stayed in the boat. He simply wanted to be nearer His Lord.

True, Peter sank when he took his eyes off the Lord, but so do we all. Peter walked on the water, not on a sea of glass. By faith he had discovered a place in Christ above the stormy, raging sea. The storm kept the waters roiling, but he walked over what threatened him—and that is the real lesson.

"When he saw that the wind was boisterous, he was afraid; and beginning to sink he cried out, saying, 'Lord, save me!'" (verse 30). Are we all not a bit afraid when strong, dark winds gather around us?

Often I have had that sinking feeling, wondering how I could stay above it all. Then I remember something my grandfather told me years ago: "David, keep your eyes on Jesus. Get as close to Him as you can. That is the secret to all victory, holiness and peace."

Recovery of Faith

I have a special word for all who face impossibilities: The recovery of your faith depends on a fuller revelation of the love our heavenly Father has toward us.

"The Lord your God in your midst, the Mighty One, will save; He will rejoice over you with gladness, He will quiet [rest] you in His love, He will rejoice over you with singing" (Zephaniah 3:17). This glorious scriptural revelation tells us God rests and rejoices in His love for us!

The Hebrew word for *quiet* here means that "God has not a single question concerning His love for us." In other words, He has settled His love for us once and for all, and He will never take it away. In fact, we are told God is so satisfied in His love for us that He *sings about it*.

Can you imagine this? There is a manifestation in heaven of God's delight over you! John Owen interprets the passage this way: "God leaps, as overcome with joy."

Moreover, Paul says, everything that is out of divine order—all that is of unbelief and confusion—is changed by the appearance of God's love. "The kindness and the love of God our Savior toward man appeared" (Titus 3:4).

In the preceding verse, Paul says, "For we ourselves were also once foolish, disobedient, deceived" (verse 3). Everything was out of order until God's love appeared.

When Paul says the love of God appeared, he uses a word from a Greek root meaning "superimposed." In short, the Lord looked down on us poor, struggling souls and He superimposed this revelation: "My love will deliver you. Rest and delight in My love for you."

I thank God for the day His love appeared to me. There is no faith that can stand against impossibilities unless everything—every problem, every affliction—is committed into the loving care of our Father. When our situations are at their worst, we must rest in simple faith.

Fully Persuaded

Abraham did not stagger in his faith. He was "fully convinced that what He [God] had promised He was also able to perform" (Romans 4:21). He recognized that God is able to work with nothing. Consider the Genesis account: Out of nothing, God created the world. With just a single word He creates.

When everything fails—when your every scheme has been exhausted—it is time for you to cast it all upon God. It is the time for you to give up all confidence in finding deliverance anywhere else. Then, once you are ready to believe, you must see God not as a potter who needs clay, but as a Creator who works from nothing. Out of nothing God will work in ways you could never have conceived.

How serious is the Lord about our believing Him in the face of impossibilities? We find the answer to this question in the story of Zacharias, the father of John the Baptist. Zacharias was visited by an angel who told him that his wife, Elisabeth, would give birth to a special child. But Zacharias, who was quite old, refused to believe it. God's promise alone was not enough for him.

Zacharias answered the angel, "I am an old man, and my wife is well advanced in years" (Luke 1:18). Simply put, Zacharias considered the impossibilities. He was saying, "This isn't possible. You have to prove to me how it will happen."

Zacharias' doubts displeased the Lord. The angel told him, "Behold, you will be mute and not able to speak . . . because you did not believe my words" (verse 20).

The message is clear: God expects us to believe Him when He speaks. Likewise, Peter writes: "Let those who suffer according to the will of God commit their souls to Him in doing good, as to a faithful Creator" (1 Peter 4:19).

In the Face of Impossibilities

"And not being weak in faith, [Abraham] did not consider his own body, already dead (since he was about a hundred years old), and the deadness of Sarah's womb" (Romans 4:19).

The essence of true faith is found in this single verse. God had just promised Abraham he would have a son who would become the seed of many nations. Remarkably, Abraham did not flinch at this promise, even though he was well past the age of siring children. Instead, when Abraham received this word, we are told he "did not consider his own body, already dead . . . [nor] the deadness of Sarah's womb."

To the natural mind, it was impossible for this promise to be fulfilled. But Abraham did not dwell on any such impossibility. He gave no thought to how God would keep His promise. The fact is, when God is at work producing a faith that is tried and better than gold, *He first puts a sentence of death on all human resources.* He closes the door to all human reasoning, bypassing every means of rational deliverance.

The faith that pleases God is born in a place of deadness. I am speaking of the deadness of all human possibilities, a place where man-made plans flourish at first and then die.

Have you been at this place of deadness? Has it seemed that you have no options left? You have no one to call for advice. The heavens are like brass when you pray, your requests falling to the ground.

I declare to you, *this is God at work.* His Spirit is working to get you to stop considering the impossibilities—to stop looking to human ways and means—to stop trying to think your way out of your situation. The Holy Spirit is urging you, "Quit hunting for help from some man. And quit focusing on how hopeless you think your situation is. Those are hindrances to your faith."

Christ Has Won the Battle for You

We receive many sad letters from believers who are still bound by sinful habits. Multitudes of struggling Christians write, "I can't stop gambling. . . . I'm in the grips of an alcohol addiction. . . . I'm having an affair and I can't break it off. . . . I'm a slave to pornography." In letter after letter, these people say the same thing: "I love Jesus and I have begged God to free me. I have prayed, wept and sought godly counsel, but I can't break free. What can I do?"

I have spent much time seeking the Lord for wisdom on how to answer these believers. I pray, "Lord, you know Your children's lives. Many are devoted, Spirit-filled saints, yet they lack Your victory and freedom. What is going on?"

At one point, I studied the biblical passages containing God's promises to His people. I was reminded that the Lord pledges to keep us from falling, to present us faultless, to justify us by faith, sanctify us by faith, keep us holy by faith. He promises that our old man is crucified by faith and that we are translated into His kingdom by faith.

The one thing common to all these promises is the phrase "by faith." Indeed, all these things are matters of faith, according to God's Word. So I came to the only clear conclusion about these struggling Christians' problems: Somewhere at the root of their bondage is unbelief. It all boils down to a simple lack of faith.

Are you struggling to gain victory by your willpower? Paul points out, "To him who works, the wages are not counted as grace but as debt. But to him who does not work but believes on Him who justifies the ungodly, his faith is accounted for righteousness" (Romans 4:4–5).

Your victory must come not through striving, but by faith that Jesus Christ has won the battle for you. God is faithful.

THE JOSEPH COMPANY

Joseph had a vision that his life would be used mightily by God, but that vision seemed like a pipe dream after his jealous brothers sold him into slavery. The following years of Joseph's life were filled with hardship and injustice. Then, when he seemed to get back on his feet, he was falsely accused of attempted rape and sent to prison.

Yet God was watching over Joseph's life the whole time. After years of turmoil, he ended up serving in Pharaoh's house and eventually was appointed ruler over all of Egypt.

That is how God works: He was preparing a man to save a remnant. Indeed, in every generation, the Lord raises up a Joseph Company. He takes these devoted servants through years of trouble and trials to prove and strengthen their faith.

What does this mean? Scripture says it is what Joseph endured: "He sent a man before them—Joseph—who was sold as a slave. They hurt his feet with fetters, he was laid in irons. Until the time that his word came to pass, the word of the Lord tested him" (Psalm 105:17–19).

The Lord also has a Joseph Company today, godly men and women He has touched and called. They do not seek fame or fortune. All they want is to live and die fulfilling the calling God has placed on them.

As Joseph looked back over his years of suffering he could testify, "God sent me on this journey. I see now that everything I have endured has led up to this moment."

What is the lesson here for God's people today? It is this: Our Lord has preserved us in the past and He will preserve us in the days ahead. He preserved you because He has a purpose for you.

You Will Survive

Happiness does not mean living without pain or hurt—not at all. True happiness is learning how to live one day at a time, in spite of sorrow and pain. It is learning how to rejoice in the Lord, no matter what has happened in the past.

You may feel rejected, abandoned and alone. Your faith may be weak and you think you are down for the count. Sorrow, tears, pain and emptiness may swallow you up at times. But God is still on the throne. He is still God!

Convince yourself that you will survive. Read His Word and meditate on it. You will come out of it; live or die, you belong to the Lord. Life does go on, and it will surprise you how much you can bear with God's help.

You cannot help yourself or stop the pain, but our blessed Lord will come to you. He will place His loving hand under you and lift you up to sit again in heavenly places. He will deliver you from the fear of dying—and He will reveal His endless love for you.

Look up! Encourage yourself in the Lord. When the fog surrounds you and you cannot see any way out of your dilemma, lie back in the arms of Jesus and simply trust Him. He has to do it all! He wants your faith and your confidence. He wants you to cry aloud, "Jesus loves me! He is with me and He will not fail me. He is working it all out right now. I will not be cast down, I will not be defeated. I will not be a victim of Satan, I will not lose my mind or my direction. God is on my side. I love Him and He loves me!"

The bottom line is *faith*. It rests on this one absolute: "No weapon formed against you shall prosper" (Isaiah 54:17).

My Promise Is All You Need

Faith is very demanding. It demands that once we hear God's Word we are to obey it, with no other evidence to direct us. It does not matter how big our obstacles may be, how impossible our circumstances—we are to believe His Word and act on it, with no other proof to go on. God says, "My promise is all you need."

Like every generation before us, we also wonder, "Lord, why am I faced with this test? It is beyond my comprehension. You have allowed so many things in my life that make no sense. Why is there no explanation for what I am going through? Why is my soul so troubled, so filled with great trials?"

Hear me again: The demands of faith are totally unreasonable to humankind. So, how does the Lord answer our cries? He sends His Word, reminding us of His promises, saying, "Simply obey Me. Trust My Word to you." He accepts no excuse, no matter how impossible our circumstances may seem.

Please do not misunderstand me. Our God is a loving Father, and He does not allow His people to suffer for no reason. We know He has at His disposal all the power and willingness to make every problem and heartbreak go away. He can merely speak a word and rid us of every trial and struggle.

Yet the fact is God will not show us how or when He will fulfill His promises to us. Why? He does not owe us any explanation *when He has already given us the answer*. He has given us everything we need for life and godliness in His Son. He is all we need for every situation life throws at us—and God is going to stand on the Word He has already revealed: "You have my Word within your reach. So, rest on my Word. Believe it and obey it."

The Unreasonableness of Faith

When God says to humankind, "Believe," He demands something that is wholly beyond reason. Faith's very definition has to do with something unreasonable, illogical.

Think about it: In Hebrews we read that faith is the substance of something hoped for, evidence that is unseen. We are being told, in short, "There is no tangible substance, no visible evidence." Yet we are asked to believe.

Right now, all over the world, multitudes of believers are bowed low in discouragement. We are all going to continue facing discouragement in this life. Yet if we understand the nature of faith—its illogical, unreasonable nature—we will find the help we need to get through.

In Genesis 12:1–4, God told Abraham, "Get up, go out, and leave your country." Surely Abraham wondered, "But where, Lord?" God would have answered simply, "I am not telling you. Just go."

This was not logical to any thinking person. I say to every Christian wife: Imagine that your husband came home one day and said, "Pack up, honey, we're moving." Of course, you would want to know why or where or how. But the only answer he gives you is, "I don't know. I just know God said to go."

"By faith Abraham obeyed when he was called to go out to the place which he would afterward receive as an inheritance. And he went out, not knowing where he was going" (Hebrews 11:8). Faith demanded that Abraham act on nothing more than this promise.

One starry night, God told Abraham, "Look up into the sky. See the innumerable stars? That is how many descendants you are going to have" (see Genesis 15:5). Abraham must have shaken his head at this. By now he was old, as was his wife, Sarah. Yet he was given a promise that he would become a father of many nations.

Abraham obeyed—and God came through in perfect Holy Ghost timing. He always does, and He will for you.

Thanksgiving in Adversities

One of the most important verses in all of Scripture is found in Peter's first epistle. The apostle speaks of the necessity of having our faith tested: "That the genuineness of your faith, being much more precious than gold that perishes, though it is tested by fire, may be found to praise, honor, and glory at the revelation of Jesus Christ" (1 Peter 1:7).

This passage suggests God is saying, "Your faith is precious to Me—more precious than all the wealth of this world, which one day will perish. In these last days—when the enemy sends all manner of evil against you—I want you to be able to stand strong with an unshakable faith."

He further says, "I will keep you and bless you through every dark day. Your part is to simply have faith in Me. You will be kept by My power, through faith!" "[You], who are kept by the power of God through faith for salvation ready to be revealed in the last time" (verse 5).

Peter tells us: "The Lord knows how to deliver the godly out of temptations" (2 Peter 2:9). The Greek word used for *temptation* here means "putting to proof by adversities."

Paul writes: "No temptation has overtaken you except such as is common to man; but God is faithful, who will not allow you to be tempted beyond what you are able, but with the temptation will also make the way of escape, that you may be able to bear it" (1 Corinthians 10:13).

Clearly, God does not want to keep us in our trials. Why would He be interested in keeping us in the midst of temptation and affliction? He does not get any glory from testing His children—but from the results of our testing!

He is God—He is faithful and protective—and He has given us promises He will keep.

Deal with Your Fears and Unbelief

Israel had fallen into idolatry but their root sin was still unbelief and fear. In His mercy, God sent them a prophet to expose their root sin.

The prophet told them, "Look at you—a bunch of wimps, hiding out, afraid to stand up and fight. You've already given up. But you have a history of God's deliverance! He gave your fathers great victories, and He has promised to deliver you too—yet you don't believe Him!" (see Judges 6:8–10).

Many Christians are terrified the devil is going to destroy them. They are afraid they will make a mistake or go back to their sin. But that is a lie from the pit of hell! The Bible says you do not have to be terrified as you walk through this life.

When you hold on to fear, it becomes contagious. When Gideon gathered his army, God told him to send home every fearful soldier: "Whoever is fearful and afraid, let him turn and depart. . . . And twenty-two thousand of the people returned" (7:3).

God is speaking the same word to His Church today, asking, "Why do you fear? Why do you sin by not trusting Me to bring victory into your life? I have promised to defeat every demonic power that comes against you."

Gideon's father, Joash, had erected statues of Baal and the goddess Asherah from huge stones for the people to worship. This became a powerful, demonic stronghold in Israel. God told Gideon, "I am not going to deliver Israel until you get rid of these idols. Lay them aside, Gideon. Cut them down."

God is giving His Church today the same message: "You are full of fear. And before I bring deliverance, you must pull down this stronghold, this besetting sin!"

"Lay aside every weight, and the sin which so easily ensnares us" (Hebrews 12:1). Victory comes by praying in faith, expecting God to answer.

Know, Believe and Keep Trusting in His Love

Anyone can keep his joy when he is riding high in the Holy Spirit. But God wants us to keep ourselves in His love at all times—especially in our temptations.

The apostle John tells us very simply how we can keep ourselves in God's love: "And we have known and believed the love that God has for us. God is love, and he who abides in love abides in God, and God in him" (1 John 4:16). In short, if we "abide in God's love," we are keeping ourselves in God.

The word *abide* here means "to stay in a state of expectancy." In other words, God wants us to expect His love to be renewed in us daily. We are to live in the knowledge that God has always loved us and will always love us.

In reality, most of us flit in and out of God's love according to our emotional ups and downs. We feel safe in His love only if we have done well, but when we are tried or tempted—or have failed Him—we become unsure of His love. He is telling us in these passages, "No matter what trial you face, or even if you fail, you must never doubt My love. If you are actively trusting in My love then you are living the way I want you to live."

Jeremiah 31 offers a wonderful illustration of God's love. Israel was in a backslidden state. The people were indulging in all kinds of wickedness, but suddenly they lost all pleasure in fulfilling their sensual appetites. When they cried out to the Lord in repentance, God heard their cry and His heart was touched. Still, He had to chasten them with His rod of correction (see Jeremiah 31:18–19).

Even when God's people sin against Him, He knows their struggle. Even though He has to chasten and speak hard words of truth, He freely forgives and restores—because He is love.

From the Battlefield of Faith

I went up . . . to Jerusalem . . . by revelation, and communicated to them that gospel which I preach" (Galatians 2:1–2). Paul went to Jerusalem to share a mystery that God wanted to reveal to His people.

This godly man had his own full, glorious revelation of Christ. He was not some isolated philosopher who dreamed up theological truths, thinking, "Someday my works will be read and taught by future generations."

Paul produced his epistles in dark, damp prison cells. He wrote them while wiping the blood from his back after being scourged, and after crawling from the sea, having survived another shipwreck.

Paul knew that all the truth and revelation he taught came from the battlefield of faith, and he rejoiced in his afflictions for the Gospel's sake. He said, "Now I can preach with all authority to every sailor who has been through a shipwreck, to every prisoner who has been locked up with no hope, to everybody who has ever looked death in the face. God's Spirit is making me a tested veteran so I can speak His truth to all who have ears to hear."

God is allowing your trial because the Holy Spirit is performing an unseen work in you. Christ's glory is being formed in you for all eternity.

I believe one of the great secrets of Paul's spirituality was his readiness to accept whatever condition he was in without complaining. He writes, "I have learned in whatever state I am, to be content" (Philippians 4:11).

Our part in every trial is to trust God for all the power and resources we need to find contentment in the midst of suffering. Don't misunderstand me—being "content" in our trials does not mean we enjoy them. It simply means we no longer try to protect ourselves from them. We are content to stay put and endure whatever is handed to us—because we know our Lord is conforming us to the image of Christ.

WHEN ALL MEANS FAIL

To believe when all means fail is exceedingly pleasing to God and is most acceptable. Jesus said to Thomas, "Because you have seen Me, you have believed. Blessed are those who have not seen and yet have believed" (John 20:29).

Blessed are those who believe when there is no evidence of an answer to prayer—who trust beyond hope when all means have failed.

You may have come to the place of hopelessness—the end of hope, the end of all means. A loved one is facing death and doctors give no hope. Death seems inevitable. Hope is gone. The miracle you prayed for is not happening.

That is when Satan's hordes come to attack your mind with fear, anger and overwhelming questions: "Where is your God now? You prayed until you had no tears left. You fasted. You stood on promises. You trusted."

Blasphemous thoughts will be injected into your mind: "Prayer failed. Faith failed. You don't have to quit on God—just do not trust Him anymore. It doesn't pay."

Even questioning God's existence will be injected into your mind. These have been the devices of Satan for centuries. Some of the godliest men and women who ever lived were under such demonic attacks.

To those going through the valley and shadow of death, hear this word: Weeping will last through some dark, awful nights—yet in that darkness you will soon hear the Father whisper, "I am with you. I cannot tell you right now why this is happening, but one day it will all make sense. You will see it was all part of My plan. It was no accident. It was no failure on your part. Hold fast. Let Me embrace you in your hour of pain."

Beloved, God has never failed to act but in goodness and love. When all means fail, His love prevails. Hold fast to your faith. Stand fast in His Word. There is no other hope in this world.

The Holy Ghost Is Received by Faith

"This only I want to learn from you: Did you receive the Spirit by the works of the law, or by the hearing of faith?" (Galatians 3:2).

This message should ignite our faith—and by faith we should lay hold of God's great promises: "Let him ask in faith, with no doubting, for he who doubts is like a wave of the sea driven and tossed by the wind. For let not that man suppose that he will receive anything from the Lord" (James 1:6–7).

Have you asked God for this gift? Are you seeking the Holy Spirit? "If you then, being evil, know how to give good gifts to your children, how much more will your heavenly Father give the Holy Spirit to those who ask Him!" (Luke 11:13).

Simply ask and you will receive. Seek your heavenly Father for the baptism of the Holy Spirit—and He will give it to you!

The devil is on the loose in our world today, unleashing all the power at his command, and legions of evil principalities are digging in for the final conflict. Yet Satan cannot stand up to a righteous, Holy Spirit-filled child of God who walks in faith and obedience.

Paul said, "Walk in the Spirit, and you shall not fulfill the lust of the flesh" (Galatians 5:16). He also said, "If we live in the Spirit, let us also walk in the Spirit" (verse 25).

Many believers tell me they walk in the Spirit, yet they cannot tell me what that truly means. *Walking in the Spirit is simply allowing the Holy Spirit to do in us what God sent Him to do.*

So, do you walk and live in the Spirit—and is this what it means to you? The Holy Spirit has come to dwell in you to seal, sanctify, empower and prepare you for each and every trial.

Claiming the Power That Is in Christ

As Jesus spent His last hours with His disciples, He said to them, "Most assuredly, I say to you, whatever you ask the Father in My name He will give you" (John 16:23). Then He told them, "Until now you have asked nothing in My name. Ask, and you will receive, that your joy may be full" (verse 24).

What an incredible statement. As this scene took place, Christ was warning His followers that He was going away and would not see them for a short time. In the very same breath, however, He assured them they had access to every blessing of heaven. All they had to do was ask in His name.

The disciples had been taught by Jesus to knock, seek and ask for the things of God. They were taught firsthand that all the blessings of the Father—all grace, power and strength—were found in Christ. They also had heard Jesus declare to the multitudes: "Most assuredly, I say to you, he who believes in Me, the works that I do he will do also; and greater works than these he will do, because I go to My Father. And whatever you ask in My name, that I will do, that the Father may be glorified in the Son. If you ask anything in My name, I will do it" (14:12–14).

I am convicted by Christ's words here to His disciples: "Until now you have asked nothing in My name" (16:24). As I read this, I heard the Lord whisper to me, "David, you have not claimed the power I have made available to you. You simply need to ask in My name."

I believe the ever-growing lack of faith in God's promises grieves His heart more than all the sins of the flesh combined. As His children, we are to ask largely—for wisdom, guidance and revelation. We are to ask in faith, doubting nothing. He wants us to live and move in His power!

He Wants It All

"Blessed are all those who wait for Him. . . . You shall weep no more. He will be very gracious to you at the sound of your cry. . . . Your ears shall hear a word behind you, saying, 'This is the way, walk in it,' whenever you turn to the right hand, or whenever you turn to the left. . . . You shall have a song as in the night . . . and gladness of heart" (Isaiah 30:18–19, 21, 29).

Isaiah was saying, "If you will just wait on the Lord—if you will cry out to Him again and return to trusting Him—He will do for you everything I have said and more."

God can speak one word and the enemy will falter: "For through the voice of the LORD Assyria will be beaten down" (verse 31). There is no matter our Father cannot solve, no battle He cannot win for us, with a mere word from His lips. Isaiah says "the breath of the Lord" will consume everything in our way (see verse 33).

This process of trusting God in all things is not easy, however. I once sought the Lord about a situation concerning our church building in New York City: "Father, I have sought You about this and I will be at peace." He answered me: "David, I am amazed that you can trust Me with your real estate, finances and other material things—yet you still will not trust Me with your physical well-being."

Yes, dear saint, He wants it all—your health, your family, your future. He wants you to live in quietness, confidence and rest. So, get alone with the Lord. He has promised, "You will hear My word behind you telling you which way to go. This is the way, now walk in it."

True faith trusts all things into His hands—and the evidence of faith is rest.

Spiritual Strength and Trust

The Holy Spirit gives us strength when we release all our needs into God's hands and trust in His might.

Ruth is an example of this kind of trust. After her husband died, Ruth lived with her mother-in-law, Naomi. Naomi was concerned about Ruth's welfare and future, so she advised Ruth to lie down at the feet of the wealthy Boaz and ask him to fulfill his obligation to her as her "kinsman."

That evening, after the day's winnowing was finished, Boaz lay down "at the end of the heap of grain" (Ruth 3:7) and pulled a blanket up over him. The next morning, he awoke startled, finding a woman lying at his feet. (There was nothing immoral about Ruth's presence; this was a common custom of the day.)

Ruth said to him, "Take your maidservant under your wing, for you are a close relative" (3:9). She was saying, in essence, "Will you take on the obligation of a relative for me? Will you provide for me?" She actually was asking, "Will you marry me?"

This was no manipulative scheme. Ruth and Naomi had done everything in divine order. We can be sure of this because Christ's lineage came through Ruth. When Ruth returned home, Naomi asked her, "Is that you, my daughter?" (3:16). She was asking, in other words, "Shall I call you 'engaged Ruth'? Or are you still 'widowed Ruth'?"

Naomi had prayed about the matter, seeking God's direction, and the Lord had given her counsel. He had reminded her of the law of the kinsman-redeemer (which was a type and foreshadowing of Christ). Naomi was confident that she and Ruth had done their part, so now it was time to sit still and trust God to perform what He had promised. These two faithful women relaxed, sang and praised the Lord—and they saw His promise fulfilled.

Have you prayed? Have you trusted? Are you ready to sit still and "see the salvation of the Lord"?

Go Ahead and Cry

When you hurt the worst, go to your secret closet and weep out all your despair. God encourages it.

Jesus wept. Peter wept—bitterly! Peter carried with him the hurt of denying the very Son of God, but he came back to shake the kingdom of Satan.

Jesus never turns away from a crying heart. The Bible says, "A broken and contrite heart . . . O God, You will not despise" (Psalm 51:17). Not once will the Lord say, "Get hold of yourself. Grit your teeth and dry your tears." No! Jesus stores every tear in His eternal container.

Do you hurt? Badly? Then go ahead and cry—and keep on crying until the tears stop flowing. Let those tears originate only from hurt, however, and not from unbelief or self-pity.

True happiness is found in learning how to live one day at a time in spite of all the sorrow and pain life brings. It is found in learning how to rejoice in the Lord no matter what has happened in the past.

You may feel rejected or abandoned. Your faith may feel weak. Sorrow, tears, pain and emptiness may swallow you up at times, but God is still on His throne. You cannot help yourself—if only you could stop the pain and hurt. But our Lord will come to you, place His loving hand underneath you and lift you up to sit again in heavenly places.

Look up! Encourage yourself in the Lord. When the fog surrounds you and you cannot see any way out of your dilemma, lie back in the arms of Jesus and simply trust Him. He wants your faith, your confidence. He will deliver you from fear—and reveal His endless love for you!

Tempting God

As Jesus stood at the highest point of the temple, Satan whispered to Him, "Go ahead—jump! If you are really God's Son, He will save you."

"Then the devil . . . said to Him, If You are the Son of God, throw Yourself down. For it is written, 'He shall give His angels charge concerning you,' and, 'In their hands they shall bear you up, lest you dash your foot against a stone'" (Matthew 4:5–6).

Do you see Satan's deviousness in this? He isolated a single promise from Scripture and tempted Jesus to cast His whole life upon it. He was suggesting, "You say God is with You—well, show me the proof. Your Father has already allowed me to harass You. Where was His presence in that? You can prove He is with You right now by jumping. If He is with You He will save You."

How did Jesus respond? He stated, "It is written again, 'You shall not tempt the Lord your God'" (4:7). What exactly does Jesus mean here by "tempting God"?

Ancient Israel is an example. Ten times the Lord proved Himself faithful to the Israelites. After every time, however, the people asked the same question: "Is God among us or not?" God calls this "tempting Him."

Jesus used this same phrase—"tempting God"—in His reply to Satan. What does this tell us? It shows us that it is a grave sin to doubt God's presence. We are not to question whether He is with us.

As with Israel, God has already given us an entire body of evidence. First, we have in His Word multiple promises of His closeness to us. Second, we have our personal history with God—a testimony of His many past deliverances in our lives. Third, we have a Bible full of witnesses to God's presence in past centuries.

The Bible is clear: We are to walk with God by faith and not by sight. Otherwise, we will end up like faithless Israel.

The New Man

As followers of Christ, we are to take God at His Word and accept as true what He says we are.

This means our "old man" represents a man who still seeks to please God in the flesh. Such a man may hate sin and not want to offend God, but his conscience continually brings him under guilt. So he pledges to overcome his sin problem: "I'm going to change! I'll start today to fight my besetting sin, no matter what the cost. I want God to see how hard I am trying."

Such a man brings to the Lord much sweat and many tears. He prays and fasts to prove to God that he has a good heart. He is able to resist sin for days at a time. So he tells himself, "If I can go for two days, then why not four, or even a week?" By the end of the month he feels good about himself, convinced he is working himself free. But then his old sin surfaces, and down he goes, deep into despair. The cycle then starts all over again.

His man-in-flesh was crucified along with Christ, killed in the eyes of God. Indeed, Paul tells us that the old man was pronounced dead at the cross. Jesus took that old man into the grave with Him, where He was left for dead and forgotten.

The new man is the one who has given up all hope of pleasing God by any effort of the flesh. He has died to the old ways of the flesh. By faith he has come to know there is only one way to please God, one way to delight him: *Christ must become all.*

This new man lives by faith alone: "The just shall live by faith." He believes God's Word so completely he leans on nothing else. He has found his source of everything in Christ, who is all-sufficient.

FULL CONTROL

There is no formula for living wholly dependent upon the Lord. All I can offer you is what God has been teaching me in this area. He has shown me two simple things about how I am to give Him full control.

First, I must be convinced the Lord is willing to make His will known to me, even in the smaller details of my life. I have to believe that the Spirit who abides in me knows God's will for me, and that He will guide me, lead me and speak to me.

"When He, the Spirit of truth, has come, He will guide you into all truth. . . . He will glorify Me, for He will take of what is Mine and declare it to you" (John 16:13–14).

You may be in the midst of an affliction that has been caused by too quick a decision. Even so, the Lord promises, "Your inner ear will hear my Spirit speaking to you, 'Go that way. Do this. Don't do that.'"

Second, we have to pray with unwavering faith for power to obey God's direction. Scripture says, "Let him ask in faith, with no doubting, for he who doubts is like a wave of the sea driven and tossed by the wind. For let not that man suppose that he will receive anything from the Lord" (James 1:6–7). When God tells us to do something, we need power to stay the course and obey Him fully.

Many of us pray, "Lord, I know what You told me, but I am not sure that was Your voice speaking."

That is not the faith response He is looking for from His children. You can pray all you want, but if you do not pray with faith, you will never have the mind of God conveyed to you. He wants to see that you are committed to accepting whatever He says, and to obeying it without question. This is how we please our faithful Father.

God's Plan: Our Testimony

By the close of the book of Genesis, God had chosen a small, insignificant people to become a teaching nation, a people who would be living examples of His goodness to the heathen world. To bring about such a testimony, God took His people into places that were beyond their control. He isolated Israel in a wilderness, where He alone would be their source of life.

Israel had no control over their survival in that desolate place. They could not control the availability of food or water or their destination. How would they eat and drink? Which direction would they travel—and where would they end up?

God would do it all for them, guiding them by a miracle cloud that glowed at night. He would feed them with angels' food from heaven and provide them with water from a rock. Yes, every single need would be supplied by the Lord, and no enemy would be able to defeat them.

"Out of heaven He let you [Israel] hear His voice, that He might instruct you" (Deuteronomy 4:36). God's people would hear His very words guiding them, and in turn they would testify, "Who among all of humankind has heard the voice of the living God?" (see verses 32–34).

The nations surrounding ancient Israel were filled with "gods" that were mute, unable to see or hear, unable to love, guide or protect the people who worshiped them. Yet the nations could see in Israel a special people whom God carried through a terrible wilderness—a living God who loved His people, answered prayers and provided miracles.

God raised up a people who would live under His authority and give Him full control of their lives—to become His testimony to the world.

Why would God want full control of His people? Because only He knows the way—and He will perform the impossible needed to get us there.

Increase Our Faith

Mark 4 relates a story of Jesus and His disciples in a boat, being tossed about on a stormy sea. As we pick up the scene, Christ has just calmed the waves with a single command. Now He turns to His disciples and asks, "How is it that you have no faith?" (Mark 4:40).

You may think this sounds harsh. It was only human to fear in such a storm. Yet Jesus was not chiding them for that reason. Rather, He was telling them, "After all this time with Me, you still do not know who I am. How could you possibly walk with Me for this long and not know Me intimately?"

Indeed, the disciples were astonished by the amazing miracle Jesus had performed. "They feared exceedingly, and said to one another, 'Who can this be, that even the wind and the sea obey Him!'" (verse 41). Can you imagine? Jesus' own disciples did not know Him. He had personally called each of these men to follow Him, and they had ministered alongside Him to multitudes. Yet they were still unaware of who their Master really was.

Tragically, the same is true today. Multitudes of Christians have ridden in the boat with Jesus, ministered alongside Him and reached multitudes in His name—but they really do not know their Master. They have not spent intimate time shut in with Him. They have never sat quietly in His presence, opening their hearts to Him, waiting and listening to comprehend what He wants to say to them.

Another time the disciples came to Jesus, requesting, "Increase our faith" (Luke 17:5). How did He answer them? "Gird yourself and serve me till I have eaten and drunk" (verse 8). Jesus was saying, in essence, "Put on your garment of patience. Then sit down with Me, open your heart and learn of Me."

Many Christians today ask the same question, but they do not seek the Lord for their answer. Will you?

The Faith of Abel

As we read Hebrews 11, we find a common denominator to the lives of the people mentioned. Each had a particular characteristic that denotes the kind of faith God loves. What was this element? *Their faith was born of deep intimacy with the Lord.*

It is impossible to have a faith that pleases God without sharing intimacy with Him. What do I mean by intimacy? I am speaking of a closeness to the Lord that comes from yearning after Him—a close personal bond, a communion. It comes when we desire the Lord more than anything else in this life.

"By faith Abel offered to God a more excellent sacrifice than Cain, through which he obtained witness that he was righteous, God testifying of his gifts; and through it he being dead still speaks" (Hebrews 11:4). Note several significant things about this verse. First, God Himself testifies of Abel's gifts or offerings. Second, Abel built an altar to the Lord, where he brought his sacrifices. Moreover, he offered not only unspotted lambs for the sacrifice, but the fat of those lambs as well. "Abel also brought of the firstlings of his flock and of their fat" (Genesis 4:4).

What does the fat signify? The book of Leviticus says, "[It is] as food, an offering made by fire for a sweet aroma; all the fat is the Lord's" (Leviticus 3:16). The fat was the part of the sacrifice that caught flame quickly, bringing about the sweet smell. The fat here serves as a type of fellowship that is acceptable to God. It represents our ministry to the Lord in the secret closet of prayer—an intimate worship that rises to Him like a sweet-smelling savor.

The Bible's first mention of this kind of worship is by Abel. It is why he is listed in the Hall of Faith in Hebrews 11 as a testimony of true, living faith. May we all aspire to the same kind of faith.

CRUMBS AND FAITH

The woman with the demon-possessed daughter persisted in seeking Jesus. Finally, the disciples urged their Master, "Lord, send her away, get rid of her. She won't stop bothering us."

Note Jesus' response to the woman's pleas: "But He answered her not a word" (Matthew 15:23). Evidently, Christ ignored the whole situation. Why would He do this?

Jesus knew this woman's story would be told to every future generation, and He wanted to reveal a truth to all who would read it. He was testing the woman's faith by saying, "I was not sent except to the lost sheep of the house of Israel" (verse 24). Christ was saying, "I came for the salvation of the Jews. Why should I waste their Gospel on a Gentile?"

This statement would have sent most of us on our way, but the woman did not budge. How many times have you grown weary in prayer and just given up? This woman did not reply with a complaint, or an accusing finger, saying, "Why are you denying me, Jesus?" Scripture says just the opposite: "Then she came and worshiped Him, saying, 'Lord, help me!'" (verse 25).

What follows next is hard to read. Once again, Jesus rebuffed the woman, only harsher. He told her, "It is not good to take the children's bread and throw it to the little dogs" (verse 26). He was testing her again.

Now the woman answered Him, "True, Lord, yet even the little dogs eat the crumbs which fall from their masters' table" (verse 27). What an incredible reply. The Lord commended her for it! "Jesus answered and said to her, 'O woman, great is your faith! Let it be to you as you desire.' And her daughter was healed from that very hour" (verse 28).

Beloved, we are not to settle for crumbs. We have been promised all the grace and mercy we need for our crises. We have been invited to come boldly to Christ's throne, with confidence. We must come that way in faith.

Beyond Human Hope

There comes a time when a situation is beyond human hope, seemingly impossible. No counsel, no doctor, no medication can help. It requires a miracle or all will end in devastation.

At such times, the only hope is for someone to take the responsibility to get to Jesus with the determination, "I am not leaving until I hear from the Lord. He has to tell me, 'It is done. Now go your way.'"

In the gospel of John we find just such a situation. A family was in crisis: "There was a certain nobleman whose son was sick at Capernaum" (John 4:46). This was a family of distinction, perhaps even royalty. A spirit of death hung over the home as the parents nursed their dying son.

Someone in that troubled family knew who Jesus was, however, and had heard of His miraculous power. Somehow word came to the household that Christ was in Cana, about 25 miles away. Scripture tells us, "When he heard that Jesus had come out of Judea into Galilee, he went to Him" (verse 47).

This desperate nobleman had a strong determination and got through to Jesus. The Bible says he "implored Him to come down and heal his son, for he was at the point of death" (same verse). What a marvelous picture of intercession. This man set aside everything to seek the Lord to provide a word.

Christ answered him, "Unless you . . . see signs and wonders, you will by no means believe" (verse 48). What did Jesus mean by this? He was telling the nobleman that a miraculous deliverance was not his most pressing need. Instead, the number-one issue was the man's faith. As a result, the whole household believed, including the servants: "[The father] believed, and his whole household" (verse 53).

Christ desired more than the son's healing for this man and his family. He wanted them to believe He was God in flesh so they would have faith in Him for salvation. Does He not want the same for us?

The Foundation of Faith

What is your faith built on? Scripture tells us faith comes by hearing, and that God's Word gives us "spiritual ears" that enable us to hear (see Romans 10:17).

The Bible talks about the wilderness experiences in our lives, in which we need spiritual ears to hear and recall His Word:

- "Let not the floodwater overflow me, nor let the deep swallow me up. . . . Hear me, O Lord, for Your lovingkindness is good. . . . Do not hide Your face from Your servant, for I am in trouble" (Psalm 69:15–17). Clearly waters of affliction flood the lives of the godly.
- "Before I was afflicted I went astray, but now I keep Your word. . . . It is good for me that I have been afflicted, that I may learn Your statutes" (119:67, 71). These verses make it perfectly clear that it is good for us—it even blesses us—to be afflicted at times.

Consider the psalmist's testimony: "I love the Lord, because He has heard my voice and my supplications. . . . The pains of death encompassed me, and the pangs of Sheol laid hold of me; I found trouble and sorrow" (Psalm 116:1–3). Here was a faithful servant who loved God and had great faith—yet he faced the sorrows of pain, trouble and death.

God's Word loudly declares that the path to faith is through the floods and fires: "When you pass through the waters, I will be with you; and through the rivers, they shall not overflow you. When you walk through the fire, you shall not be burned" (Isaiah 43:2). "For I, the Lord your God, will hold your right hand, saying to you, 'Fear not; I will help you'" (41:13).

This last verse holds an important key: In every wilderness experience we face, our Father is holding us by the hand. Yet, only those who go through the wilderness or are caught in raging rivers get this hand of comfort.

The Heathenism of Worry

"Therefore do not worry, saying, 'What shall we eat?' or, 'What shall we drink?' or, 'What shall we wear?' For after all these things the Gentiles seek" (Matthew 6:31–32).

Jesus tells us that worry—about the future of our family, about jobs, about how we are to survive—is a heathen's way of thinking. Jesus is talking here about those who have no heavenly Father. They do not know God as He wants to be known—as a caring, providing, loving Father in heaven.

"Therefore do not worry about tomorrow" (verse 34). In these plain words, Jesus commands us, "Do not give a thought, do not give a worry, about what might or might not happen tomorrow. You cannot change anything. When you worry, you are doing as the heathen do."

"But seek first the kingdom of God and His righteousness, and all these things shall be added to you" (verse 33). In other words, we are to go on loving Jesus. We are to move on, casting all our cares on Him, resting in His faithfulness. Our heavenly Father will see to it that we are supplied with all the essential things of life.

I wonder if the angels are baffled by all the worrying and anxiousness of those who claim to trust in God. To them it must seem so degrading, so insulting to the Lord that we worry as if we had no caring Father in heaven. What perplexing questions the angels must ask among themselves:

"Do they not believe their Father in heaven loves them? Did He not tell them He knows all about their needs? How can they fret and worry if they know He owns all power and wealth and can supply the needs of all creation? Why would they accuse their heavenly Father of neglect as if He were not true to His word?"

You have a heavenly Father. He is faithful—trust Him!

THE ULTIMATE TEST OF FAITH

There comes a time in the life of every believer—as well as in the Church—when God puts us to the ultimate test of faith. It is the same test Israel faced on the wilderness side of the Jordan.

This test is to look at all the dangers ahead—the giant issues facing us, the high walls of affliction, the principalities and powers that seek to destroy us—and cast ourselves totally on God's promises. The test is to commit ourselves to a lifetime of trust and confidence in His Word. It is a commitment to believe that God is bigger than all our problems and enemies.

Our heavenly Father is not looking for a faith that deals with one problem at a time. He is looking for a lifetime faith, a lifelong commitment to believe Him for the impossible. This kind of faith brings a calm and rest to our soul, no matter what our situation.

Our Lord is loving and longsuffering, but He will not allow His people to dwell in unbelief. You may have been tested time after time, but now the time has come for you to make a decision. God wants faith that endures the ultimate test, a faith that will not allow anything to shake you from trust and confidence in His faithfulness.

We simply cannot conjure up faith. We cannot create it by repeating, "I believe, I really believe." No, faith is a commitment we make to *obey* God.

As Israel faced Jericho, the people were told not to say a word but simply to march. In short, God asked one thing of them: to obey His Word and go forward. They did not whisper, "Help me to believe, Lord." Instead, they simply obeyed.

That is faith. It means setting your heart to obey all that is written in God's Word, without questioning it or taking it lightly.

Peace and Safety

One thing I dread above all others is that I would drift away from Christ. I shudder at the notion that I would become slothful, spiritually neglectful, caught up in prayerlessness, going for days without seeking God's Word.

In my travels around the world I have witnessed a "spiritual tsunami" of sinful drifting. Entire denominations have been caught up in the waves of this tsunami, leaving in their wake the ruins of apathy in their churches. The Bible warns clearly that it is possible for devoted believers to drift from Christ.

For example, a Christian who goes after "peace and safety at any cost," merely hanging on to salvation, pays a high spiritual price. So how can we guard against drifting from Christ and neglecting "so great a salvation"? Paul tells us: "Therefore we must give the more earnest heed to the things we have heard, lest we drift away" (Hebrews 2:1).

God is not interested in our being able to "speed-read" through His Word. Reading many chapters a day or trying to get through the Bible quickly may give us a good feeling. More important, however, is that we "hear" what we read with spiritual ears and meditate on it.

Staying steadfast in God's Word was no small matter for Paul. He lovingly warns us to be very careful to stay in the Word because it is an anchor to keep us from drifting. Paul urges, "As lovers of Christ, take a spiritual inventory. You know enough about your walk with Jesus to know you are loved by Him, that He has not turned from you, that you are redeemed."

Do you see a bit of drifting in your life? Are you praying less and less? Are you neglecting His Word? Is your walk with the Lord as it should be?

"For we have become partakers of Christ if we hold the beginning of our confidence steadfast to the end" (3:14).

The Hermit Crab

King David grew weary of his struggles. He was so tired in soul, so beset by troubles, all he wanted was to escape to a place of peace and safety: "Oh, that I had wings like a dove! For then I would fly away and be at rest. . . . I would hasten my escape from the windy storm and tempest" (Psalm 55:6–8).

A lesson from nature reveals what happens when we walk away from our struggle. Crabs are creatures that live in a rough, dangerous environment among jagged rocks. Daily they are dashed about by waves and attacked on every side by creatures from deeper waters. They battle continually to protect themselves, and over time they develop a strong shell and powerful instincts for survival.

Amazingly, some in the crab family, known as hermit crabs, give up the struggle. Searching for a safe haven, they take up residence in the cast-off shells of other ocean creatures. They retreat from the battle and escape into secondhand houses that are ready-made.

Yet hermit crabs' "safe houses" prove to be costly and ruinous. Through their lack of struggle, crucial parts of their bodies deteriorate. Over time hermit crabs lose all power of motion; their limbs simply fall off, leaving them out of danger but useless to do anything except exist.

Meanwhile, crabs that continue the struggle flourish. Their five pairs of legs become meaty and strong from resisting the powerful tides. They learn to hide from predators by scuttling under rock formations.

This law of nature illustrates the law of the Spirit. As believers, we get tossed and pounded by wave after wave of difficulties. Yet as we fight on, holding on to faith, we grow stronger. We also come to recognize the devil's wiles when he employs them against us. We discover our true refuge, the "cleft in the rock," by trusting in Jesus. Only then are we truly safe in the midst of our battle.

Jesus Had a Plan

Then Jesus lifted up His eyes, and seeing a great multitude coming toward Him, He said to Philip, 'Where shall we buy bread, that these may eat?' But this He said to test him, for He Himself knew what He would do" (John 6:5–6).

Jesus took Philip aside, and said, "Philip, there are thousands of people here. They are all hungry. Where are we going to buy enough bread to feed them? What do you think we should do?"

How incredibly loving of Christ. Jesus knew all along what He was going to do—the verse above tells us so. Yet the Lord was trying to teach Philip something, and the lesson He was imparting to him applies to each of us today.

Consider how many of us in Christ's Body sit up half the night trying to figure out our problems. We think, "Maybe this will work. No, no, maybe that will solve it."

Philip and the apostles did not have just a bread problem. They had a bakery problem, and a money problem, and a distribution problem, and a transportation problem, and a time problem. Add it all up and their situation seemed absolutely impossible.

Jesus knew all along exactly what He was going to do—He had a plan. Beloved, the same is true of your troubles and difficulties today. There is a problem but Jesus knows your whole situation. He comes to you, asking, as he did Philip, "What are we going to do about this?"

The correct answer from Philip would have been, "Jesus, You are God. Nothing is impossible with You. I am giving this problem over to You. It is no longer mine but Yours."

That is just what you need to say to the Lord today in your crisis: "Lord, I trust in Your power. I surrender it all to You."

I Am Power and Compassion

Then Jesus called His disciples to Himself and said, 'I have compassion on the multitude, because they have now continued with Me three days and have nothing to eat. And I do not want to send them away hungry, lest they faint on the way'" (Matthew 15:32).

Christ was saying to His disciples, "I am going to do more for the people than heal them. I will make sure they have enough bread to eat. You must see that I am more than just power—I am also compassion. If you only see Me as a healer or miracle worker, you will fear Me—but if you also see Me as compassionate, you will love and trust Me."

This message is for all who are on the brink of exhaustion, about to faint, overwhelmed by your present situation. You have been a faithful servant, feeding others, confident that God can do the impossible for His people. Yet you have some lingering doubts about His willingness to intervene in your struggle.

I wonder how many readers of this message have spoken words of faith to others who are facing distressing, seemingly hopeless situations. You have urged them, "Hold on! The Lord is able. He is a miracle-working God and His promises are true. Do not lose hope!"

The Holy Spirit asked me, *"Do you really believe in miracles?"*

I answered, "Yes, of course, Lord. I believe in every miracle I have read about in Scripture." Beloved, this answer is not good enough. The Lord's question to each one of us really is: "Do you believe I can work a miracle *for you?*" And not just one miracle, but a miracle for every situation we face. We need more than Old Testament miracles, New Testament miracles, bygone miracles. We need up-to-date, personal miracles that are designed just for us and our situation.

Rest in the Father's care—and trust Him for your miracle.

FOUR EXPECTATIONS

God is a promise maker and a promise keeper, and He has spoken to my heart about four things His people are to trust Him for. These expectations are based on God's promises.

1. Expect to be rewarded as you diligently seek the Lord. "[God] is a rewarder of those who diligently seek Him" (Hebrews 11:6).

God is always on time, and He knows you need a ray of hope and good news in your testing time. Expect Him to keep His promise to reward you when you are in greatest need. God says He rewards those who diligently seek Him—and He cannot lie.

2. Expect to see evidence of a progressive miracle in your life. "With God all things are possible" (Mark 10:27).

I believe in instantaneous and progressive miracles. Progressive miracles start in unseen, quiet ways and unfold little by little, one small mercy at a time. Expect to see God working in mysterious ways, unseen to the human eye.

3. Expect to enter into God's promised place of rest. "There remains therefore a rest for the people of God . . . enter that rest" (Hebrews 4:9, 11).

In the last few years the world has seen an outpouring of incredible calamities, problems and trials. In the midst of this, the Lord desires that you believe Him to bring you into His promised rest. God never intended that His children live in fear and despair.

4. Expect the Holy Spirit to be always in His temple. "Do you not know that your body is the temple of the Holy Spirit?" (1 Corinthians 6:19).

The Holy Spirit abides in the heart of every believer. Face each day knowing He is in His temple to comfort you, guide you, encourage you, anoint you and reveal the glory of Jesus Christ in you. He wants to bring you into unshakable faith. Believe these promises! Lay hold of these expectations and you will see God do marvelous things.

A Good Report

By [faith] the elders obtained a good testimony" (Hebrews 11:2).

The Greek word for *obtained* here means "to bear witness, to become a testimony." Our ancestors in the Lord had a settled, unwavering faith that became a testimony to God's faithfulness in troubled times.

They had trusted God through floods, mockery, bonds, imprisonment, torture, warfare, lions' dens, fires. After it all, they knew the Lord was smiling at them and saying, "Well done! You believed and trusted Me."

"Without faith it is impossible to please Him, for he who comes to God must believe that He is, and that He is a rewarder of those who diligently seek Him" (verse 6). Whenever we hold our faith position through hard times, we have the same affirmation from the Holy Spirit: "Well done!"

Indeed, Scripture says that when I cast every burden on Christ, I obtain a "good report." Those who watch my life may not respond openly, but they will know there is hope and redemption available to them. They can look at me in my hour of crisis and say, "There is hope! There stands someone who has not lost faith in his God."

As calamities increase and the world falls into great distress, the believer's response must be a testimony of unwavering faith. We have the Holy Spirit abiding in us, and we have the Bible as the fully revealed Word of God. We cannot boast in our own flesh, but we can lean on His Word.

Over the years, I have gone out fully armed, determining, "I will set my heart and I will not fear. I will not listen to the doubts and fears of my flesh. I will not waver and I will not turn back. I will not pout, fret or wallow in self-pity." I still have so much to learn, but I have tasted the victory that comes when I trust the Lord and lay all my burdens on Christ.

"Setting" Our Faith

I am convinced people lose hope because they have lost faith. Christians who once espoused faith are giving up their trust in God in the midst of their hard times.

Where are God's people to turn for hope? The Spirit spoke a clear word to me: "You have to anchor your faith. Set your heart to trust God in everything, at all times."

To "set" our faith means to stabilize, make unshakable, set down roots, put pillars underneath, lay a foundation. James writes, "He who doubts is like a wave of the sea driven and tossed by the wind. For let not that man suppose that he will receive anything from the Lord" (James 1:6–7).

In this passage, the Lord lays the whole responsibility on the believer. God is telling us, "When the world looks at My people in these days of trembling and anxiety, they have to be able to see faith. While everything is shaking, faith is what must remain solid and unshakable. So anchor your faith and take a fixed position."

The world needs to see an illustrated sermon—that is, the life of a man or woman who is living out faith. They need to see servants of God go through the same calamities they are facing and not be shaken by them.

David described this when he spoke of "those who trust in You in the presence of the sons of men!" (Psalm 31:19). He was talking about believers whose strong trust and faithful lives are beams of hope to those in darkness.

I once received a phone call with news that shook me. For a moment, a flood of fear swept over me, but the Holy Spirit gently whispered, "Hold your faith position. I have everything under control. Just stand steadfast."

Peace flooded through me at that moment. By day's end, my heart was full of joy as I realized, "I trusted You, Lord. I did not waver—and You came through. Thank You!" God is faithful.

A WAY KNOWN ONLY TO GOD

"The steps of a good [righteous] man are ordered by the Lord" (Psalm 37:23). The Hebrew word for *ordered* in this verse means "fixed, preplanned." God does not plan out our path a day ahead or a week or a year ahead. No, He has an entire life-plan laid out for every believer, a plan that goes into operation the moment we are saved.

What is this preplanned path? Jesus answers very simply, "*I am the way*" (John 14:6). Christ Himself is the path to glory and eternal life. He leads us toward our final destination in heaven. The book of Hebrews tells us Jesus is "bringing many sons to glory" (Hebrews 2:10).

We cannot know the specific route that Jesus will take us or what the rest of our journey will look like. That path is known only to God. Take my own life, for example. I have been en route to glory for more than seventy years. Along the way God has given me some goals, some dreams and some visions, which I have pursued. But the Lord has never outlined the entire path to me. In fact, even after all these years I am not sure where the path will lead me tomorrow.

When Jacob was old, he described his own path to Pharaoh: "The days of the years of my pilgrimage are one hundred and thirty years; few and evil have been the days of the years of my life" (Genesis 47:9). The Hebrew word for *evil* here signifies calamities, afflictions, sorrows, troubles, adversities.

I can identify with Jacob. I would not want to relive certain periods of my own pilgrimage. Of course, I praise God for all blessings and I am grateful for the faith He has built in me. Yet I would want to know how everything turns out, of course—but that is not the way God works. The path of every believer is one of faith.

Days of Excitement

God, in His love and mercy, is allowing disasters to strike the earth. These are warnings to all who would hear that Jesus is coming back. His message is, "It is time to get ready."

The Lord loves His children too much to bring His new Kingdom to pass without warning. He knows that humankind is hard of hearing and that it takes disasters of massive proportions to get our attention. These disasters are a kind of countdown, too painful to ignore and allowed by God to set the stage for the final moments of time.

According to Jesus, these labor pains will become more frequent and intense as we approach the last hour. "Now when these things begin to happen, look up and lift up your heads, because your redemption draws near" (Luke 21:28).

Does it all sound scary? Is the truth frightening? Is it really possible the end of the world is upon us? Is this the very point in time that all the prophets in the Bible predicted would come? Can even the most devout Christian remotely understand how terribly close this earth is to the midnight hour? One thing is certain—everything appears to be falling apart, as far as the natural eye can discern.

Dearly beloved, I offer you what the Holy Spirit spoke to me about these days. It is contained in just five little words, but the words are so powerful they awakened in me a glorious new hope and faith. Those five little words are: *God has everything under control.*

If you trust God, you can look every disaster in the face and proclaim with confidence, "My God is speaking to this universe and is demonstrating His power. I will stand still in faith and see the salvation of the Lord."

Yes, our God has everything under control. His message for this hour is: "For God has not given us a spirit of fear, but of power and of love and of a sound mind" (2 Timothy 1:7).

Earthen Vessels

One of the most encouraging passages in the Bible comes from Paul in 2 Corinthians 4:7: "But we have this treasure in earthen vessels, that the excellence of the power may be of God and not of us."

Paul goes on to describe these earthen vessels as dying men from biblical history—men troubled on every side, perplexed, persecuted, cast down. Even though never in despair, these men who were used by God were constantly groaning under the burden of their bodies, waiting anxiously to be clothed with new ones.

You see, God mocks man's power. He laughs at our egotistical efforts at being good. He bypasses the high and mighty and uses the weak things of this world in order to confound the wise.

> For you see your calling, brethren, that not many wise according to the flesh, not many mighty, not many noble, are called. But God has chosen the foolish things of the world to put to shame the wise, and God has chosen the weak things of the world to put to shame the things which are mighty; and the base things of the world and things which are despised God has chosen . . . that no flesh should glory in His presence.
>
> 1 Corinthians 1:26–29

Wow, does this ever describe me! Weak thing, foolish thing, despised thing, base thing, a thing not very noble, not very smart, not very mighty. What insanity to think God could use such a creature! Yet that is His perfect plan—and it is the greatest mystery on earth.

God calls us in our weaknesses, even when He knows we will do things wrong. He puts His priceless treasure in earthen vessels, because He delights in doing the impossible with nothing.

God has determined to accomplish His goal on earth through men and women with weaknesses. As it is written of Abraham, who had many weaknesses but had faith, he "believed God, and it was accounted to him for righteousness" (Romans 4:3).

All He Wants Is Your Faith

So you have turned everything over to the Lord's hands. You are trusting Him, casting all your cares upon Him. You are believing in His promises to keep you, protect you and cause you to walk uprightly before Him. You declare, "I believe God's Word. I may not have arrived yet, but I know it is not my job to make that happen. It is the Lord's. I know that somehow, by His Spirit working in me, He is going to get me there."

God does not want your home, your car, your furniture, your savings, your possessions. All He wants is your faith—your strong belief in His Word.

This may be the one thing lacking in others who appear "more spiritual." You may look at another person as being more spiritual than you, but that person may actually be struggling hard to keep up an appearance of righteousness. The truth is that as God looks at you He declares, "There is a righteous man or woman." Why? Because you have trusted in the Lord to give you *His* righteousness.

Paul tells us we are deemed righteous in God's eyes for the same reason Abraham was: "Therefore it was accounted to [Abraham] for righteousness. Now it was not written for his sake alone that it was imputed to him, but also for us. It shall be imputed to us who believe in Him who raised up Jesus our Lord from the dead" (Romans 4:22–24).

You may claim, "I believe this. I have faith in the God who resurrected Jesus." When everything looks hopeless—when you are in an impossible situation, with no resources and no hope before you—do you believe God will be your Jehovah Jireh, seeing to your need?

Believe He is committed to keeping His eternal promises to you. Trust that if only a single word of His fails, the heavens would melt and the universe collapse. That is how committed He is to keeping His promises to His children!

A Prayer of Faith . . . about Sin

Let me give you an example of a prayer of faith. Daniel told Israel why their prayers had not been answered for seventy years: "All this disaster has come upon us; yet we have not made our prayer before the Lord our God, that we might turn from our iniquities and understand Your truth" (Daniel 9:13).

According to righteous Daniel, Israel's prayers were hindered for decades by sin. Daniel was saying, "I see now why God was not listening to us. It is because we refused to deal with sin. We did not make our iniquity a matter of prayer—and it has cost us God's favor and blessing."

So Daniel prayed this prayer of faith: "I set my face toward the Lord God to make request by prayer and supplications, with fasting, sackcloth, and ashes. And I prayed to the Lord my God, and made confession, and said, 'O Lord, great and awesome God, who keeps His covenant and mercy with those who love Him, and with those who keep His commandments, we have sinned and committed iniquity, we have done wickedly and rebelled, even by departing from Your precepts and Your judgments'" (verses 3–5).

Before Daniel could even finish praying, God sent the angel Gabriel to him: "Now while I was speaking, praying, and confessing my sin and the sin of my people Israel . . . the man Gabriel, whom I had seen in the vision at the beginning, being caused to fly swiftly, reached me about the time of the evening offering" (verses 20–21).

Beloved, Daniel was touched by God Himself. And immediately Israel was back in relationship with the Lord.

I ask you, why was this man's prayer answered so quickly? Because it was a true prayer of faith. Simply put, Daniel believed that God judges sin but He also shows mercy.

The Lord is ready to answer your prayer today, but you must face your sin. Then He will come to you quickly!

Having a Perfect Heart

Do you know it is possible to walk before the Lord with a perfect heart? If you are hungering for Jesus, you may already be trying—desiring earnestly—to obey this command of the Lord.

Having a perfect heart has been part of the life of faith from the time God first spoke to Abraham: "I am Almighty God; walk before Me and be blameless [perfect]" (Genesis 17:1). I want to encourage you: Having a perfect heart is possible. Otherwise, God would not have given us such a call.

In the Old Testament we see that some succeeded. David, for instance, determined to obey God's command to be perfect. He said, "I will behave wisely in a perfect way. . . . I will walk within my house with a perfect heart" (Psalm 101:2).

To come to grips with the idea of perfection, we first must understand that perfection does not mean a sinless, flawless existence. Perfection in the Lord's eyes is something entirely different—it means having completeness, maturity.

The Hebrew meanings of *perfection* include "uprightness, having neither spot nor blemish, being totally obedient." It means "to finish what has been started, to make a complete performance." John Wesley called this concept of perfection "constant obedience." That is, a perfect heart is a responsive heart, one that answers quickly and totally all of God's wooing, whispering and warning. Such a heart says at all times, "Speak, Lord, for your servant is listening. Show me the path, and I will walk in it."

The perfect heart cries out with David, "Search me, O God, and know my heart" (Psalm 139:23). God does indeed search our hearts: "I, the Lord, search the heart" (Jeremiah 17:10).

The perfect heart seeks to be in God's presence always, to dwell in communion, talking with the Lord, sharing sweet fellowship with Him, seeking His face and knowing His presence in our daily walk. Ask in faith for this kind of heart today.

The Exceeding Danger of Unbelief

"Beware, brethren, lest there be in any of you an evil heart of unbelief in departing from the living God. . . . And to whom did He swear that they would not enter His rest, but to those who did not obey? So we see that they could not enter in because of unbelief" (Hebrews 3:12, 18–19).

Hebrews warns the New Testament Church: "Take heed to Israel's example. If you do not, you may fall as they did. You will descend into evil unbelief, and it will turn your life into one long wilderness."

God told this unbelieving generation pointedly, from the leaders to the Levites on down, that His hand would be against them. From then on, they would know distress and leanness of soul. They would not see His glory. Instead, they would become focused on their own problems and consumed by their own lusts.

The same thing happens with all unbelieving people. They end up consumed with their own welfare, with no vision, no sense of God's presence and no prayer life. They no longer care about their neighbors or a lost world. Instead, the entire focus of their lives is on their problems, their troubles, their illnesses. They go from one crisis to another, shut up in their own pain, their days filled with confusion, strife, envy and division.

Without faith, it is simply impossible to please God. After God walled up the waters of the Red Sea and let the Israelites walk through safely, they danced and rejoiced. Yet just three days later these same Israelites grumbled against God, questioning His very presence in their midst. For 38 years Moses watched as one by one every Israelite in that unbelieving generation died—their lives wasted.

Likewise today, some Christians are content to merely exist until they die, risking nothing to believe God. They refuse to believe His Word, and are just living to die. Beloved, take the warning of Hebrews to heart: "Beware, brethren, lest there be in any of you an evil heart of unbelief in departing from the living God."

PART 4

The Life of Prayer

He Delights in Intimacy with Us

Hell-Shaking Prayer

When the book of Daniel was written, Israel was in captivity to Babylon. By chapter 6, after a long life in ministry, Daniel was eighty years old.

Daniel had always been a praying man, and now in his old age he had no thoughts of slowing down. On the contrary, Daniel was just beginning. Scripture shows that even as this man turned eighty, his prayers shook hell, enraging the devil.

King Darius promoted Daniel to the highest office in the land. He became one of three co-equal presidents, ruling over princes and governors of 120 provinces. Darius favored Daniel over the other two presidents, putting Daniel in charge of forming government policy and teaching all the court appointees and intellectuals (see Daniel 6:3).

Obviously, Daniel was one busy prophet with a busy schedule and pressure-filled, time-consuming meetings. Nothing, however, could take Daniel away from his times of prayer, which remained his central occupation, taking precedence over all other demands. Three times a day he stole away from all his obligations, burdens and demands as a leader to spend time with the Lord. He simply withdrew from all activities and prayed—and God answered him. Daniel received all his wisdom, direction, messages and prophecies while on his knees (see verse 10).

The prayer that shakes hell comes from the faithful, diligent servant who sees his nation and the Church falling deeper into sin. He falls on his knees, crying, "Lord, I do not want to be a part of what is going on. Let me be an example of Your keeping power in the midst of this wicked age."

Too busy to pray? Do you say, "I just take it by faith"? You may think to yourself, "God knows my heart—He knows how busy I am. I give Him 'thought prayers' throughout the day."

I believe the Lord wants quality, unhurried time alone with us. Prayer then becomes an act of love and devotion, not just petition time. Daniel is our example—and his prayers saw results!

A CLEAR WORD, AND DARKNESS VANISHES

Paul said, "For in Him we live and move and have our being" (Acts 17:28). Every servant of God lives within a very small circle. Our life, our every move, our very existence is wrapped up only in the interests of Christ.

To know nothing but Christ there must be a continual flow of revelation from the Holy Spirit. If the Holy Spirit knows the mind of God—if He searches the deep and hidden things of the Father, if He is to be living water springing up—then the well of flowing water must be a continual, never-ending revelation of Christ. It awaits every servant of the Lord who is willing to wait on Him—quietly in faith, believing and trusting the Holy Spirit to manifest the mind of God.

Today we need to hear God's word to His Church—a word "in season," a true and living revelation that speaks to our times. Samuel had that kind of word from God, and all of Israel knew it. When Samuel spoke, out of all the voices in the land his alone came through powerfully, and not one word fell to the ground.

Today multitudes are trying to sift through all the voices to hear the clear word of God. The whole world lies in darkness, and light alone will dispel that darkness. Christ alone is the light, as Peter says: "And so we have the prophetic word confirmed, which you do well to heed as a light that shines in a dark place" (2 Peter 1:19).

"For it is the God who commanded light to shine out of darkness who has shone in our hearts to give the light of the knowledge of the glory of God in the face of Jesus Christ" (2 Corinthians 4:6).

Your good works alone will not dispel the darkness, and our preaching on social issues will not cut through it. Even your personal experiences will not do it. All darkness vanishes in the light of God's glory reflected in the face of Jesus Christ!

The Making of a Worshiper

Exodus 14 describes an incredible moment in Israel's history. The Israelites had just left Egypt under God's supernatural direction and were being hotly pursued by Pharaoh's army. They had been led into a valley surrounded on both sides by steep mountains, and ahead of them was a forbidding sea. They were about to experience the darkest, stormiest night of their souls—an agonizing time of panic and despair that would test them to their very limits.

I believe this portion of Scripture has everything to do with how God makes His people into worshipers. Indeed, no other chapter in the Bible demonstrates this more strongly. You see, worshipers are not made during revivals—in the good, sunny times, or periods of victory and health. Worshipers of God are made during dark, stormy nights. How we respond to our storms in turn determines what kind of worshipers we are.

Hebrews 11 gives us this image of Jacob in his old age: "By faith Jacob, when he was dying, blessed each of the sons of Joseph, and worshipped, leaning upon the top of his staff" (Hebrews 11:21). Why was Jacob portrayed this way in his dying days?

Jacob knew his life was about to end. That is why we see him giving his blessing to his grandchildren. So, what does Jacob do as he looks back on the events of his life? He is moved to worship. Not a word is spoken by this man. We are told that as he leans on his staff, marveling at the life God had given him, "he worshiped."

Jacob worshiped God in that moment because his soul was at rest. He had proven God faithful beyond any shadow of a doubt. Now the patriarch concluded, "It never mattered what battle I went through—God proved Himself faithful to me. He has always been faithful. O Lord, Almighty God, I worship you!"

May the same be true of us!

Do Three Things

In the midst of Israel's trial, God told them to do three things: "Fear not. Stand still. See the salvation of the Lord."

God's call to Israel was, "I am going to fight for you. You are simply to be quiet and put everything into My hands. Right now, I am doing a work in the supernatural realm. Everything is under My control, so do not panic. Trust that I am fighting your enemy. This battle is not yours" (see Exodus 14:13–14).

Dusk soon fell over the camp. This was the beginning of Israel's dark and stormy night—but it was also the beginning of God's supernatural work. He sent an awesome, protective angel to stand between His people and their enemy, the Egyptians. I believe God still sends protective angels to camp around all who love and fear Him (see Psalm 34:7).

The Lord also moved the supernatural cloud He had given Israel to guide them. The cloud suddenly shifted from the front of Israel's camp to the rear, looming as a pitch-black wall before the Egyptians. On the other side, the cloud provided a supernatural light, giving the Israelites clear visibility all night long (see Exodus 14:20).

Even though Pharaoh's army was in total darkness, they could still raise their voices—and all night long they spewed forth threats. It did not matter how loudly the enemy threatened Israel, however. An angel was on guard to protect them, and God had promised His people He would bring them through.

What possible reason did God have for permitting this awful night to take place? There was but one reason: The Lord was making worshipers.

Likewise today, He has put a warrior-angel between you and the devil. He also commands you, as He did Israel, "Do not fear. Stand still. Believe in My salvation."

Satan may come against you, but at no time during your dark night will he be able to destroy you. The Lord stands watch over His own!

Our Intercessor

"Therefore He is also able to save to the uttermost those who come to God through Him, since He always lives to make intercession for them" (Hebrews 7:25).

What does Scripture mean when it says Jesus makes intercession for us? This subject is so deep, so beyond human understanding, I tremble even to address it. Bible scholars have varying views on the subject.

Through prayer and trust in the Holy Spirit's guidance, I am beginning to grasp just a little of this incredible subject. Recently, I prayed very simply, "Lord, how does Your intercession in heaven affect my life? Your Word says that You appear before the Father on my behalf. What does this mean in my daily walk with You?"

The English word *intercession* means "to plead on another's behalf." This speaks of a figure who takes your place before others to plead your cause. When you hear such a definition, do you picture Christ continually pleading to God for you, asking for mercy, forgiveness, grace and blessings?

I believe this image makes our heavenly Father appear tight-fisted—and I refuse to believe that grace has to be pried out of our loving God. If we limit ourselves to such a narrow definition of intercession, we will never understand the deeper spiritual meaning of what Christ does for us.

The Bible declares that God knows my needs before I can ask Him. Often, He supplies those needs even before I pray. Therefore, I find it difficult to accept that God's own Son has to plead with Him for anything.

I do not claim to know everything about Christ's intercession for us, but I do believe that whatever our High Priest is doing in His intercession, it is a very simple matter. I also believe that intercession has to do directly with the growth of His Body here on earth. He is at work supplying every joint and part with might and strength. *That* is our generous Father's way!

PEACE WITH GOD

Jesus died on the cross to purchase peace with God for us—and He is in heaven now to maintain that peace, for us and in us. The peace we have with God through Christ distinguishes our faith from all other religions.

In every other religion besides Christianity, the sin question is never settled. Sin's dominion simply has not been broken. Therefore there can be no peace: "'There is no peace,' says the Lord, 'for the wicked'" (Isaiah 48:22). Yet we have a God who provides peace by pardoning sin. Jesus came to earth to bring peace to troubled, fearful humankind.

How does Jesus maintain God's peace for me? He does it in three ways:

- Christ's blood *removed the guilt of my sin*. In this sense, Paul says, "He Himself is our peace" (Ephesians 2:14). Jesus made peace for me through His blood.
- Christ *maintains my peace and joy in believing*: "Now may the God of hope fill you with all joy and peace in believing, that you may abound in hope by the power of the Holy Spirit" (Romans 15:13).
- Jesus *causes me to rejoice at the hope of entering glory*: "[We] rejoice in hope of the glory of God" (Romans 5:2).

When Jesus ascended to heaven, He did not just bask in the glory that God bestowed on Him. No, He went to the Father to maintain the hard-won peace He achieved for us at Calvary. Simply put, a life without fear is a life full of His peace.

Our Savior is alive in glory right now, and He is both fully God and fully human. He has never discarded His humanity. Right now, our Man in eternity is working to make sure we are never robbed of the peace He gave us when He left. When He comes again, He wants us to "be found by Him in peace" (2 Peter 3:14).

"These Men Have Been with Jesus"

In Acts 3, we find Peter and John going to the Temple to worship. Just outside the Temple gate sat a beggar who had been crippled from birth. When he saw Peter and John, he asked them for alms and Peter answered him, "Silver and gold I do not have, but what I do have give I you" (Acts 3:6). Peter then prayed for the beggar, saying, "In the name of Jesus Christ of Nazareth, rise up and walk" (same verse).

Instantly, the man was healed. In utter joy, he began running through the Temple, jumping and shouting, "Jesus healed me! Jesus healed me!" (see verse 8).

Everyone in the Temple marveled at the sight because they recognized the man as the cripple. When Peter and John saw the crowds gathering, they began preaching Christ and thousands were saved. Yet, while Peter and John were preaching, the synagogue rulers "came upon them, being greatly disturbed" (4:1–2). These high and mighty men asked the disciples, "By what power or by what name have you done this?" (4:7).

Peter, emboldened by the Holy Spirit, answered the rulers, "His name is Jesus Christ of Nazareth, the man you crucified just three weeks ago. God raised Him from the dead—and now He is the power that healed this man. No one can be saved by any other name. You will be lost if you do not call on Christ's name" (see 4:10–12).

The rulers sat stunned. Indeed, Scripture says "they marveled [admired them]. And they realized that they had been with Jesus" (4:13). The word *realized* comes from a root word meaning "known by some distinguishing mark."

What was this mark that distinguished Peter and John? *It was the presence of Jesus.* They had Christ's own likeness and Spirit.

Those who spend time with Jesus cannot get enough of Him. Their hearts continually cry out to know the Master better, to draw closer to Him—and the world knows it!

"GOD IS WITH THEM"

"Now when they saw the boldness of Peter and John, and perceived that they were uneducated and untrained men, they marveled. And they realized that they had been with Jesus" (Acts 4:13).

In Acts 4, as Peter and John stood waiting for judgment to be pronounced, the man who had just been healed stood alongside them. There, in flesh and blood, was living proof that Peter and John had been with Jesus. Now, as the synagogue rulers looked on, "seeing the man who had been healed standing with them, they could say nothing against it" (verse 14).

What did Peter and John do when they were released from their accusers? "They went to their own companions and reported all that the chief priests and elders had said to them" (verse 23).

The saints in Jerusalem rejoiced with the two disciples. They prayed, "Now, Lord, look on their threats, and grant to Your servants that with all boldness they may speak Your word, by stretching out Your hand to heal, and that signs and wonders may be done through the name of Your holy Servant Jesus" (verses 29–30). These believers were praying, "God, thank You for the boldness You have given our brothers. Help us all to speak with holy boldness, and provide visible evidence that You are with us."

No doubt, Peter and John had seen the look of resignation on the high priest's face when he realized they had been with Jesus. Peter must have winked at John and said, "If they only knew! They only remember that we were with Jesus weeks ago—but we were with Him also in the Upper Room, and again this morning as we prayed in our cell. As soon as we get out of here, we're going to meet Him again!"

This is what happens with men and women who spend time with Jesus. When they come away from their time with Christ, it is clear to all that He is with them wherever they go.

GIVING THANKS ALWAYS

"Giving thanks always for all things to God the Father in the name of our Lord Jesus Christ" (Ephesians 5:20).

This matter of giving thanks was so important in Paul's theology that he repeats it three times in Ephesians 5:19–20.

1. "Speaking to one another in psalms and hymns and spiritual songs"
2. "Singing and making melody in your heart to the Lord"
3. "Giving thanks always for all things to God the Father in the name of our Lord Jesus Christ"

We are pressed down by so many problems and distresses that without faith we cannot give thanks as we ought. It seems to me Paul has given us the key to it all when he tells us, "Do it unto the Father."

Sometimes our grief is so great that we do not feel like giving thanks. The heart cries, "Lord, do You really expect me to sing and make melody when I hurt so badly? I can barely lift my head, much less praise and worship."

Our Lord says, *"Give thanks always."* It is not always easy to respond to this important command. God is not severe with us when we hurt—we are His children, after all—but these words are given that we might find solace in such times. We become so focused on our difficulties that we lose more than our song. We get swallowed up in praying only for ourselves, our needs and families, and we do not lift up our eyes to others' suffering.

I want to face tomorrow determined to sing to my Lord and give thanks—for all things! Oh, that ten thousand reading this message would endeavor to sing along with me—what a joy it would bring to the Father's heart. Then to follow up by resting in the truth that God has heard our cry—hallelujah!

Our precious Lord is working out the solution even now—so we are never to stop singing love songs to Him.

WILL MY PRAYERS EVER BE ANSWERED?

I believe in Holy Spirit timing. In God's own time, all our prayers will be answered, one way or another. The trouble is, we are afraid to submit our prayers to Holy Spirit scrutiny.

Some of our prayers need to be purged because often our faith is misspent on immature requests. We do not know how to pray believing, "Thy will be done." Most of us do not want God's will as much as those things permitted by His will!

Abraham exercised his faith to keep reminding himself he was a stranger on this earth. At first the blessing-pact he received from God produced only a tent to dwell in. Yet Abraham was content, because he put all his faith in that city to come "whose builder and maker is God."

Were some of the faith warriors of old not living in faith? Did God refuse to answer some of their prayers? After all, not all of them were delivered and not all lived to see answers to their prayers. Some were tortured; others wandered about destitute, afflicted and tormented (see Hebrews 11:36–38).

Indeed, some who had a reputation for having great faith "did not receive the promise" (verse 11). Those who did "obtain promises" used their faith to work righteousness and to put the enemy to flight.

What is the message for us today? It is this: Do not worry about whether God is saying "yes" or "no" to your request—and stop concentrating on faith formulas and methods. Instead, commit every prayer to Jesus and go about your business with confidence. He will answer in His time. If He does not fulfill the request, He must have a perfect reason for not doing so. No matter what happens, we are always to have faith in His faithfulness.

Will you rest in His love while patiently waiting for the promise?

Preserved for a Purpose

King David prayed, "Preserve me, O God, for in You I put my trust" (Psalm 16:1). The Hebrew word for *preserve* used by David here is packed with meaning: "Put a hedge around me, a wall of protective thorns. Guard me and keep me."

David fully believed that God preserves the righteous. This blessed man declared, "He who keeps Israel shall neither slumber nor sleep. The Lord is your keeper . . . your shade at your right hand. The sun shall not strike you by day, nor the moon by night. The Lord shall preserve you from all evil; He shall preserve your soul" (Psalm 121:4–7).

The same Hebrew word for *preserve* appears in this passage as well. Once again, David is speaking of God's divine hedge, the supernatural wall of protection. He is assuring us, "God keeps His eye on you everywhere you go."

The Lord is indeed with us in all places: at work, at church, while running errands. He is with us in our cars, on buses, on subways—and all the while, David says, God is preserving us from evil.

Time after time, God has proved Himself a preserver to His people—and that includes the reason for His commandments. "The Lord commanded us to observe all these statutes, to fear the Lord our God, for our good always, that He might preserve us alive, as it is this day" (Deuteronomy 6:24). Moses says God gave the people commandments for one reason: to preserve and keep them.

Beloved, the Lord has preserved you so *He can take you someplace*. You see, He wants to accomplish something in your life beyond miracles. The Lord preserved Israel and put a wall around them for a specific purpose: *to bring them into a place of usefulness*. He was leading them to the Promised Land. He wants the same for His people today!

Delayed Answers to Prayer

Most of us pray as David did: "In the day that I call, answer me speedily" (Psalm 102:2). "I am in trouble; hear me speedily" (69:17).

The Hebrew word for *speedily* suggests "right now, hurry up, in the very hour I call on You, do it!" David was saying, "Lord, I put my trust in You—but, please, hurry!"

God is in no hurry. He does not jump at our commands. In fact, at times you may wonder if He will ever answer. You may cry out, weep, fast and hope—but days go by, weeks, months, even years, and you do not receive even the slightest evidence that God is hearing you.

Over time you question yourself: "Something must be blocking my prayers." You become perplexed, and your attitude toward God slowly becomes something like this: "Lord, what do I have to do to get this prayer answered? You promised in Your Word to give me an answer, and I prayed in faith. How many tears must I shed?"

Why does God delay answers to sincere prayers? It certainly is not because He lacks power. Moreover, He is most willing for us to receive from Him. No, the answer is found in this verse: "He spoke a parable to them, that men always ought to pray and not lose heart" (Luke 18:1).

The Greek word for *lose heart* means "to relax, become weak or weary in faith, give up the struggle, no longer wait for completion." Galatians 6:9 advises, "Let us not grow weary while doing good, for in due season we shall reap, if we do not lose heart."

The Lord is seeking a praying people who will not relax or grow weary of coming to Him. These will wait on the Lord, not giving up before His work is completed—and they will be found waiting when He brings the answer.

Knowing God

I am going to make a shocking statement, and I mean every word of it: *I really do not know God!* That is, I do not know Him in the way He wants me to know Him.

I know this because the Holy Spirit whispered to me, lovingly, "David, you really don't know God in the way He wants you to. You don't allow Him to be God to you."

In the Old Testament, God took a people unto Himself—a people no richer or smarter than the rest—only so He could be God to them: "I will take you as My people, and I will be your God" (Exodus 6:7). God was saying, in essence, "I am going to teach you to be My people, so that I can be God to you."

The Lord revealed Himself to His people over and over again. He sent angels, spoke to them audibly and fulfilled every promise with great deliverances. Yet after forty years of miracles, signs and wonders, God's estimation of His people was: "You don't know Me—you don't know My ways!"

God is still looking for a people who will let Him be God to them—to the point that they truly know Him. We trust God in most areas of our lives, but our faith always has boundaries and limits. This has to do with not knowing God's ways—His nature and character, especially toward His beloved children.

Jesus says that God does not hear our prayers and praises simply because we utter them over and over, for hours at a time. That is not the prayer posture of a child who knows his Father loves him. It is possible to pray, fast and do righteous things, and still not reach the place where we hunger to know our Father's nature and understand His ways.

In order to know God's ways you must spend much time with Him in prayer. But prayer must include quality time in which we let God be God to us—laying every need and request in His hands and leaving them there. That is the relationship of a child and Father.

Thanksgiving Time

I remember that the subject of thanksgiving came to me during a time of great personal heaviness. At the time, our church building needed major work. Parishioners' problems were piling up. Everyone I knew seemed to be going through some kind of trial—and I was feeling the burden of it all.

I went into my office, feeling sorry for myself. I began to complain to God: "Lord, how long will You keep me in this fire? How long do I have to pray before You do something? When are You going to answer me, God?"

Suddenly, the Holy Spirit fell upon me—and I felt ashamed. The Spirit whispered to my heart, "Just begin to thank Me right now, David. Bring to Me a sacrifice of thanksgiving—for all the past things I have done for you, and for what I am going to do in the future. Give Me an offering of thanksgiving. Suddenly, everything will look different."

As those words settled in my spirit, I wondered: "What does the Lord mean by a sacrifice of thanksgiving?" I looked up the phrase in Scripture and was amazed at all the references I found:

- "Let them sacrifice the sacrifices of thanksgiving, and declare His works with rejoicing" (Psalm 107:22).
- "I will offer to You the sacrifice of thanksgiving, and will call upon the name of the Lord" (116:17).
- "Let us come before His presence with thanksgiving; let us shout joyfully to Him with psalms" (95:2).
- "Enter into His gates with thanksgiving, and into His courts with praise. Be thankful to Him, and bless His name" (100:4).

We are to bring God a sacrifice of praise and thanksgiving from our lips: "Therefore by Him let us continually offer the sacrifice of praise to God, that is, the fruit of our lips, giving thanks to His name" (Hebrews 13:15).

What is the "fruit of our lips"? It is gratitude and thanks. That will change our outlook every time!

Right Song—Wrong Side

When the children of Israel were going through their terrible testing, were they really expected to express gratitude and thanksgiving in the midst of it? When they were surrounded by enemies in a hopeless situation, did God want them to have that kind of reaction?

Yes, absolutely! In fact, that was the secret to getting out of their difficulty. You see, God wants something from all of us in our times of overwhelming troubles and testing. He wants us to offer Him a sacrifice of thanksgiving in the midst of it all.

I believe James had discovered this secret when he admonished, "Count it all joy when you fall into various trials" (James 1:2). He was saying, "Don't give up! Make an altar in your heart, and offer up joyous thanksgiving in the midst of your trials."

Of course, the children of Israel did offer the Lord praise and thanksgiving—but they did it on the wrong side of the Red Sea. The people rejoiced all night after their deliverance, but God had no pleasure in it. Anybody can shout in gratitude *after* the victory comes. The question God put to Israel was, "Will you praise Me *before* I send help—while you are still in the midst of the battle?"

I believe if Israel had rejoiced on the "trial side" of the Red Sea, they would not have had to be tested again at the waters of Marah. Had they passed the Red Sea test, the waters at Marah would not have tasted bitter but sweet. Israel would have seen water springing up everywhere in the desert, rather than having to go thirsty.

God help us to sing the right song on the testing side of trials. This brings the highest delight to our heavenly Father!

Are you in a most difficult time? Then sing! Praise! Say to the Lord, "You can do it—You delivered me before, You can deliver me now. I rest in joy."

HOW TO STAND UP AND FIGHT

With all the talk going on in churches about spiritual warfare, Christians still have not learned how to stand up to the enemy. We are pushovers for the devil!

I do not believe every misfortune that befalls a Christian comes from the enemy. We wrongly blame Satan for a lot of our own carelessness, disobedience and laziness.

Let me tell you something of Satan's strategy: If he cannot pull the Almighty out of His throne, he will try to tear God's image out of you—turning worshipers into murmurers and blasphemers.

Satan cannot attack you at will. God has put a wall of fire around His children, and the devil cannot go beyond that wall without God's permission.

Satan cannot read a Christian's mind. Some people are afraid to pray because they think the devil can read their every thought. Not so! Only God is omnipresent and omniscient.

Scripture commands us to stand up, be strong and do battle against our flesh and the devil: "Watch, stand fast in the faith, be brave, be strong" (1 Corinthians 16:13). "Brethren, be strong in the Lord and in the power of His might" (Ephesians 6:10). Simply put, we have to become fed up with being held down by the devil—fed up with being depressed, joyless, empty, harassed.

In Judges 6:1–6 we see the Israelites at their lowest point ever. They were driven to living in dark caves, starving, scared and helpless. Then something happened. It started with Gideon and spread throughout the whole camp: Israel got sick and tired of hiding in those dark caves!

Something rose up within Gideon—and he finally said what God was waiting to hear: "We serve a mighty, victorious God. Why do we go on, day after day, taking this abuse?"

God will not do anything until you are thoroughly disgusted with being oppressed by the enemy—until you are sick and tired of being sick and tired. You have to do as Gideon did—cry out to the Lord!

The Prayer of Unbelief

You have heard of the prayer of faith. I believe there is a mirror image of this prayer, a prayer that is based on flesh. I call this the prayer of unbelief.

Let me pose a question to you: Have you ever heard the Lord say, "Quit praying—get up off your knees"?

The Lord spoke these very words to Moses: "And the LORD said to Moses, 'Why do you cry to Me?'" (Exodus 14:15). The literal Hebrew meaning of the verse is, "Why are you shrieking at Me? Why all the loud pleading in My ears?"

Why would God say this to Moses? Here was a godly, praying man, in the crisis of his life. The Israelites were being chased by Pharaoh, with no escape. Most Christians would probably react as Moses did. He got alone with the Lord and poured out his heart in prayer.

Yet when God heard Moses shrieking, He told him, "Enough!" Scripture is not explicit about what follows, but at that point God might have said, "You have no right to agonize before Me, Moses. Your cries are an affront to My faithfulness. I have already given you My solemn promise of deliverance, and I have instructed you specifically on what to do. Your tears are not the cry of a broken heart now—they are tears of self-pity. It is time to stop crying."

As we face our own crises, we may convince ourselves, "Prayer is the most important thing I can do right now"—but a time comes when God calls us to act, to obey His Word in faith. At such a time, He will not allow us to retreat to a wilderness to pray. That would be disobedience—and any prayers would be offered in unbelief.

The prayer of unbelief takes into account only God's goodness; it ignores the severity of His holy judgments. Paul writes, "Therefore consider the goodness and severity of God" (Romans 11:22). There is a reason the apostle purposely mentions God's goodness and severity in the same breath here. It is to turn our eyes away from the prayer of unbelief—and toward true belief!

Our Part in Communion

Walking in God's glory means not only that we receive the Father's love, but that we love Him back as well. It is about mutual affection, both giving and receiving love. "You shall love the Lord your God with all your heart, with all your soul, and with all your strength" (Deuteronomy 6:5).

God says in Proverbs, "My son, give me your heart" (Proverbs 23:26). His love demands that we reciprocate, that we return to Him a love that is total, undivided, requiring all our heart, soul, mind and strength.

Yet the Lord tells us in no uncertain terms, "You cannot earn My love. The love I give to you is unmerited." John writes, "In this is love, not that we loved God, but that He loved us and sent His Son to be the propitiation for our sins," and, "We love Him because He first loved us" (1 John 4:10, 19).

Just as God's love for us is marked by rest and rejoicing, so our love for Him must have these same two elements:

1. David expresses a rest in his love for God when he writes, "Whom have I in heaven but You? And there is none upon earth that I desire besides You" (Psalm 73:25). The heart that loves the Lord finds full contentment in Him. God's loving-kindness is better than life itself.
2. Such a heart also rejoices in its love for God. It sings and dances in joyous ecstasy over the Lord.

We read in Proverbs these prophetic words of Christ: "I was daily His delight, rejoicing always before Him, rejoicing in His inhabited world, and my delight was with the sons of men" (Proverbs 8:30–31).

Who are the sons being mentioned here? It is us! Jesus testifies, "I was my Father's delight, the joy of His being. Now all who turn to Me in faith are His delight as well."

A Life of Communion

I am convinced that multitudes of God's offspring know very little of true communion with Him. Why is this so?

I believe such Christians have a sad, distorted concept of the heavenly Father. I recall Jesus' parable about the servant who hid his talent because he had a twisted image of his master. That servant said, "Lord, I knew you to be a hard man" (see Matthew 25:24). The master rightly upbraided this servant for his attitude.

Likewise, many believers today think, "There is no way God could ever be glad over me, rejoicing and singing in love. I've failed Him so miserably at times, bringing reproach on His name. How could He possibly love me?"

One powerful reason so many Christians do not want to get close to their heavenly Father is because they sense they continually fail Him. Their concept of Him is that He is ready to judge and condemn them.

How can we not want to be near a Father who writes love letters to us, who is always ready to embrace us? In spite of our foolishness, He assures us, "Satan may tell you that you are useless, but I say you are My joy!"

You may be thinking, "Surely the Lord doesn't rejoice over someone who continues in sin, someone who cannot overcome a bondage."

Yes, God does love His people, though He does not love their sin. The Bible says He reproves every child who continues in iniquity, but He always does it with longsuffering.

I trust you are able to say, "My heavenly Father is in love with me. He says I am lovely in His eyes, and I believe Him. No matter what I go through, no matter how tempted or tried I become, He will rescue me and hover over me through it all."

This is when true communion begins. We are to be convinced each day of God's unchanging love for us—and we are to show Him we believe His revelation about Himself!

TRUE COMMUNION

Many Christians talk about intimacy with the Lord—walking with Him, knowing Him, having fellowship with Him. Yet we cannot have true communion with God unless we receive into our hearts the full revelation of His love, grace and mercy.

Communion with God consists of two things: receiving the love of the Father, and loving Him in return. You can spend hours each day in prayer telling the Lord how much you love Him, but that is not communion. If you have not received His love in turn, you have not had communion with Him. You simply cannot share intimacy with the Lord unless you are secure in His love for you.

God is not a hard, fierce, demanding Father. He does not wait for me with an angry countenance. Nor does He trail me, waiting for me to fail so He can say, "I caught you!"

No, my Father has revealed Himself to me as kind and tenderhearted, full of grace and mercy, anxious to lift all my cares and burdens. I know He will never turn me down when I call on Him.

The prophet Zephaniah says something incredible about God's love for us: "The LORD your God in your midst, the Mighty One, will save; He will rejoice over you with gladness, He will quiet you in His love, He will rejoice over you with singing" (Zephaniah 3:17).

To *rejoice* means "to have joy and delight." It is an outward expression of internal gladness and the highest expression of love. The Hebrew word Zephaniah uses for *rejoice* here is *tripudiare*, meaning "to leap, as one overcome with joyful ecstasy."

Can you conceive of your Father leaping for joy at the very thought of you? That He loved you before the world was created, before you were even born? Can you accept that He loved you even after you fell into Adam's sinful ways and became an enemy to Him?

Love and Hate

If anyone comes to Me and does not hate his father and mother, wife and children, brothers and sisters, yes, and his own life also, he cannot be My disciple" (Luke 14:26).

The Greek word for *hate* means "to love less by comparison." Jesus is calling us to have a love for Him that is so all-inclusive, fervent and absolute that our earthly affections cannot come close.

Do we know what it is like to come into His sweet presence and ask nothing? To reach out to Him only because we are grateful that He loves us so completely? Mostly we are self-centered in our prayers: "Give us—meet us—bless us—use us—protect us." All this may be scriptural, but *the focus remains on us.*

Even our work for the Lord has become selfish. We want Him to bless our service to Him so we can know our faith is genuine. Yet the Lord is more interested in what we are becoming in Him than in what we are doing for Him.

You may be hurting because doors of ministry have closed. You may feel "put on the shelf." Or you may think you would be more useful to the Lord on some needy mission field. I say we cannot be more useful to the Lord than when we minister love to Him in the secret closet of prayer.

When we seek the Lord and search His Word to know Him, we are at the peak of our usefulness. We do more to bless God by being shut up with Him in loving communication than by doing anything else.

The person who is often with the Lord in prayer will be given wisdom, Holy Spirit timing and supernatural power to do the will of God. Whatever work He might open up for us to do, at home or abroad, will flow effortlessly out of our communion with Him.

A PERSONAL REVELATION OF CHRIST

If you are a preacher, missionary or teacher, ask yourself: What are you teaching? Is it what a person taught you, a rehashing of the revelation of some great teacher? Or have you experienced your own personal revelation of Jesus Christ? If you have, is that revelation ever-increasing? Is heaven being opened to you?

Paul said, "For in Him we live and move and have our being" (Acts 17:28). True men and women of God live within this very narrowly defined yet vast circle. Their every move is wrapped up only in the interests of Christ.

Years ago I knew the Holy Spirit was drawing me into such a ministry, one that preached Christ alone. Oh, how I yearned to preach nothing but Him! But my heart was unfocused, and I found the circle too narrow. As a result, I had no flow of revelation to sustain my preaching.

Paul said Christ was being revealed *in* him, not just *to* him (see Galatians 1:16). In God's eyes it is unfruitful to preach a word that has not already worked its power in the preacher's life and ministry. It may seem all right for certain shallow ones to preach Christ with contention—but not so for the man or woman of God. We must preach an ever-increasing revelation of Christ—yet only as that revelation effects a deep change in us.

Without a continuous flow of revelation from the Holy Spirit, we will end up repeating a stale message. Our words will fall to the ground. We must stay filled up with a never-ending revelation of Christ. Such revelation awaits every servant of the Lord who is willing to wait on Him, believing and trusting the Holy Spirit to manifest to him the mind of God.

How Can You Obtain a Walk in the Spirit?

I say then: Walk in the Spirit" (Galatians 5:16). The command to walk in the Spirit is given to all, not just to a few "supersaints."

Here are three things every follower of Jesus may do to obtain this walk:

1. *You must go after this walk with everything in you.* Ask the Holy Spirit to be your guide and friend. "Ask, and it will be given to you; seek, and you will find; knock, and it will be opened to you" (Luke 11:9).

If you are saved, the Holy Spirit has already been given to you. Now ask Him to take over—surrender to Him! You have to determine in your heart that you want Him to lead and guide you. Moses, speaking of the latter days, said, "But from there you will seek the Lord your God, and you will find Him if you seek Him with all your heart and with all your soul" (Deuteronomy 4:29).

2. *Focus on knowing and hearing the Spirit—and get your eyes off your trouble and temptation.* Paul, Silas and Timothy would have wallowed in fear and depression if they had focused on their troubles. Instead, they focused on the Lord, praising and worshiping Him.

Most of the time when we go to prayer, we focus on past failures. We replay our defeats, saying, "Oh, how far up the road I would be if I hadn't failed God and messed up."

Forget everything in your past—it is all under the blood! Forget about the future, too. Instead, focus only on the Holy Spirit, with your whole mind and heart.

3. *Give quality time to communion with the Holy Spirit.* Wait patiently on the Lord and minister praises to Him. Take authority over every other voice that whispers thoughts to you. Believe that the Spirit will not let you be deceived or blinded.

"He who is in you is greater than he who is in the world" (1 John 4:4).

"Abba, Father"

The Holy Spirit has a way of simplifying our relationship with God the Father and Jesus. He is the One who teaches us to say, "Abba, Father!" (Galatians 4:6).

This phrase refers to an oriental custom of Bible days regarding the adoption of a child. Until the adoption papers were signed and sealed by the adopting father, the child saw this man only as *a* father. He had no right to refer to him as *Abba*, signifying *my*.

Yet, as soon as the papers were signed and sealed, the child was presented to the adopting father—and for the first time the child could say, "Abba, Father!"

This is the work and ministry of the Holy Spirit. He presents you to the Father and keeps reminding you, "I have sealed the papers. You are no longer an orphan—you now have a very loving, powerful Father."

Our cry should be one of exceeding joy and thanksgiving. The Spirit in us literally cries out, "You are an heir of all that Jesus won." What an inheritance you have, because your Father is the wealthiest in the whole universe. You are not forsaken—so enjoy Him!

Not only are we not forsaken, but the Holy Spirit is there with us during moments of confusion and suffering. The Holy Spirit's mission is to comfort Christ's Bride in the absence of the Bridegroom: "And He will give you another Helper [Comforter], that He may abide with you forever" (John 14:16).

Comforter signifies "one who soothes in a time of pain or grief—one who eases pain, consoles and encourages." By calling the Holy Spirit the Comforter, Jesus made an infallible prediction that His people would suffer and need comfort—that there would be a lot of pain among His people in the last days. The comfort brought by the Holy Spirit is the very comfort of a father to a child—of "Abba, Father!"

Benefits to Both

"Therefore, brethren, having boldness to enter the Holiest by the blood of Jesus, by a new and living way which He consecrated for us, through the veil . . . Let us draw near with a true heart in full assurance of faith" (Hebrews 10:19–20, 22).

There are two sides to Christ's work at Calvary. One side is to the benefit of man, the other to the benefit of God. One benefits the sinner while the other benefits the Father.

We are well acquainted with the benefit on the human side. The cross of Christ has provided us with forgiveness of our sins. We are given the power of victory over all bondages and dominion over sin. We are supplied with mercy and grace and, of course, we are given the promise of eternal life. I thank God for this benefit of the cross and for the wonderful relief it brings.

Yet there is another benefit of the cross, one that we know very little about. This one is to the benefit of the Father. You see, we understand very little about the delight of the Father made possible by the cross. It is a delight that comes to Him whenever He receives a prodigal child into His house.

If all we focus on about the cross is forgiveness—if that is the end-all of our preaching—we miss an important truth that God has meant for us about the cross. There is a fuller understanding to be had—and it has to do with His delight.

I believe most Christians have learned to come boldly before God for forgiveness, for supply of needs, for answers to prayer. But they lack boldness in this aspect of faith—an aspect that is just as crucial in their walk with the Lord. This truth provides God's people with much more than just relief. It brings liberty, rest, peace and joy. Seek to know the benefit of the cross to the Father—and double your joy!

In the Secret Place

The Holy Spirit came to Ananias, a godly man living in Damascus, instructing him to go to Judas's house on Straight Street, lay hands on Saul and restore his sight.

Because of Saul's reputation, Ananias knew this was going to be dangerous. Yet here is how the Holy Spirit referred to Saul when instructing Ananias: "He is praying" (Acts 9:11).

The Lord was saying, "Ananias, Saul knows you are coming, and you will find him on his knees. He even knows your name and why you're being sent to him. He wants his eyes opened."

So, when Ananias arrived, how did Saul receive this vision, this pure word from God? It came through fervent prayer. The Spirit's words to Ananias reveal what moved God's heart about Saul: "He is praying."

At the time, Saul had been shut in with God for three days, refusing all food and water. All he wanted was the Lord, so he stayed on his knees, praying and seeking God.

My preacher father taught me, "God always makes a way for a praying man." As a young pastor, I felt a deep hunger rise up in me that caused me to pray diligently. I spent months on my knees—weeping and praying for hours at a time—when finally the Lord called me to go to New York City to minister to gangs and drug addicts.

I was also on my knees, seeking God with tears, when He called me back to New York in the 1980s to start a church in Times Square.

Whenever I have heard from God—and whenever I have received any revelation of Christ—it came not through Bible study alone. It came through prayer and seeking God in the secret place.

Make your abode the secret place of prayer. God always makes a way for the praying servant!

Go "in the Spirit"

You can go "in the Spirit" to any nation on earth, touching an unreached people while on your knees. Your own secret closet may become the headquarters for a move of God's Spirit over an entire nation.

I think of Abraham's example. He prayed over godless, wicked Sodom and the Lord answered him, "If I find in Sodom fifty righteous within the city, then I will spare all the place for their sakes" (Genesis 18:26).

When Abraham heard this, he began to negotiate with the Lord. He asked, "Suppose there were five less than the fifty righteous; would You destroy all of the city for lack of five?" (verse 28).

Abraham was asking, "Lord, what if there are 45 righteous people among those 50 believers? What if only that many are praying seekers? Or, what if there are only 10 upright people who seek You? If only 10 call on You, will You spare the city?" God answered Abraham, "I will not destroy it for the sake of ten" (verse 32).

This passage tells us something about the Lord. He is willing to save entire societies if He can find a band of righteous people who seek His face for the sake of their nation.

God goes even further in Ezekiel 22. In this passage He speaks of finding just one praying believer who will stand in the gap: "So I sought for a man among them who would . . . stand in the gap before Me on behalf of the land, that I should not destroy it; but I found no one" (Ezekiel 22:30).

At the time of Ezekiel's prophecy, Israel was polluted spiritually. The prophets were profane, violating God's law left and right. The people were oppressed, vexed on all sides, and some turned to robbing one another. Not one person among them cried out to the Lord—yet God would have saved the entire nation for the sake of just one intercessor.

Will you "go in the Spirit," interceding for a community, as Abraham did? All it takes is one.

They Had the Life and the Light

The Church of Jesus Christ lacks spiritual authority in society because it lacks spirituality. Why are our government leaders and the media so condescending to Christians? Why has the Church lost all meaning and purpose in the world's eyes? Why have young people written off Christianity as totally irrelevant to their lives?

At such times it is because, for the most part, the Church is no longer a light. Christ is not ruling in our society because He does not reign in His people's lives.

As I look around today, I see few in God's house who are truly in union with Christ. There is so little fellowship with heaven. It seems that few ministers refuse worldly methods to wholly trust God for their direction. In short, we have lost our light because we have lost Christ's *life*. In order for God's authority to have any impact, it must be lived out in yielded, obedient vessels.

The kingdom of Babylon during the time of Nebuchadnezzar was the mightiest, most powerful empire on earth. Daniel prophesied that every succeeding king would be inferior, less powerful, far less influential. Why would this be? Because Nebuchadnezzar was not the real ruler in Babylon.

The power behind that great empire was not in the golden statue that the king erected. No, Babylon's authority rested in the hands of a small group of God-possessed men. The Lord had set up a secret, heavenly government—and it was ruled by Daniel and the three Hebrew men.

These men were God's governing instruments because they operated in the heavenly realm. Even as leaders in a secular society, they lived their lives in purity, refusing to have anything to do with the world system. Instead, they shut themselves in with God.

As a result, those holy men knew the times. They could tell the people what God was up to at any given time. They were bright, shining lights to the whole nation, because they had the life of God within them.

So, do you—and does your church—have the light and the life?

Friend of God

Consider the way God Himself described His relationship with Abraham: "Abraham My friend" (Isaiah 41:8). Likewise the New Testament tells us, "Abraham believed God. . . . And he was called the friend of God" (James 2:23).

What an incredible commendation, to be called the friend of God. To have the Creator of the universe call a man His friend seems beyond human comprehension—yet it happened with Abraham!

The Hebrew word that Isaiah uses for friend here signifies affection and closeness. In the Greek, James' word for *friend* means "a dear, close associate." Both imply a deep, shared intimacy.

The closer we grow in intimacy to Christ, the greater our desire becomes to live wholly in His presence. Moreover, we begin to see more clearly that Jesus is our only true foundation.

The Bible tells us Abraham "waited for the city which has foundations, whose builder and maker is God" (Hebrews 11:10). To Abraham, nothing in this life was permanent. Scripture says the world was "a strange place" to him, definitely not a place to put down roots.

The heavenly country Abraham yearned for is not a literal place. Rather, it is being home with the Father. The Hebrew word for this phrase, "heavenly country," is *pater*. It comes from a root word meaning "Father." So the heavenly country Abraham sought was, literally, a place where he would be with the Father.

Yet, Abraham was no mystic. He was not an ascetic who put on holy airs and lived in a spiritual haze. This man lived an earthly life, heavily involved in the world's affairs. After all, he was the owner of thousands of head of livestock, and he had enough servants to form a small militia. Abraham had to be a busy man, directing his servants and buying and selling his cattle, sheep and goats.

Yet, somehow, despite his many business affairs and responsibilities, Abraham found time for intimacy with the Lord.

Do you have that kind of intimacy with the Lord—the kind where He calls you "My friend"? It can be yours.

A LIVING SACRIFICE

Paul was rejected, tempted, persecuted, beaten, jailed, shipwrecked and stoned. On top of this, he had all the cares of the Church laid on him. Yet Paul testified, "In every condition, I have been content."

Paul might have asked, "So, do you want to know how I came into the knowledge of this heavenly walk, how I found true contentment in Christ? Here is the secret: Present your body as a living sacrifice to the Lord. I come into contentment only by the sacrifice of my own will."

"Present your bodies a living sacrifice, holy, acceptable to God, which is your reasonable service" (Romans 12:1).

The Greek root for *living* here suggests "lifelong." Paul is talking about a binding commitment, a sacrifice that is made once in a lifetime. This sacrifice does not have to do with propitiation for sin. Christ's sacrifice on the cross is the only worthy propitiation: "But now, once at the end of the ages, He has appeared to put away sin by the sacrifice of Himself" (Hebrews 9:26).

Paul is talking about a different kind of sacrifice, one that God takes great pleasure in precisely because it involves the heart. This sacrifice is one of death to our will, of laying aside our self-sufficiency and abandoning our ambitions.

When Paul exhorts, "Present your body," he is saying, "Draw near to the Lord." This means drawing near to God for the purpose of offering our entire selves to Him. It means coming to Him not in our own sufficiency, but as a resurrected child, as holy in Jesus' righteousness, as being accepted by the Father through our position in Christ.

The moment you resign your will to Him, the sacrifice has been made. This act of faith is the "reasonable service" Paul refers to. It is all about trusting Him with our will, believing He will provide all the blessings we need.

Make that sacrifice today. Then you will find contentment—for God will be pleased!

Seated with Jesus

According to Paul, we who believe in Jesus have been raised up from spiritual death and are seated with Him in a heavenly realm. "Even when we were dead in trespasses, [God] made us alive together with Christ . . . and raised us up together, and made us sit together in the heavenly places in Christ Jesus" (Ephesians 2:5–6).

Where is this heavenly place where we are seated with Jesus? It is none other than God's own throne room—the throne of grace, the dwelling place of the Almighty. Two verses later we read how we were brought to this wonderful place: "For by grace you have been saved through faith, and that not of yourselves; it is the gift of God" (verse 8).

This throne room is the seat of all power and dominion. Here in the throne room, God the Father monitors every move of Satan and examines every thought of man—with Christ seated at His right hand.

Scripture tells us, "Without Him [Jesus] nothing was made that was made" (John 1:3). "For in Him dwells all the fullness of the Godhead bodily" (Colossians 2:9). In Jesus resides all wisdom and peace, all power and strength, everything needed to live a victorious and fruitful life.

Paul is telling us, "As surely as Christ was raised from the dead, we have been raised up with Him by the Father. Jesus was taken to the throne of glory, and because we are in Him, we are also where He is. That is the privilege of all believers. It means we are seated with Him in the same heavenly place where He dwells."

All the riches of Christ are available to us there: steadfastness, strength, rest, ever-increasing peace. "Blessed be the God and Father of our Lord Jesus Christ, who has blessed us with every spiritual blessing in the heavenly places in Christ" (Ephesians 1:3).

He is pleased when we ask—therefore, make His riches yours today.

THE SECRET CLOSET

But you, when you pray, go into your room [closet], and when you have shut your door, pray to your Father who is in the secret place; and your Father who sees in secret will reward you openly" (Matthew 6:6).

I have written that because of the demands of making a living, we may have a "secret closet of prayer" anywhere: in the car, on the bus, during a break at work. In measure, this is true—but there is more to it.

The Greek word for *closet* in this verse means "a private room." This was clear to Jesus' listeners, because the homes in their culture had an inner room that served as a sort of storage closet.

Jesus set the example as He went to private places to pray. "Now in the morning, having risen a long while before daylight, He went out and departed to a solitary place; and there He prayed" (Mark 1:35). "And when He had sent the multitudes away, He went up on a mountain by Himself to pray. Now when evening came, He was alone there" (Matthew 14:23).

We all have excuses for why we do not pray in a special place alone. Thomas Manton, a godly Puritan leader, wrote: "We say we have no time to pray secretly. We yet have time for all else: time to eat, to drink, for children, yet not time for what sustains all else. We say we have no private place, but Jesus found a mountain; Peter a rooftop; the prophets a wilderness. If you love someone, you will find a place to be alone."

Do you see the importance of setting your heart to pray in a secret place? It is not about legalism or bondage but about love. It is about God's goodness toward us. He sees what is ahead—and He knows we need tremendous resources, daily replenishing. All of that is found in the secret place with Him.

Family Prayer

If two of you agree on earth concerning anything that they ask, it will be done for them by My Father in heaven" (Matthew 18:19). Some Christians call the principle of this verse "agreement praying." You are deeply blessed if you have a devoted brother or sister to pray with. Indeed, the most powerful intercessors I have known have come in pairs or more.

The place where this kind of prayer takes place most powerfully is the home. My wife, Gwen, and I pray together daily, and I believe it holds our family together. We prayed for each of our children during their growing-up years, that not one of them would be lost. We prayed about their friendships and relationships and for their future mates. Now we are doing the same with our grandchildren.

Very few Christian families take time for prayer in the home. I personally can testify that I am in the ministry today because of the power of family prayer. When I was a child, every day, no matter where my siblings and I were playing—in the front yard or down the street—my mother would call very loudly out the front door of our home, "David, Jerry, Juanita, Ruth—it's prayer time!" (My brother Don was not born yet.)

The whole neighborhood knew about our family prayer time. Sometimes I hated to hear that call, and I griped and groaned about it. But something clearly happened in those times of prayer, with the Spirit moving amid our family and touching our souls.

Maybe you cannot see yourself holding family prayer. Maybe you have a spouse who is not cooperative or a child who is rebellious. Yet it does not matter who chooses not to be involved. You can still come to the kitchen table and bow your head and pray. That will serve as your household's prayer time—and every family member will know it. God will honor it as "family prayer"!

PRAYER IN TROUBLED TIMES

In perilous times such as these in which we live, is the Church powerless to do anything? Are we to sit and wait for Christ's return? Or are we called to take drastic action of some kind? When all around us the world is trembling, with men's hearts failing them for fear, are we called to take up spiritual weapons and do battle with the adversary?

The prophet Joel saw a similar day approaching Israel, one of "thick darkness and gloom." According to Joel, that day of darkness approaching Israel would be one such as never seen in their history. The prophet cried, "Alas for the day! For the day of the Lord is at hand; it shall come as destruction from the Almighty" (Joel 1:15).

What was Joel's counsel to Israel in that dark hour? He brought this word: "'Now therefore,' says the LORD, 'Turn to Me with all your heart, with fasting, with weeping, and with mourning.' So rend your heart, and not your garments; return to the LORD your God, for He is gracious and merciful, slow to anger, and of great kindness" (2:12–13).

As gross darkness fell over Israel, God appealed to His people: "Even now, at the hour of My vengeance—when you have pushed Me out of your society, when the world has mocked My warnings, when fear and gloom are covering the land—even now, I urge you to come back to Me.

"I am slow to anger, and I have been known to hold back My judgments for a season, as I did for Josiah. My people can pray and petition for My mercy. But if you say there is no mercy, the world will not repent."

Do you see God's message to us in this? As His people, we can plead in prayer and He will hear us. We can make requests of Him and know He will answer the sincere, effectual, fervent prayers of His saints.

Ever-Present Help

God has promised us, "In your time of trouble—when you face a persistent, ever-present evil—I will be your ever-present help" (see Psalm 46:1).

Ever present means "always here, always available, with unlimited access." In short, the abiding presence of the Lord is always in us, and He wants continual conversation with us. He wants us to talk with Him no matter where we are: on the job, with family, with friends, even with nonbelievers.

I refuse to accept Satan's lie that the Lord has stopped speaking to His people. The enemy wants us to think God has allowed him to grow in power and influence, but that the Lord has not equipped His own people with greater authority. No, never! Scripture says, "When the enemy comes in like a flood, the Spirit of the Lord will lift up a standard against him" (Isaiah 59:19).

It does not matter what the devil brings against us. God's power in His people will always be greater than Satan's assaults. His help comes in the gift of His Holy Spirit, who dwells in us and works the Father's will in our lives. Paul tells us again and again that our body is the temple of the Holy Spirit. We are the Lord's dwelling place on earth.

Of course, we repeat this truth often, in our worship and testimonies. Yet many of us still simply do not understand the power that resides in this truth. If we did grasp it and trust in it, we would never again be afraid or dismayed.

Even after all my years as a minister, I am still tempted to think I have to work up some emotion in order to hear from God. No, the Lord is saying, "You do not have to spend hours waiting for Me. I abide in you. I am present for you, night and day. I am your ever-present help!"

Binding Precedent

A precedent is a preceding case that serves as an example in subsequent cases. Then there is a binding precedent—a legal decision made in the past that becomes an authoritative rule for similar cases in the future. For judges, this means having to stand by a decision that has already been made.

Good lawyers regularly rely on binding precedents for their cases, because they know a precedent will stand up in court. So they search their law books to find favorable cases from the past that can fortify their argument in court. They also seek the counsel of skilled legal advisors who can point out precedent decisions.

All through the Bible, we find holy men and women who seek out this kind of binding precedent. They come into the Lord's presence to make a request and they bind Him to His Word. These bold saints do not show up unprepared—they come carrying, as it were, a spiritual briefcase loaded with precedents of how God answered the prayers of His people in times past. They remind Him of all the promises He made, and point out case after case of how He fulfilled His Word to those in similar need.

I ask you: How does someone obtain the confidence to enter God's presence boldly and make such a request? He does it by preparing, by going to God's Word to find precedent cases. He does not enter God's court nonchalantly, but with an airtight history of example after example when the Lord bound Himself to His Word.

Now let me ask you: Who knows God's decrees and immutable laws better than the Holy Spirit? The Spirit takes each of us into God's Word, shows us the Lord's dealings in history, and prepares us with case histories that build our confidence. Indeed, this is how we obtain boldness for prayer: by knowing and standing on God's promises and laying claim on them in our present case.

Let the Spirit be your spiritual counselor—reminding you of binding precedents in God's Word. The Lord your Father is pleased to hear them!

Boldly

"Let us therefore come boldly to the throne of grace, that we may obtain mercy and find grace to help in time of need" (Hebrews 4:16). "In whom we have boldness and access with confidence through faith in Him" (Ephesians 3:12). These verses speak of coming to God boldly with our pressing needs—an act that pleases Him.

When God tells us to come boldly to His throne, with confidence, it is not a suggestion. It is His preference and it is to be heeded. How do we obtain this boldness, this access with confidence?

"The effectual fervent prayer of a righteous man availeth much" (James 5:16, KJV). The word *effectual* here comes from a Greek root word that means "a fixed position." It suggests an immovable, unshakable mindset. Likewise, *fervency* speaks of a boldness built on solid evidence, absolute proof that supports your petition. Together these two words—*effectual fervency*—suggest "coming into God's court fully convinced that you have a well-prepared case." It is beyond emotional, pumped-up enthusiasm.

Such prayer can only come from a servant who searches God's Word and is fully persuaded that the Lord is bound to honor it. It is important that none of us goes into God's presence without bringing His Word with us. The Lord wants us to bring His promises, remind Him of them, bind Him to them and stand on them.

We have been given help to approach God's throne of grace. The Bible says we are petitioners at His throne and that Christ is there as our advocate. We also have the Holy Spirit standing beside us in the Father's court. The Spirit is our *Paraclete*, one who serves as our advisor. He stands by to remind us of the eternal decrees that make up God's Word.

We have been given incredible promises—of an advocate and an advisor, standing beside us—to give us boldness and assurance in coming to God's throne.

Lord Jesus, Come Quickly, Come Soon!

In Revelation, Jesus announces, "Behold, I am coming quickly! Blessed is he who keeps the words of the prophecy of this book" (Revelation 22:7). Five verses later Christ says, "Behold, I am coming quickly, and My reward is with Me, to give every one according to his work" (verse 12).

Here is the cry of all who look expectantly for Jesus' return: "The Spirit and the bride say, 'Come!'" (verse 17). This refers to the Bride of Christ, made up of a worldwide body of believers under His lordship.

You may ask, "I understand this is the believer's heart-cry. But why would the Spirit also cry out for Jesus to come?"

It is because this is the Holy Spirit's last prayer, knowing His work on earth is almost completed. Like Paul or Peter who were told by God their time was short, the Spirit likewise cries, "Come, Lord Jesus."

Where do we hear this cry of the Spirit today? It comes through those who are seated with Christ in heavenly places—who live and walk in the Spirit, their bodies the temple of the Holy Spirit. The Spirit cries in and through them, "Hasten, Lord, come!"

When was the last time you prayed, "Lord Jesus, come quickly, come soon"? Personally, I cannot remember praying this prayer. I never knew I could hasten Christ's coming by allowing the Spirit to pray this prayer through me.

Yet Peter gives us proof of this incredible truth: "Looking for and hastening the coming of the day of God" (2 Peter 3:12). In Greek, the phrase "hastening the coming of [that] day" means "to speed up, to urge on." Peter says our expectant prayers are hastening, speeding up, urging the Father to send back His Son quickly.

The Lord's merciful patience dictates the timing of His return. Just imagine what might happen if, all over the world, Christ's Bride woke up and prayed in the Spirit, "Jesus, come!"

My Soul's Boast

In 1958, I was brokenhearted over a news story about seven teenage boys who stood trial for murdering a physically disabled boy. The Holy Spirit stirred me so strongly that I felt led to go to the New York courthouse where the trial was taking place. I entered the courtroom convinced the Spirit had prompted me to talk to those youngsters.

As the day's session came to a close, however, a realization began to dawn on me. I thought, "Those boys are going to be led out that side door in chains, and I will never see them again." So I got up and made my way down the aisle toward the judge's bench, where I asked to be allowed to talk with the boys before they returned to their cells.

In an instant, policemen pounced on me, and I was unceremoniously escorted from the courtroom. Flashbulbs popped all around me, and I was besieged with questions from reporters who were covering the trial. I could only stand there speechless, utterly dumbfounded, in a humiliating situation. I thought, "What will my church back home think? People are going to see me as crazy. I've been so naïve."

In the midst of all this chaos, I prayed inside, "Lord, I thought You told me to come here. What went wrong?" I could not pray out loud, of course, because the media would have thought I was even crazier than I appeared.

God heard the cry of this poor man that day, and He has honored my silent cry ever since. You see, from that very pitiful scene in the courthouse, the Teen Challenge ministry was birthed, with a reach today that extends worldwide. I happily share in David's humble testimony from Psalm 34: "My soul shall make its boast in the Lord; the humble shall hear of it and be glad" (verse 2).

Praying Inaudibly

Of all the Psalms, Psalm 34 is my absolute favorite. It is all about our Lord's faithfulness to deliver His children from great trials and crises. David declares, "I sought the Lord, and He heard me, and delivered me from all my fears. . . . The angel of the Lord encamps all around those who fear Him, and delivers them. . . . The righteous cry out, and the Lord hears, and delivers them out of all their troubles. . . . Many are the afflictions of the righteous, but the Lord delivers him out of them all" (Psalm 34:4, 7, 17, 19).

Note David's claim in this Psalm: "I sought the Lord. . . . This poor man cried out " (verses 4, 6). When did David do this crying out?

It had to have happened when he was feigning madness in Gath and could not pray audibly in the Philistines' presence. This brings us to a great truth regarding God's deliverance. Sometimes the loudest cry is made without an audible voice.

I know what this kind of "inner crying out" is like. Many of the loudest prayers of my life—my most important, heart-wrenching, deepest cries—have been made in total silence.

At times I have been overwhelmed by situations so beyond me that I could not think clearly enough to pray. On occasion, I have been unable to say anything to the Lord, but the whole time my heart was crying out: "God, help me! I don't know how to pray just now, so hear the cry of my heart."

I believe this is exactly what David went through when he was captured by the Philistines. It seems he was saying, "This poor man cried out from within, not knowing what or how to pray—and the Lord heard me and delivered me."

It was a deep cry from David's heart, and the Lord heard him. He is faithful to hear every whimper, from all of His servants, no matter how faint.

THE FACE OF GOD

"One thing I have desired of the LORD, that will I seek" (Psalm 27:4). King David knew there had to be more to knowing God and he would not rest until he found it. He said, in short, "There is a beauty, a glory, an excitement about the Lord I have not yet seen in my life. I want to know what it is like to have uninterrupted communion with my God. I want my life to be a living prayer. Only that will see me through the rest of my days."

In answering the cry of David's heart to have intimacy with Him, God told him to seek His face. The "face of God" is His likeness, His reflection. David's response was, "When You said, 'Seek My face,' my heart said to You, 'Your face, LORD, I will seek'" (Psalm 27:8).

In answering as He did, the Lord revealed to David that his longings could be satisfied by reflecting God in his own life. He was instructing David, "Learn of me. Search my Word and pray for understanding through the Spirit, so you can be like Me. I want your life to reflect My beauty to the world."

This was not merely a call to prayer, as David had already been praying seven times a day. In fact, David's prayers are what created this passion in him to know the Lord. No, this call from God was to hunger for a lifestyle that totally reflects who Jesus is.

Jesus came to earth as a human so He could feel our pain, be tempted and tried as we are, and show us the Father. Today, when God says, "Seek My face," His words have greater implications than at any other time in history. With all that is going on in the world around us, how should we respond? We should seek His face for one purpose: that we may be like Him and reflect His beauty.

Dwelling in the House of the Lord

In Psalm 27, David beseeches God in an intense, urgent prayer. He pleads in verse 7, "Hear, O Lord, when I cry with my voice! Have mercy also upon me, and answer me."

David's prayer is focused on one desire, one ambition, one all-consuming longing or need: "One thing have I desired of the Lord, that will I seek" (verse 4). He is testifying, "I have one prayer, Lord, one request. It is my single most important goal in life, my constant prayer, the one thing I desire. I will seek after it with all that is within me."

What was this one thing that David desired above all else? He tells us: "That I may dwell in the house of the Lord all the days of my life, to behold the beauty of the Lord, and to inquire in His temple" (same verse).

Make no mistake: David was no ascetic, shunning the outside world, nor a hermit, seeking to hide away in a desert place. On the contrary, David was a passionate man of action. He was a great warrior, with huge throngs singing of his victories in battle. He was also passionate in his prayer and devotion, with a heart that yearned after God.

The Lord had blessed David with many of the desires of his heart. Indeed, David tasted everything a man could want in life. He had riches, wealth, power and authority, and he had the respect, praises and adulation of men. God had given him Jerusalem as the capital for the kingdom, and he was surrounded by devoted men who were willing to die for him.

Most of all, David was a worshiper, a praising man who gave thanks to God for all his blessings. He testified, "The Lord laid blessings on me daily."

After all these blessings were showered on him, still David sought one thing. He was saying, "There is a way of living I seek now. My soul longs for uninterrupted spiritual intimacy with my God."

May it be so for us as well!

Take the Lowest Seat

In Luke 14, Jesus was invited by a certain chief Pharisee to "eat bread" in his house. Other Pharisee leaders had been invited as well. When the host called his guests to be seated, there was a sudden scramble for the best seats at the head table. It was a brazen display of pride, a need to be seen and recognized.

When Christ Himself sat down to eat, He gave that roomful of Israel's top religious leaders this word of rebuke: "But when you are invited, go and sit down in the lowest place, so that when he who invited you comes he may say to you, 'Friend, go up higher.' Then you will have glory in the presence of those that sit at the table with you. For whoever exalts himself will be humbled, and he who humbles himself will be exalted" (Luke 14:10–11).

Christ's words in this scene apply to all of His followers. In short, He says, there are men and women who do good works only to be seen by others. These people love the spotlight and are constantly blowing their own trumpet. Jesus then instructed, "Take the lowest seat in the house."

What, exactly, does Jesus mean by this? He is inviting us—all of us—to "come up higher" into a place of true honor. This call to come up higher is a call to enter into the fullness of God's touch. It is a call to have a richer intimacy, and to become a more convincing, sure oracle of the Lord.

Choosing to take a higher seat before man is prideful and perilous. But when we seek honor from God, we are blessed—and so is He!

Pour It Out

The following word is for those who need an answer to prayer, who need help in a time of trouble, and who are ready and willing to move God's heart according to His Word.

First, lay hold of this covenant promise in Psalm 46:1: "God is our refuge and strength, a very present help in trouble." The phrase *very present* means "always available, immediate."

Faith must rest in the assurance that God's Spirit is abiding in you all hours of the day and night, continually. Because He took up a habitation in you, He listens to your every prayerful thought and cry. The Holy Spirit will move heaven and earth for any child of God who takes time to pour out his heart to the Father with unhurried time in His presence.

Next, read and believe Psalm 62:5–7. This is the prayer of David that touched God's heart. David says, "Wait on God only. Expect help from no other source. He alone must be your source, your only hope and defense. Only He can supply you with the strength to keep going until your answer comes."

When you become wholly dependent on the Lord alone—when you stop looking for man to help you and trust God to supernaturally meet you—nothing will be able to shake you. Nothing can move you into depression and pits of despair. David declared, "He is my defense; I shall not be moved" (Psalm 62:6).

Now comes the heart of it all, the secret to prevailing prayer that every saint throughout history has learned—*the pouring out of the heart before the Lord.* "Trust in Him at all times, you people; pour out your heart before Him; God is a refuge for us" (Psalm 62:8).

God will hear and answer you when He sees you are willing to shut off all outer distractions for a season, pour your heart out before Him and trust that He will respond.

To Be a Wise Virgin

"Then the kingdom of heaven shall be likened to ten virgins who took their lamps and went out to meet the bridegroom. Now five of them were wise, and five were foolish" (Matthew 25:1–2).

Does this parable describe you? You may answer, "Yes, I have grown lazy. I don't want to become a foolish virgin. I want to be ready as the day of the Lord approaches."

If you want to be as a wise virgin, you must take two simple steps that cannot be overlooked.

1. Make Christ the center of your thought life. Let the Lord be in all your thoughts. When you wake up in the morning, whisper His name. At night as you are going to bed, call out to Him in thought and on your knees.

> Finally, brethren, whatever things are true, whatever things are noble, whatever things are just, whatever things are pure, whatever things are lovely, whatever things are of good report, if there is any virtue and if there is anything praiseworthy—meditate on these things.
>
> Philippians 4:8

Let this verse be the basis of a simple prayer for you throughout the day: "Jesus, You are true, honest, just, pure, lovely. You are my Good News."

Paul writes, "The Lord knows the thoughts of the wise" (1 Corinthians 3:20). God records all your thoughts. He knows every time you think of Him, so give Him all your "thank you" thoughts.

2. Pray throughout the day, "Lord, have mercy on me, a sinner" (see Psalm 6:2).

This simple prayer is the oil for your lamp. You are telling God, "Father, I am not worthy to be called by Your name. I need Your mercy. I thought I was a pretty good person, yet whatever meager goodness I may possess gains me nothing.

"I know I can't be saved by my good works. I need Your grace. I humble myself before You now. Lord, have mercy on me, a sinner."

Jonah Gave Thanks and Was Delivered

Listen to the words of Jonah: "You cast me into the deep . . . and the floods surrounded me; all Your billows and Your waves passed over me. . . . The deep closed around me. . . . I went down to the moorings of the mountains; the earth with its bars closed behind me forever" (Jonah 2:3–6).

Jonah had hit rock bottom, entombed in the belly of a whale. He was in a battle for his life—filled with despair, shame and guilt. He was heavy of heart, as low as a person could get, and he thought God had abandoned him.

How did Jonah get out of his pit? Simply put, he passed the test: "When my soul fainted within me, I remembered the LORD. . . . I will sacrifice to You with the voice of thanksgiving" (verses 7, 9).

Jonah was in a hopeless situation, yet he said, "I am going to praise the Lord." In the midst of the worst troubles of his life, Jonah entered the Lord's presence and offered up thanks.

God answered him, "That is what I have been waiting to hear from you, Jonah. You just passed the test!" Then Scripture says, "So the LORD spoke to the fish, and it vomited Jonah onto dry land" (verse 10).

When you have no place to turn, turn to thanksgiving. Thank the Lord for His forgiveness—for releasing you from all past sins. Thank Him for delivering you from the teeth of the lion, for giving you a new home in glory, for all His past blessings, for all that He is going to do. In everything, give thanks!

"It is good to give thanks to the LORD, and to sing praises to Your name, O Most High" (Psalm 92:1).

"Offer to God thanksgiving, and pay your vows to the Most High. Call upon Me in the day of trouble; I will deliver you, and you shall glorify Me" (Psalm 50: 14–15).

The Guiding Holy Spirit

When Scripture says the Holy Spirit "abides" in us, it means God's Spirit comes in and possesses our bodies, making us His temple. Moreover, because the Holy Spirit knows the mind and voice of the Father, He speaks God's thoughts to us: "However, when He, the Spirit of truth, has come, He will guide you into all truth: for He will not speak on His own authority, but whatever He hears He will speak; and He will tell you things to come" (John 16:13). The Holy Spirit is the voice of God in and to us!

If you have the Holy Spirit abiding in you, He will instruct you personally. He does not speak only to pastors, prophets and teachers, but to all followers of Jesus. This is evident all through the New Testament, as the Holy Spirit led and guided His people, constantly saying to them, "Go here, go there, enter this town, anoint that person, speak deliverance to that person." The early believers were led everywhere and in everything by the Holy Spirit!

The Holy Spirit never speaks a single word contrary to the Scriptures. Instead, He uses the Scriptures to speak clearly to us. He never gives us a "new revelation" apart from God's Word. He opens up to us His revealed Word to lead, guide and comfort us, and to show us things to come.

I am convinced God speaks only to those who discipline themselves to "come and stand by Him," just as Moses did. This means we have to spend quality time with the Lord daily—waiting on Him to open our hearts fully to hear His voice. He will not keep anything from us—and He will never allow us to be deceived or left in confusion. Even in the most difficult times, we will enjoy a time of great rejoicing—because He will reveal Himself to us as never before.

GO AHEAD AND CRY

When you hurt the worst, go to your secret prayer closet and weep out all your bitterness. We know that Jesus wept. Peter wept—bitterly—yet his bitter tears worked a sweet miracle in him and he came back to shake the kingdom of Satan.

Years ago Betty Rollin, a woman who had endured a mastectomy, wrote a book entitled *First You Cry.* How true is that title! Recently I talked with a friend who was just informed he had terminal cancer. "The first thing you do," he said, "is cry until there are no more tears left. Then you begin to move closer to Jesus, until you know His arms are holding you tight."

Jesus never looks away from a crying heart. He said, "A broken heart I will not despise" (see Psalm 51:17). Not once will the Lord say, "Get hold of yourself. Stand up and take your medicine. Grit your teeth and dry your tears." No! Jesus hears our every cry and bottles our every tear.

Do you hurt? Then go ahead and cry. Keep on crying until the tears stop flowing, as my friend said.

Then encourage yourself in the Lord. When the fog surrounds you and you cannot see any way out of your dilemma, lie back in the arms of Jesus and simply trust Him. He has to do it all.

He only wants your faith, your confidence. He wants you to cry aloud, "Jesus loves me! He is with me, and He will not fail me. He is working it all out, right now. I will not be cast down. I will not be defeated. I will not become a victim of Satan. I will not lose my mind or my direction. I love God, and He loves me—that is all I need. I know He is on my side!"

Lord, Walk Me Home

As we read in Daniel 3:15–17, the three Hebrew men went into the fire with their bodies already dead to the world. They were able to offer their bodies joyfully, as living sacrifices—and Jesus literally met them in their crisis.

What do you think they said to Jesus when He showed up in the furnace? "Thank You for not letting us feel the pain. Thank You for giving us another chance, to have a few more years!"

No, never! I believe they said, "Lord, take us with You. Don't leave us here. In Your presence we have touched the ecstasy, the glory, and we don't want to go back. Walk us home to be with You." They would have preferred to be with Him.

Jesus knows this kind of heart—and it is to such that He commits Himself.

Are you able to say, "Lord, walk me home"? Perhaps you have never learned to commit your body, your business, your marriage, your crisis into God's hands. Yes, we are always to pray in faith, believing that God will answer. Yet we are also to trust Him completely with our situation, saying in our hearts, "But if not, Lord, I will still trust You."

Can you pray the following prayer? "Lord, You are able to deliver me from this fiery furnace—but even if You don't, I will still believe. Even if I have to go on in this horrible trial—if I have to face more suffering, more testing—I commit everything to You. Just come and walk through it with me."

I promise you—Jesus Christ will come into your crisis. He will take you by your hand and lead you through the fire.

The greatest possible answer to any prayer is having Him come. His presence lifts us above all our pain, all our hurt, all our confusion. When Jesus appears at our side, He takes us by the hand and makes us stand strong.

Prayer—the Long and Short of It

"Do not be rash with your mouth, and let not your heart utter anything hastily before God. For God is in heaven, and you on earth; therefore let your words be few" (Ecclesiastes 5:2).

There is often a pretense in long prayers. It is a desire to build up "credit power" with God; an ambition to duplicate the prayer lives of men used greatly of God; a subtle attempt to overwhelm the Lord with enough words to weary Him into action.

I wonder if God ever gets bored. Does He long for more prayers and petitions framed with brevity and thoughtfulness? Some of us go to the secret closet and just "run off at the mouth." We become rash and wordy, parroting clichés, meaningless petitions and praise patterns.

God deserves an intelligent, concise presentation of our needs—a clear-minded offering of sincere praise, and a dignity based on our respect for the King of all kings.

I believe if you are specific with God in prayer, He will be specific with you in regard to the answer. Nonchalance and casualness have no place in His courts.

The true purpose of prayer is that we enjoy much personal communion with the Lord. The heart is reluctant to dwell in God's presence and satisfies itself with "devotions." Too often a "quickie" prayer is offered and a hurried portion of Scripture is partly absorbed. But Jesus said to His disciples, "Stay here and watch with Me" (Matthew 26:38).

All the ministry and evangelizing in the world cannot excuse a servant from his duty and privilege of prayer in the secret closet. God wants us locked in with Him until the carnal soul is transformed. No one should pray without plowing, and no man should plow without praying.

Still Standing

Every victory we win over the flesh and the devil will soon be followed by an even greater temptation and attack. Satan simply will not give up in his war against us. If we defeat him once, he will double his forces and come right back at us.

We see this in the life of David. Scripture tells us, "The Syrians set themselves in battle array against David and fought with him" (2 Samuel 10:17). Suddenly, David was facing the same old enemy—one he thought he had defeated soundly.

It is important to note that David was not living in sin at this time. He was a godly man who walked in the fear of the Lord. Yet David was also human, and he must have been awfully confused about what was happening. Why would God allow this enemy to come against him again?

Have you stood in David's shoes? You may have prayed, "Lord, all I want is to please You—to obey Your Word and do what is right. You know that I fast, I pray and I love Your Word. Why am I still facing the same battle with an old enemy?"

Let us consider the promise God made to David: "Since the time that I commanded judges to be over My people Israel, and have caused you to rest from all your enemies. Also the Lord tells you that He will make you a house. When your days are fulfilled, and you rest with your fathers, I will set up your seed after you, who will come from your body, and I will establish his kingdom" (2 Samuel 7:11–12).

In the midst of his confusion and soul searching, David remembered the promise God had made to him. While the devil was throwing every weapon in hell at David, the Lord was showing him that even before he entered battle he would emerge a victor.

This is what God intends for every one of His children when the enemy comes in like a flood.

PART 5

God's Healing Hand

He Delights in Restoring Us

David Encouraged Himself in the Lord

Then David was greatly distressed" (1 Samuel 30:6). These are familiar words in Scripture about David.

He had just returned from Gath, where King Achish had said to him, "I know that you are as good in my sight as an angel of God" (29:9). With those praises ringing in his ears, David and his men returned to Ziklag, anxious to be reunited with their wives and children. When they got there, however, they found their city burned to the ground, their homes destroyed, their children and wives gone. The Amalekites had invaded while David was in Aphek and taken captive all that was precious to him and his men.

What a horrible day of infamy in the life of this anointed man of God. "Then David and the people who were with him lifted up their voices and wept, until they had no more power to weep" (30:4).

The people rose up in anger because of their overwhelming grief. There was even talk of stoning David. David himself was torn with grief: "Then David was greatly distressed" (30:6). They all had come to the end of their rope, hopeless and swallowed up in despair.

Believe it or not, God's hand was in this apparent tragedy. He had incredible blessings ahead—and He alone could solve this situation. David knew this was true of the Lord in so many situations.

So, what did this child of God do when discouragement had set in and he felt useless, like a complete failure, abandoned by God and rejected by those who once cared? "David strengthened [encouraged] himself in the Lord his God" (30:6).

David had learned to stand alone, dependent only on God. What a victorious sight now—David standing amid the ruins of his life, rejoicing in God's faithfulness and encouraging himself in the presence of the Lord.

Once the lesson was learned, God opened the heavens and spoke clearly to David. "So David inquired of the Lord . . . and He [God] answered him . . . 'Without fail [you will] recover all'" (30:8).

It was true: David and his men recovered all, with nothing lacking. It could only happen by the hand of God!

The Secret of Spiritual Strength

For thus says the Lord God, the Holy One of Israel; 'In returning and rest you shall be saved; in quietness and confidence shall be your strength.' But you would not" (Isaiah 30:15).

Here is God's secret to spiritual strength: "Quietness and confidence shall be your strength." The word for *quietness* in Hebrew signifies repose. And *repose* means "calm, relaxed, free from all anxiety; to be still, to lie down with support underneath, to lounge."

Not many Christians today have this kind of quietness and confidence. Multitudes are involved in a frenzy of activity, rushing madly to obtain material goods, possessions and pleasures. Even in the ministry, God's servants run about worrying, fearing, looking for answers in conferences, seminars and bestselling books.

Everyone wants answers, guidance, solutions, something to calm their spirit. Yet they seek it in every source except the Lord. They do not realize God has already spoken a word for them, through Isaiah: "If they don't turn to Him as their source, their striving will end in sorrow and confusion."

Isaiah describes what God's righteousness is supposed to accomplish in us: "The work of righteousness will be peace, and the effect of righteousness quietness and assurance forever" (32:17). If we are truly walking in righteousness, our lives will bear the fruit of a calm spirit, quietness of heart and peace with God.

As Isaiah looked around, he saw God's people fleeing to Egypt for help, trusting in men, relying on horses and chariots. Ambassadors were coming and going. Leaders were holding emergency strategy meetings. Everyone was in a panic, wailing, "What can we do?"

Isaiah assured them, "It doesn't have to be this way. Return from your backsliding. Repent of your rebellious trusting in others. Turn to the Lord, and He will cover you with a blanket of peace. He will give you quietness and rest in the midst of everything you are facing."

That is the secret to spiritual strength!

An Outpouring of the Holy Spirit on Households

"While Peter was still speaking these words, the Holy Spirit fell upon all those who heard the word. . . . For they heard them speak with tongues and magnify God" (Acts 10:44, 46).

This passage speaks of the household of Cornelius. Think of it, a "private Pentecost" falling upon an entire household—with everyone there lifted into the heavenlies. It was miraculous!

The praises were thrilling as all the relatives and children were getting saved and filled with God's Holy Spirit. It was all because one man set his heart to seek God until an answer came.

Here we sit today, in the time of the outpoured Holy Spirit, with so many Christian homes having little or no evidence of His working and presence. Many such homes are instead influenced by the spirit of the world rather than the Spirit of God. Not surprisingly, there is much strife, confusion and dissension.

Where the Spirit of the Lord is, there is unity. Where He abides there is rest, peace, unspeakable joy and victory over the spirit of this world.

We need to take back the spiritual authority in our homes. If a Christian husband and wife are not in total unity, flowing together in the Spirit and love of Jesus, there is extreme danger ahead. When both are seeking God in private prayer and devotion to God, however, the Spirit works His wonders.

God is doing something new in the land right now. It is something so powerful it is terrorizing hell. The Holy Spirit has come to separate a people unto the Lord, away from the love of this world.

Being successful is not nearly as important as hearing from God. To newly baptized saints, prospering means seeing Jesus in a new and living way. Houses, land, furniture, cars, clothes—all these things have lost their charm to a people now passionately in love with the Lord of glory.

The Holy Spirit has come to reveal Christ as the Savior—in our homes! Pray this for yours.

Deeper Roots

Whenever opposition arises, God's grace thrives in us. Think about what happens to a tree when a great storm beats violently against it. The wind threatens to uproot the tree and carry it away. It breaks off branches and blows away its leaves. It loosens its roots and blows off its buds. Once the storm is over, things look hopeless.

Yet look closer: The same storm that opened crevices in the earth around the trunk of the tree has helped the roots go deeper. The tree now has access to new sources of nutrition and water. It has also been purged of all its dead branches. The buds may be gone, but others will grow back more fully.

I tell you, that weather-beaten tree is now stronger, growing in unseen ways. Just wait till harvest, when it will bear much fruit!

Maybe you are in a storm right now. The wind is blowing hard, shaking you violently, and you think you are going down. Do not panic: you must know that in the midst of the tempest, you are putting down deep spiritual roots. God is developing in you a deepening humility, a greater mourning and sorrow for sin, a heightened hunger for His righteousness.

"Tribulation produces perseverance [patience]" (Romans 5:3). The word *produces* means "to accomplish." In 2 Corinthians 4:17 we read, "For our light affliction, which is but for a moment, is working for us a far more exceeding and eternal weight of glory." The word *working* in this verse is the same word used for *produces* in Romans 5:3.

God is making you a seasoned soldier of the cross—battle-scarred, but battle-smart and courageous. You may get down on yourself at times, but the Lord never does. The fact is, He could have acted sovereignly at any time to pluck you out of your struggle. But He did not—because He saw it producing in you a greater thirst for Him.

His Word Sees Us Through

Over and over, the psalmist asks, "Why is my soul cast down? I feel useless, forsaken. There is such a restlessness inside me. Why, Lord? Why do I feel so helpless in my affliction?" (see Psalm 42:11; 43:5.) These questions speak for multitudes who have loved and served God.

Take godly Elijah, for example. We see him under a juniper tree, begging God to kill him. He is so downcast he has come to the point of giving up his own life.

We also find righteous Jeremiah cast down in despair. The prophet cries, "Lord, You have deceived me. You told me to prophesy all these things, but none of them has come to pass. I have done nothing but seek You all my life. Is this how I am repaid? Now I will no longer mention Your name."

Each of these servants was under a temporary attack of unbelief. Yet the Lord understood their condition in times of confusion and doubt. After a period, He always pointed the way out. It was in the midst of their afflictions that the Holy Spirit turned on the light.

Consider Jeremiah's testimony: "Your words were found, and I ate them, and Your word was to me the joy and rejoicing of my heart" (Jeremiah 15:16). "The word of the LORD came to [Elijah]" (1 Kings 19:9). At some point each of these servants remembered God's Word. It became the joy and rejoicing of their lives, pulling them out of the pit.

The truth is, the whole time these people were struggling, the Lord was sitting by, waiting. He heard their cries, their anguish. After a certain time had passed, He told them, "You have had your time of grief and doubt. Now I want you to trust Me. Will you go back to My Word? Will you lay hold of My promise to you? My Word will see you through."

In all our trials, may we remember His Word. It will see us through.

An Invitation and a Warning

Jesus stood in the Temple and invited everyone to come under His merciful wings of protection. He called out to the blind, the sick, the leprous, the poor, the lost, everyone to come and find healing and forgiveness.

The religious crowd refused His offer. Christ then testified of them, "You were not willing!" (Matthew 23:37).

As I read this, a question arises. Here in the New Testament, would God cast off those who reject His offers of grace and mercy? Would He dispose of an old work the same way He did in the Old Testament?

Yes, He would. Jesus answered those who rejected Him, "See! Your house is left to you desolate" (verse 38). He told them, "This Temple is now your house, not Mine. I am leaving what you wasted and deserted."

Christ then added, "I say to you, you shall see Me no more till you say, 'Blessed is He who comes in the name of the LORD'" (verse 39). He was declaring, "My glory is no longer in this old work."

Think of it: Here stood mercy and grace Incarnate, saying, "This old thing isn't Mine anymore." Afterward, Jesus moved on to Pentecost, to the beginning of a new thing. He was about to raise up a new Church, not a replica of the old.

Let me ask you: Is what you see going on in your church today representative of who Jesus is? Does it reveal the very nature of God? Is this the best that God's Spirit can produce in these last days?

If so, be thankful. If not, pray that your pastor and church will accept Jesus' invitation and offer to come under His wings, for healing and forgiveness. That is His desire in these last days!

He Will Restore Your Wasted Years

So I will restore to you the years that the swarming locust has eaten, the crawling locust, the consuming locust, and the chewing locust, My great army which I sent among you" (Joel 2:25).

How many years did you waste before you repented and surrendered all to Jesus? How many years were eaten up by the locust of sin and rebellion?

You know you are forgiven and your past is forgotten. Yet wouldn't you also love to get back those years and live them for the glory of the Lord?

Perhaps you think, "I could have been so much deeper in Christ. I could have brought such joy to His heart. I could have saved myself and my family so much pain and suffering. How blind I was! How close I came to losing my soul and my sanity. I can never make up for all those wasted years."

Consider how Paul looked back over his life in his final days. He testified, "I have fought the good fight . . . I have kept the faith. Finally, there is laid up for me the crown of righteousness" (2 Timothy 4:7–8).

Paul counsels us, "Forgetting those things which are behind and reaching forward to those things which are ahead, I press toward the goal for the prize of the upward call of God in Christ Jesus" (Philippians 3:13–14). In other words, "Forget your past. Lay it down before the Lord in His mercy. Now, press on in Jesus!"

Satan's favorite form of harassment is bringing up your past to scare you. He will try to persuade you that an old addiction or lust is going to rise up and take you back to the old life.

The fact is, you might feel the pangs of remorse as long as you live. Yet, according to Paul, you are to take those old wounds and let God restore you. He will restore to you years that were taken away, just as He did with Paul. Then press on toward the prize of your high calling in Him!

A Cry from the Heart

I believe God's merciful love is revealed in response to a cry from the heart—not just any cry, but a humble cry for deliverance. "In my distress I called upon the LORD, and cried out to my God; He heard my voice from His temple, and my cry came before Him, even to His ears" (Psalm 18:6).

"Many times He delivered them; but they rebelled in their counsel, and were brought low for their iniquity. Nevertheless He regarded their affliction, when He heard their cry" (106:43–44).

You can be sure that no one is too wicked or hopeless if he reaches out to God in humility. The story of the wicked King Manasseh proves it. The Bible says he was one of the most wicked kings of Israel.

> And he did evil in the sight of the LORD. . . . For he rebuilt the high places which Hezekiah his father had destroyed; he raised up altars for Baal . . . and he worshipped all the host of heaven, and served them. . . . Also he made his son pass through the fire . . . used witchcraft, and consulted spiritists and mediums. He did much evil in the sight of the LORD.
>
> 2 Kings 21:2–6

"So Manasseh seduced Judah and the inhabitants of Jerusalem to do more evil than the nations. . . . And the LORD spoke to Manasseh and his people, but they would not listen" (2 Chronicles 33:9–10).

Is there hope for someone who gets so far from God? Yes, if he will humble himself, and confess and believe Christ's victory at the cross. Manasseh ended up in prison, bound with chains. But in his affliction he cried out—and God heard him and restored him.

"Now when he was in affliction, he implored the LORD his God, and humbled himself greatly" (2 Chronicles 33:12).

This word of hope and restoration is for you, too, beloved! No matter how far you have fallen, heed His Word. He will hear your cry—and you will be made whole.

Rise and Walk

Jesus said to him, 'Rise, take up your bed, and walk'" (John 5:8).

The cripple at the Pool of Bethesda may have thrilled to stories of Jesus going about the land healing, but he did not know Christ personally. Jesus knew all about him, however—and the Lord was touched with the feelings of this poor man's infirmity.

All Jesus asked of this man was to believe His Word and act on it. "Rise! Take up your bed! Walk away from this scene!"

Later, after being healed, the man would talk with Jesus in the Temple and come to know and trust Him. But when he was still crippled, lying by the pool and encountering Jesus, he faced the biggest decision of all his painful years. A word of hope had come to him and he was being challenged: "Rise by faith and be made whole—or lie here and die!"

The man could have continued to lie by the pool, thinking, "Why would God pick me to heal? I'm destined to die in this condition."

The fact is, Jesus would not have raised him up against his will. The man had to believe his cries had been heard and that his time for deliverance had come. It was now or never.

"Then Jesus answered and said to them [Jews], 'Most assuredly, I say to you, the Son can do nothing of Himself, but what He sees the Father do; for whatever He does, the Son also does in like manner'" (verse 19).

In essence, Jesus was saying to the doubters within earshot, "My Father wanted this man healed, so I healed him. I do only what my Father wills." It was God's will, God's love, God's desire to make the man completely whole.

Beloved, I know better than anyone how difficult it is to believe God loves you when you are down and weak. That is why He comes to us in that very condition—when we are weak—with His command: "Rise up and walk!"

It takes childlike faith to accept that love, step out in faith and say, "Lord, on Your Word alone I will arise and walk—with You!" That is the response He is looking for.

RESTORATION

The "days of the Gentiles" are almost over. God has given us plenty of warning that the Spirit will not forever strive with the rebellious. Before this generation comes under the retribution of Almighty God, a great restoration is prophesied.

"So I will restore to you the years that the swarming locust has eaten . . . My great army which I sent among you" (Joel 2:25).

David said, "[The righteous] shall be like a tree planted by the rivers of water, that brings forth its fruit . . . whose leaf also shall not wither; and whatever he does shall prosper" (Psalm 1:3). Yet this promise is only to those who have totally separated themselves from the wicked. It is only for those who are devoted students of God's Word, meditating in it day and night.

"The ungodly are not so," said David (verse 4). They become weak and withered, blown about by every wind of doctrine. Such compromisers are likened to withered trees, diseased and corrupted with worms.

This is a picture of many professing Christians in God's house today. They neglect their Bible reading; they become too preoccupied to pray and build themselves up in the faith; they become cozy with the ungodly and take their seat among the scornful.

An army of cankerworms has been eating away at their inner man. Outwardly they appear as trees planted by the water—but inwardly they are corrupted and diseased. They are drying up spiritually, no longer bearing fruit. The cankerworm does its destructive work in the bark of trees, and so it is with sin. It is eating away deep within those who have strayed from the presence of the Lord.

A powerful revelation of the Lord's new covenant will restore God's people to spiritual health. Sin will lose its power as God's people get back to His Word. Pray for His restoration in this generation.

A Perfect Heart Is Trusting

The psalmist wrote, "Our fathers trusted in You; they trusted, and You delivered them. They cried to You, and were delivered: they trusted in You, and were not ashamed" (Psalm 22:4–5).

The Hebrew root word for *trust* suggests "to fling oneself off a precipice." This means being like a child who has climbed up into the rafters and cannot get down. He hears his father say, "Jump!" and he obeys, throwing himself into his father's arms.

Are you in such a place right now? Are you on the edge, with no option but to fling yourself into the arms of Jesus? You have resigned yourself to your situation and think you are trusting, but that is not trust—it is nothing more than fatalism.

As we hunger for Jesus more intensely, we will find that our trust in Him is well founded. At some point in our lives we may have thought that we could not totally trust Him—that He did not really have control over the big picture, and that we had to stay in charge. Growing closer to Him and getting to know Him changes that.

The trusting heart always says, "All my steps are ordered by the Lord. He is my loving Father, and He permits my sufferings and temptations—but never more than I can bear, for He always makes a way of escape. He is Lord—not just over me, but over every situation that touches me."

The trusting heart is also a broken heart. The psalmist David said, "The LORD is near to those who have a broken heart, and saves such as have a contrite [crushed] spirit" (Psalm 34:18).

Brokenness means more than sorrow and weeping, more than a crushed spirit, more than humility. When we are truly broken before God, He gives us a power that restores ruins, a power that brings a special kind of glory and honor to Him. It causes us to trust—and that is where we find our peace. We can face any precipice, knowing He is there to catch us!

Growth in Grace Can Be Stunted

Paul warned the Ephesians, "No longer be children, tossed to and fro and carried about with every wind of doctrine" (Ephesians 4:14).

You may think, "This verse doesn't apply to me. My foundation is biblically solid. I'm not taken in by all the new Christian fads and frivolous gimmicks that are distracting people from Jesus. I am grounded in God's Word."

Yet listen to the rest of this verse: "carried about . . . by the trickery of men, in the cunning craftiness . . . to deceive." Perhaps you cannot be fazed by false doctrine—but Paul says you could still be carried away by another means. He is asking, "Are you tossed about by the evil plans of those who oppose you?"

Paul's message calls us to examine ourselves again. How do we react to people who call themselves our brothers and sisters in Christ, yet spread falsehoods about us?

When Paul commands, "No longer be children," he is saying, "Those enemies of yours—the ones who use gossip and slander, manipulation and craftiness, deception and underhandedness—I tell you, they are all rebellious children, devious and spoiled. They have not allowed God's grace to work in them. So do not fall for their wicked, childish games. They want you to react to their meanness, but you are not to answer them in childishness."

In the next verse, Paul urges us to move on to maturity: "Speaking the truth in love, may [you] grow up in all things into Him who is the head—Christ" (verse 15).

He is saying, "You cannot help the slights you receive, the hurts done to you, the gossip spoken against you, the fraud and deception aimed at you. Yet you can use these things to grow in grace. View them as opportunities to become more Christlike. Respond softly, with a meek spirit. Forgive those who spitefully use you."

Do not allow your growth to be stunted by those who oppose you. Always grow in grace—responding softly, forgiving deeply.

God's Special Forces

You have heard of the U.S. Army's Special Forces—a highly trained army-within-an-army, an elite unit of dedicated soldiers. These special units are made up completely of volunteers, fighters who have been noticed and called out by their superiors.

Before the war in Afghanistan, Osama bin Laden had said American soldiers were weak, cowardly, not trained for mountain warfare. He predicted the Taliban would send U.S. troops home in shame, but he had not counted on America's Special Forces. This fearless unit invaded Afghanistan with a mere two thousand soldiers. Within days, it had located all the enemy's strongholds.

I believe God is doing something similar in the spiritual realm. While in prayer, I was impressed by the Holy Spirit with the concept that God has been at work in the heavenlies on a covert operation. He is raising up an army-within-an-army to form an elite unit of volunteers made up of warriors He can touch and stir, to do battle with the enemy.

We see a picture of this in the Bible, with Saul's special militia. The Word tells us, "and valiant men went with him, whose hearts God had touched" (1 Samuel 10:26).

God's elite unit today includes the young, the middle-aged, even the elderly. They have been training in their secret closets of prayer. What has intimacy with Jesus taught them? They have learned how to do battle on any spiritual plane, whether in the mountains or in valleys.

God's army-within-an-army is in place in every nation. Its activity may be covert now, but soon we will see it doing exploits in the name and power of Christ.

"But the people who know their God shall be strong, and carry out great exploits" (Daniel 11:32).

"But those who wait on the Lord shall renew their strength; they shall mount up with wings like eagles; they shall run and not be weary, they shall walk and not faint" (Isaiah 40:31).

WE ARE FAMILY

Claiming the power that is in Christ's name is not some complicated, hidden theological truth. In my library are books written solely on the subject of Jesus' name. The authors wrote them to help believers understand the deep implications hidden in Christ's name. Yet most of these books are so "deep," they go right over readers' heads.

I believe the truth we are meant to know about Jesus' name is simply this: When we make our requests in Jesus' name, we are to be fully persuaded that it is the same as if Jesus Himself were asking the Father.

God loved His Son and answered every request He made. Jesus testified to this, saying, "He hears me always." Simply put, the Father never denied His Son any request.

Today, the heavenly Father receives us as intimately as He receives His own Son. This is because of our spiritual union with Christ. Through His crucifixion and resurrection, Jesus has made us one with the Father. "That they all may be one, as You, Father, are in Me, and I in You; that they also may be one in Us . . . I in them, and You in Me" (John 17:21–23).

We are now *family*—one with the Father and one with the Son. We have been adopted, with the full rights of inheritance possessed by any child. This means all the power and resources of heaven are made available to us, through Christ.

Praying "in the name of Jesus" is not a formula. It is not the phrase that has power in simply speaking it. The power is in believing that Jesus takes up our cause and brings it to the Father on His own merits. He is the Advocate—He is doing the asking for us. The power is in fully trusting that God never denies His own Son—and that we are the beneficiary of the Father's faithfulness to His Son.

Becoming People of Prayer

In Jeremiah 5, God pleaded, "Run to and fro through the streets of Jerusalem and . . . if you can find a man, if there is anyone who executes judgment, who seeks the truth; and I will pardon her" (Jeremiah 5:1). The Lord was saying, "I will be merciful, if I can find just one person who will seek Me."

During the Babylonian captivity, God found such a man in Daniel. Today, more than ever, the Lord is searching for the same kind of godly men and women who are willing to "stand in the gap"—through prayer.

When the Holy Spirit came to Daniel, he was reading the book of Jeremiah. At that time the Spirit revealed that God's time of deliverance for Israel had come—and Daniel was provoked to pray: "Then I set my face toward the Lord God to make request by prayer and supplications, with fasting, sackcloth, and ashes. And I prayed unto the LORD my God" (Daniel 9:3–4).

Daniel knew God's people were not ready to receive His restoration. Yet did the prophet lambaste his peers for their sins? No—Daniel identified himself with the moral decay all around him, declaring, "We have sinned. . . . To us belongs shame of face . . . because we have sinned against You" (Daniel 9:5, 8).

God strongly desires to bless His people today—but if our minds are polluted with the spirit of this world, we cannot receive His blessings. Daniel made this powerful statement: "All this disaster has come upon us; yet we have not made our prayer before the LORD our God, that we might turn from our iniquities and understand Your truth. Therefore the LORD has kept the disaster in mind, and brought it upon us" (Daniel 9:13–14).

Let us examine our walk with the Lord. Let Him show us areas of compromise so that we can set our faces to pray for the deliverance of our families and our nation.

DAY 41

Suppose you came upon Jesus on day 41—the day immediately after His temptation in the wilderness. You would see His face shining, and He would be exuding life and confidence. He would be rejoicing, praising the Father, because He had won a great victory.

Now Jesus was ready to face the powers of hell—and He set off boldly for the great cities that lay in darkness. He preached the Gospel, sure of God's Word, and He healed the sick, knowing His Father was with Him.

As you examine your life, you may be facing your own dry, wilderness experience. You have endured fiery attacks from Satan and your soul is cast down. You cannot help thinking, "Jesus never went through trials like mine. He was above all this."

You may see a minister who appears strong in faith, sounding so assured of God's presence that you think, "He has never had problems like mine." If you only knew! You were not there when God called this man to preach and then led him into a wilderness to be sorely tempted. You were not there when he was reduced to nothing, cast down in despair. You cannot know that often his best sermons come out of the testings of his own life.

Paul warns us not to measure our righteousness against others: "We dare not . . . compare ourselves with those who commend themselves. But they, measuring themselves by themselves, and comparing themselves among themselves, are not wise" (2 Corinthians 10:12).

Who would have known on day 41 that Jesus had just emerged from a long, horrible temptation? Who would have known that the glory they saw in Him sprang from a struggle worse than any they would ever endure?

God's Spirit has led you into the wilderness. Let Him complete His work of building into you utter dependence and trust. You will come out with confidence—and you will have godly compassion and strength to help others.

Resist and He Will Flee

Satan tempted Jesus with this offer: "All these things I will give You if You will fall down and worship me" (Matthew 4:9). When most Christians read this they think, "This sounds so outlandish, so ridiculous. How could it ever be considered a temptation to Jesus?"

Believe it or not, this was a powerful, enticing offer. Satan was challenging Jesus, saying, "I promise that if You will merely bow down at my feet, in a single act of worship, I will quit the fight and give up all my power over these realms. I will not possess, oppress or enslave anyone else. I know that You love humankind enough to be accursed by God for their sake. So, why wait? You can sacrifice Yourself right now and free the world from this moment on."

Why was the devil willing to give up all his power for this? It was because he was trying to save his own skin. Satan knew his eternal destiny would be sealed at Calvary—therefore, if he could just keep Jesus from going to the cross, he might spare himself that fate.

You may wonder, "How does this story relate to me?" Satan still tempts the righteous with a similar offer. He comes to us with threats and accusations, telling us, "You don't have to worship me, because I already have access to your flesh. I know all your weaknesses.

"Go ahead and testify about your freedom in Christ. At the moment you are singing your loudest praises, I will overpower your mind with evil. I will bring up your sin to you so powerfully you will be publicly exposed. You are powerless."

How do we answer Satan's accusations? "Resist the devil and he will flee from you" (James 4:7). What a truth—and Jesus proved it for us!

No matter how many temptations Satan throws at you, you need not fear any sin from your past. If Christ's blood has covered it, the devil cannot do anything to separate you from the Father.

Healing Afflictions

"Before I was afflicted I went astray, *but now* I keep Your word" (Psalm 119:67).

I believe in healing, I believe in affliction and I believe in "healing afflictions." Any affliction that keeps me from going astray—that drives me deeper into God's Word—is healing. Indeed, His most gracious healing force spiritually and physically can be affliction.

To suggest that pain and affliction are of the devil is to suggest that David was driven by the devil to seek God's Word. For each time David was in great pain and suffering, he sought the Lord.

I have suffered great pain, and I have called on God for deliverance, believing Him for complete healing. Yet while I go on trusting, I continue to thank God for the present condition. I let it serve to remind me how dependent on Him I really am. With David I can say, "It is good for me" (Psalm 119:71).

Pain and affliction are not to be despised as coming from the devil. Such burdens have produced great men of faith and insight. "Casting *all* your care upon Him" (1 Peter 5:7).

Paul spoke of the "concern [care]" of the churches that were thrust upon him (see 2 Corinthians 11:28). Every newborn church was another "care" on Paul's shoulders.

Any person used by God must have broad shoulders because growth always involves new burdens. Every new step of faith brings with it numerous new cares and problems.

God knows just how many cares He can trust us with. It is not that He seeks to break us—it is that willing laborers are few, and the harvest is so great.

It is time for us to forget the load of cares we carry and cast them all on Him. Then we will be ready laborers for His great harvest!

Healing through Repentance

Jesus declares, "My church is a place of shameless, open repentance." Indeed, the apostle Paul attests: "If you confess with your mouth the Lord Jesus and believe in your heart that God has raised Him from the dead, you will be saved. For with the heart one believes unto righteousness; and with the mouth confession is made unto salvation. For the Scripture says, 'Whoever believes on Him will not be put to shame'" (Romans 10:9–11).

Simply put, we are brought to salvation through our open confession of repentance. Jesus states, "For I did not come to call the righteous, but sinners, to repentance" (Matthew 9:13). Moreover, He says, repentance is how we are healed and restored: "Those who are well have no need of a physician, but those who are sick. I have not come to call the righteous, but sinners, to repentance" (Luke 5:31–32).

This is good news! Jesus is telling us, in essence, "In My Church, everyone is healed through repentance. It does not matter who you are—the physically broken, the mentally ill, the spiritually sick—everyone must come to Me the same way. All find healing through repentance."

How many churches still open their altars for heart-smitten people to come forward and repent? How many pastors have stopped giving invitations for this all-important spiritual work? How many believers have lost all sense of their need to confess sin?

What is the central message of Christ's Gospel? It is clear in all four gospels: "Jesus came . . . preaching the gospel of the kingdom of God, and saying, 'The time is fulfilled, and the kingdom of God is at hand. Repent, and believe in the gospel'" (Mark 1:14–15). This was Jesus' first recorded message—He preached repentance!

Let repentance be your source of healing and strength. Jesus promises you will never be put to shame.

THE POWER OF THE SPIRIT TO DELIVER

"Who delivered us from so great a death, and does deliver us; in whom we trust that He will still deliver us" (2 Corinthians 1:10). What an incredible statement. Paul is saying, "The Holy Spirit delivered me out of a hopeless situation. In fact, He is delivering me even now. He will continue to deliver me in all my afflictions."

Receiving the Holy Spirit is not evidenced by some emotional manifestation (yet, I do believe there are physical manifestations of the Spirit). I am talking about receiving the Spirit through an ever-increasing knowledge about His delivering power, His burden-bearing, His provision.

See Peter's words: "His divine power has given to us all things that pertain to life and godliness, through the *knowledge* of Him who called us by glory and virtue" (2 Peter 1:3). According to Peter, the divine power of the Spirit does not come as a manifestation. He comes first "through the knowledge of Him who has called us."

"And of His fullness we have all received" (John 1:16). Moreover, the Holy Spirit is not fully received until He is fully in charge. We simply have not received Him if we have not given Him complete control. We have to cast ourselves totally into His care.

A good illustration of this is found in Genesis 19, where Lot and his family were in a terrible crisis. Judgment was about to fall on their city, Sodom, and God had sent His angels to deliver them. These messengers had the power to deliver the entire family, but they were not received. They had to force their will on Lot and his family to get them out of Sodom.

The message is clear: "If you want God to be in control and to deliver you, you must let go of your plans and be willing to go His way. Only the Spirit has power to deliver you."

The Ministry of Refreshing

Acts 27 says that Paul was on a ship headed for Rome when the vessel came to a stop at Sidon. Paul asked the centurion in charge for permission to visit some friends in the city. Scripture says that "Julius . . . gave him liberty to go to his friends to receive care [refresh himself]" (Acts 27:3). Here is yet another instance of God using believers to refresh other believers.

Another time, Paul writes of a certain believer: "The Lord grant mercy to the household of Onesiphorus, for he often refreshed me and . . . he ministered to me" (2 Timothy 1:16–18).

Onesiphorus was one of Paul's spiritual sons. He loved Paul so deeply and unconditionally that he sought out Paul whenever the apostle was suffering. Once, when Paul was jailed, Onesiphorus went through the city looking for him until he found him. His motivation was simply, "My brother is hurting and I have to encourage him."

The ministry of refreshing includes seeking out those who are hurting. Yes, there is power in the Church to heal the sick, win the lost and overcome sin—but I say that great, healing power flows out of a refreshed and renewed person. Depression, mental anguish or a troubled spirit can cause all kinds of physical sickness. A spirit that is refreshed and encouraged, however—one that is made to feel accepted, loved and needed—is the healing balm needed most.

When David was being hunted down by King Saul, he was exhausted and hurting, forced to run day and night. At a crucial moment, David's friend Jonathan came to him: "Jonathan . . . went to David . . . and strengthened his hand in God. And he said to him, 'Do not fear. . . . You shall be king over Israel, and I shall be next to you'" (1 Samuel 23:16–17). That was all David needed to hear. Immediately his spirit was refreshed to go on.

May we all have the ministry of refreshing, and see God's saints empowered anew.

COMFORT AND REFRESHING

How did the Holy Spirit bring comfort to Paul during his downcast times? The apostle himself tells us: "Nevertheless God, who comforts the downcast, comforted us by the coming of Titus" (2 Corinthians 7:6).

Titus arrived in Macedonia with a refreshing spirit, and suddenly Paul's heart was lifted. As the two men fellowshipped, joy flooded through Paul's body, mind and spirit. He wrote, "I am filled with comfort, I am exceedingly joyful in all our tribulation" (verse 4). Paul was declaring, "I still face problems, but the Lord has given me what I need for the battle. He has refreshed me through Titus."

Throughout my years in the ministry I have seen men and women of God come to the end of their endurance, cast down and utterly confused. I have anguished over these dear brothers and sisters in their pain, asking the Lord, "Father, how will Your servants ever get out of such a pit of suffering? Where is the power that will bring them out? What can I say or do to help them?"

I believe the answer is found in Paul's testimony. He was at the darkest time of his ministry—yet within a few short hours he was completely out of that dark place, reveling in joy and gladness. Once again, the beloved apostle felt loved and needed.

How did this happen? When Titus arrived in Corinth to meet with the church leaders, God was blessing them mightily and he received his own glorious refreshing. Titus returned to Macedonia with the encouraging news: "Paul, the brethren in Corinth send their love! They heeded your instruction and removed the sin that was in their midst. They no longer despise your sufferings but instead rejoice in your testimony."

"Nevertheless God who comforts the downcast, comforted us [me] by the coming of Titus" (verse 6). Do you see? God uses people to refresh people!

In the Midst of a Miracle

You may be in the middle of a miracle right now and simply not see it. It may be that you are waiting for a miracle and are discouraged because things seem to be at a standstill. You do not see any evidence of God's supernatural work on your behalf.

Consider what David said: "In my distress I called upon the Lord, and cried out to my God; He heard my voice from His temple, and my cry came before Him, even to His ears. Then the earth shook and trembled; the foundations of the hills also quaked and were shaken . . . smoke went up from His nostrils, and devouring fire from His mouth. . . . He bowed the heavens also, and came down. . . . The Lord also thundered in the heavens, and the Most High uttered His voice. . . . He sent out His arrows and . . . lightnings in abundance" (Psalm 18:6–9, 13–14).

None of these things literally happened, of course. It was all something that David saw with his spiritual eye. Yet, beloved, that is faith. It is when you believe God has heard your cry, that He has not delayed, that He is not ignoring your petition—that, instead, He quietly began your miracle immediately when you prayed, and even now He is doing supernatural work on your behalf.

David understood the foundational truth beneath it all: "He brought me out into a broad place; He delivered me, because He delighted in me" (Psalm 18:19). David declared, "I know why the Lord is doing all this for me. It is because He delights in me."

I truly believe in instantaneous miracles. God is still working glorious, instant wonders in the world today. Jesus reminds His disciples of this in Matthew 16:9–11 and Mark 8:19–21, with the miraculous feeding of the five thousand and the four thousand. He was asking them—and asks us today—to take note of His miracles. He is working them in our lives this very day.

Progressive Miracles

The Old Testament is filled with God's miracle-working power. From the opening of the Red Sea, to God's speaking to Moses from the burning bush, to Elijah's calling down fire from heaven—all were instantaneous miracles. The people involved could see them happening, feel them and thrill to them. They are the kinds of miracles we want to see today, causing awe and wonder.

Yet much of God's wonder-working power in His people's lives comes in what are called "progressive miracles." These are miracles that are hardly discernible to the eye. They are not accompanied by thunder, lightning or any visible movement or change. Rather, progressive miracles start quietly, without fanfare, and unfold slowly but surely, one step at a time.

Both kinds of miracles—instantaneous and progressive—were performed by Christ. The healings He performed were immediate, visible, easily discerned by the people present. I think of the crippled man with a gnarled body, who suddenly had an outward, physical change so that he could run and leap. This miracle had to astonish and move all who saw it.

The feedings that Christ did were progressive miracles. Jesus offered up a simple prayer of blessing, with no fire, thunder or earthquake. He merely broke the bread and the dried fish, never giving a signal that a miracle was taking place. Yet to feed that many people, there had to be thousands of breakings of that bread and those fish, all through the day. Every single piece of bread and fish was a part of the miracle.

This is how Jesus performs many of His miracles in our lives today. We pray for instantaneous, visible wonders, but often our Lord is quietly at work, forming a miracle for us bit by bit. We may not be able to hear it or touch it, but He is at work, shaping our deliverance beyond what we can see.

Finding New Strength

How quickly we forget God's great deliverances in our lives. How easily we take for granted the miracles He has performed. Yet the Bible tells us over and over, "Remember your deliverances" (see Exodus 13:3).

We are so like the disciples. They did not understand Christ's miracles when He supernaturally fed thousands with just a few loaves and fishes. Jesus performed this miracle twice, feeding five thousand people one time and four thousand another time. Yet within a few days the disciples had dropped these events from memory.

When Jesus warned them about the leaven of the Pharisees, the disciples thought He said this because they had forgotten to bring bread for their journey. But Christ answered them, "Do you not . . . remember the five loaves and how many baskets you took up? Nor the seven loaves of the four thousand and how many large baskets you took up?" (Matthew 16:9–10).

According to Mark, Christ was overwhelmed by how quickly His disciples had forgotten (see Mark 8:17–19). What do these passages tell us? Clearly, none of the disciples stopped to consider what was happening as those miraculous feedings took place.

As they walked among the crowds carrying their baskets, passing out loaves and fishes that multiplied miraculously before their eyes, I imagine them falling on their knees, crying, "How is this possible? Oh, Jesus, You truly are Lord!" I can see them urging the people they served, "Here, feast on miracle food sent from glory. Jesus has provided it."

The disciples saw these miracles with their own eyes—yet somehow the significance did not register with them. They did not understand the miracles. Likewise today, you and I forget God's miracles in our lives. Yesterday's deliverances are quickly erased from memory amid the crises of today.

Throughout both Testaments, we are told to, "Remember the powerful arm of the Lord, to perform miracles on your behalf. He is your deliverer."

Seeds of Jealousy and Envy

We all have seeds of jealousy and envy in us. The question is, who among us will acknowledge it?

A Puritan preacher named Thomas Manton said of the human penchant for envy and jealousy: "We are born with this Adamic sin. We drink it in with our mother's milk." It is that deeply a part of us.

Such sinful seeds keep us from rejoicing in the blessings and accomplishments of the ministries or works of others. The effect of such sin is to erect powerful walls between us and our brothers and sisters: "Wrath is cruel and anger a torrent, but who is able to stand before jealousy?" (Proverbs 27:4). James adds, "If you have bitter envy and self-seeking in your hearts, do not boast and lie against the truth" (James 3:14).

In plain terms, this sin of jealousy and envy is a bitter poison. If we hold on to it, it will not only cost us spiritual authority but open us to demonic activity.

King Saul provides the clearest example of this in all of Scripture. In 1 Samuel 18, we find David returning from a battle in which he slaughtered the Philistines. As he and King Saul rode into Jerusalem, the women of Israel came to celebrate David's victories, dancing and singing, "Saul has slain his thousands, and David his ten thousands" (1 Samuel 18:7).

Saul was wounded by this joyous celebration. Immediately he was consumed by a spirit of jealousy and envy. We read the deadly effect it had on him: "Saul eyed [envied] David from that day forward" (verse 9). Tragically, after this, "Saul became David's enemy continually" (verse 29).

Saul was deluded by his jealousy and could not humble himself to repent. Had he plucked it from his heart, God would have heaped honors on him. Instead, he stayed in his sin and God departed from him: "Saul was afraid of David, because the Lord was with him, but had departed from Saul" (verse 12).

Let us allow the Holy Spirit to rid us of all jealousy and envy. It is the first step in restoring relationships in the Body of Christ.

Above All That We Ask or Think

God always desires to pour out more of His glory on His people. He longs to do for us "exceedingly abundantly above all that we ask or think" (Ephesians 3:20). This is why He wants a people who have a ravenous appetite for more of Him. He wants to fill them with His awesome presence, beyond anything they have experienced in their lifetime.

Jesus said, "I have come that they may have life, and that they may have it more abundantly" (John 10:10). Yet to obtain this abundant life, we must abound more and more in pleasing the Lord.

Paul writes, "We . . . exhort in the Lord Jesus that you should abound more and more, just as you received from us how you ought to walk and to please God" (1 Thessalonians 4:1). "Therefore, my beloved brethren, be steadfast, immovable, always abounding in the work of the Lord" (1 Corinthians 15:58).

The Greek word *abound* means "to exceed, excel—to have enough and to spare, over and above, excessive, exceeding abundantly above, beyond measure." Paul is saying, "God's glory in your life is going to exceed the little moments you have had up till now. Yet your prayers have to be more than just asking a quick blessing over your meals."

"So walk in Him, rooted and built up in Him and established in the faith, as you have been taught, abounding in it with thanksgiving" (Colossians 2:6–7). Paul is instructing us, "To have this abundant life of God's glory and presence, you must serve Him above measure—with a love and commitment exceeding that of lazy, slumbering servants."

"Which He made to abound toward us in all wisdom and prudence" (Ephesians 1:8). God wants to mete out to you glory and revelation beyond any previous measure—to open to you a deeper understanding of His ways. Open yourself to the revelations of His mysteries in His Word!

DAVID'S SURPRISING ADMISSION

After exalting God's Word at length, David concludes Psalm 119 with this verse: "I have gone astray like a lost sheep; seek Your servant" (verse 176).

David is saying, "Please, Lord, seek me out, the way a shepherd searches for a lost sheep. In spite of all my biblical knowledge, preaching, and long history with You, somehow I have strayed from Your love. I have lost the sense of rest I once had in You.

"All my plans have failed. I realize now I am totally helpless. Come to me, Father. Seek me out in this awful, dry place. I can't find You on my own—You must find me. I still believe Your Word is true."

David knew he had strayed from God's rest. He knew the Lord's love should have been imprinted on his heart during his previous crises. Yet now, once again, he had forgotten about God's love for him. So he cried out to the Lord, begging Him to seek out His lost servant.

The Shepherd had come after David again. As David heard his name called, his heart was comforted. He realized, "My Shepherd knows me by name." David found himself being led down the hill into the green valley and once he reached the green pasture below, Jehovah Rohi (the Lord my Shepherd) said to him, "Lie down now. Go to sleep, and rest your weary soul. Do not worry—I will take care of everything."

Note that David's circumstances had not changed. In fact, his enemies had increased (see Psalm 3:1). But David had been restored to God's love. Now he could say, "Salvation [deliverance] belongs to the Lord" (verse 8). He testified, "No more self-made plans. No more trying to work things out. I eagerly enter into my Shepherd's love. And I am going to lie down in His rest and sleep peacefully in His unconditional love for me."

May we make the same humble admission that David did. Lord, we have forgotten You. Restore us!

Dealing with Our Strongholds

Many Christians quote 2 Corinthians 10:3–4: "We do not war according to the flesh. For the weapons of our warfare are not carnal but mighty in God for pulling down strongholds." Most of us think of strongholds as bondages such as sexual trespasses, drug addiction, alcoholism—outward sins we put at the top of a "worst sins" list. Paul, however, is referring to something much worse than our human measuring of sins.

First of all, he isn't speaking of demonic possession. In my opinion, the devil cannot enter the heart of any overcoming Christian and claim a place in that person. Rather, the figurative meaning of Paul's word *stronghold* in Greek is "holding firmly to an argument." A stronghold is an accusation planted firmly in your mind. Satan establishes strongholds in God's people by implanting in their minds falsehoods and misconceptions, especially regarding God's nature.

The enemy may plant in your mind the lie that you are unspiritual, totally unworthy of God's grace. He may whisper to you repeatedly, "You will never be free because you have not tried hard enough. In all this time you have not changed. Now God has lost patience with you because of your continual ups and downs." Satan is the accuser of the brethren, coming against us time after time with his army of accusers, planting demonic lies in our minds.

The only weapon that scares the devil is the same one that scared him in the wilderness temptations of Jesus: the living Word of God.

Here is the promise of Micah we are to cling to: "Who is a God like You, pardoning iniquity . . . ? He does not retain His anger forever, because He delights in mercy. He will again have compassion upon us, and will subdue our iniquities. You will cast all our sins into the depths of the sea" (Micah 7:18–19).

A Heart to Know Him

God has sworn by an oath to give us a new heart—one that is inclined to obey. "I will give them a heart to know Me, that I am the Lord; and they shall be My people, and I will be their God, for they shall return to Me with their whole heart" (Jeremiah 24:7). "Then I will give you a new heart and put a new spirit within you; I will take the heart of stone out of your flesh and give you a heart of flesh" (Ezekiel 36:26).

God promises not only to give us a new heart, but to write on our hearts His commands. In other words: *He promises to cause us to know Him*. Again, the Holy Spirit is the one who accomplishes this work in us. He teaches us about the Father's nature and way—and in the process, He transforms us into Christ's divine image.

Our Lord has sworn a sovereign oath to be merciful to us in our struggles against sin. Until full victory comes, He will be patient and loving with us, never casting us aside. He promises, "No matter what I demand of you, I will supply you with all the power you need to accomplish it. I will not ask anything of you for which I have not made provision."

The same power that raised Jesus from the dead—and enabled Him to fulfill God's law through a perfect, sinless life—now abides in us. God's own Spirit is alive in us, providing all power over every work of the enemy.

When the enemy comes flooding into your soul, enticing you toward an old lust, call upon the Holy Spirit. Listen to His every whisper, and obey His every command. "Therefore, if anyone is in Christ, he is a new creation; old things have passed away; behold, all things have become new" (2 Corinthians 5:17).

Victory over Your Besetting Sin

Sin causes Christians to live in humiliating defeat. They cannot stand up with courage against sin because of the secret sin in their own lives. They excuse the sins of others because of the disobedience in their own hearts. Simply put, they cannot preach victory because they live in defeat.

King David had enemies, but when he was right with the Lord none of his enemies could stand before him. When David sinned and became estranged from the Lord, however, his enemies grew bold and triumphed over him.

David's sin of adultery immediately followed one of his greatest victories. This great man of God, basking in the glory of a great victory, began to lust after Bathsheba. He ended up committing adultery with her, impregnating her and killing her husband, Uriah, to cover it up. Scripture says, "The thing that David had done displeased the LORD" (2 Samuel 11:27).

The Lord sent the prophet Nathan to David. Nathan did not come to counsel David on how to handle his guilt and condemnation—rather, he got right to the heart of the matter. "You have despised the commandment of the Lord. You have done evil in the sight of the Lord—you are guilty of secret sin." David fled into the wilderness—a weeping, barefoot, cowardly man, stripped of his power and courage because of sin.

We have had enough teaching on how to cope with our problems and fears and not enough about how to deal with sin in our lives. Where is the victory over a sin that almost becomes a part of your life?

I have no formulas, no simple solutions—but I do know there is much comfort in the Bible for those fighting battles between the flesh and the spirit. Paul fought the same kind of battle, against the same kind of enemy. He confessed, "For the good that I will *to do,* I do not do; but the evil I will not *to do,* that I practice" (Romans 7:19).

Paul makes it clear: The solution is not within us. May we all seek the Lord for *His* strength to do battle—and not to rely on our own.

Resigned into God's Care

Jesus said, "And there will be on the earth distress of nations, with perplexity . . . men's hearts failing them from fear and the expectation of those things which are coming on the earth, for the powers of heaven will be shaken" (Luke 21:25–26).

Christ is warning us, "Without hope in Me, multitudes of people are literally going to die of fright."

For Jesus' followers, however—those who trust in God's promises to preserve His children—there is glorious freedom from all fear. In fact, all who come under the Lordship of Christ never need to fear again. They need only lay hold of the following secret: *True freedom from fear consists of totally resigning one's life into the hands of the Lord.*

Resigning ourselves into God's care is an act of faith. It means putting ourselves completely under His power, wisdom and mercy. It means being led and preserved according to His will alone. If we do this, the God of the universe promises to be totally responsible for us, to feed, clothe and shelter us, and to guard our hearts from all evil.

Jesus provided the ultimate example of this kind of holy resignation when He went to the cross. Just before He gave up His spirit, He cried aloud, "Father, into Your hands I commend My spirit" (Luke 23:46).

Christ literally placed the keeping of both His life and His eternal future into the custody of the Father. In doing so, He set an example for us and placed the souls of every one of His sheep into the Father's hands.

If we are being asked to trust our lives to someone, then we have to know that this Someone has the power to keep us from all danger, threats and violence. Paul writes, "I know whom I have believed and am persuaded that He is able to keep what I have committed to Him until that Day" (2 Timothy 1:12).

PART 6

Holy Before the Lord

He Delights in Our Obedience

Following Holiness

God's Word tells us in no uncertain terms: "Pursue . . . holiness, without which no one will see the Lord" (Hebrews 12:14).

Here is the truth, plain and simple. Without the holiness that is imparted by Christ alone—a precious gift we honor by leading a life devoted to obeying His every word—none of us will see the Lord. This refers not just to heaven, but to our present life. Without holiness, we will not see God's presence in our daily walk, our family, our relationships, our witness or our ministry.

No matter how many Christian conferences we attend, how many preaching tapes we listen to, how many Bible studies we are involved in, if we harbor a cancerous sin—if the Lord has a controversy with us over our iniquity—then none of our efforts will produce godly fruit.

Of course, this issue goes beyond all lusts of the flesh to corruption of the spirit. Paul describes the same destructive sin when he says, "Nor complain, as some of them also complained, and were destroyed of the destroyer" (1 Corinthians 10:10).

Dearly beloved, will you allow the Holy Spirit to deal with any hidden sin you are harboring? Will you trust in the escape that God has provided for you? I urge you to cultivate a holy fear and trust in these last days. It will keep you pure, no matter how loudly wickedness rages around you. It will also enable you to walk in God's holiness, which holds the promise of His enduring presence.

It is all a matter of faith. Christ has promised to keep you from falling, and to give you sin-resisting power—if you simply believe what He has said. You cannot break free from the death-grip of besetting sin by willpower, by promises, or by any human effort alone. "Not by might nor by power, but by My Spirit, says the Lord of hosts" (Zechariah 4:6).

HOLINESS

When I speak of total trust in Christ, I mean not only trust in His *saving* power but trust in His *keeping* power. We have to trust His Spirit to make our life conform to His—that is, to keep us in Christ.

Think about it—at one time you were alienated, cut off from God by wicked works. What good work did you do to make things right with Him? None! No one has ever been able to make himself holy. Rather, we are brought into Christ's holiness by faith alone.

Yes, He wants your practical, daily walk to measure up to your faith walk. Yet the fact is, we have to believe Him even for that. We must trust in Him to give us the Holy Spirit, who will conform us to Christ's likeness in our daily walk.

"And you, who once were alienated and enemies in your mind by wicked works, yet now He has reconciled in the body of His flesh through death, to present you holy, and blameless, and above reproach in His sight—if indeed you continue in the faith" (Colossians 1:21–23).

Note the phrase, "*if* you continue in the faith." Jesus is saying, "Just continue trusting in Me, living by faith, and I will present you as clean, faultless and holy before the Father." That is the sanctifying work of the Holy Spirit.

There is but one holiness, and it is Christ's. It is foolish to measure yourself against some other person you picture as being holy. Never look at another Christian and say, "Oh, I wish I were as holy as he." You may struggle more often and make more mistakes—but he is no more accepted by the Father than you are.

Dearly beloved, here is the ground upon which you are to live: "I claim my holiness that is in Christ Jesus. My Father sees me as holy because I am in Christ."

Finishing the Race

"For which of you, intending to build a tower, does not sit down first and count the cost, whether he has enough to finish it—lest, after he has laid the foundation, and is not able to finish it, all who see it begin to mock him, saying, 'This man began to build and was not able to finish'" (Luke 14:28–30).

Jesus spoke these words near the close of His ministry on earth. He was warning His followers that good intentions would not be enough to see them through hard times. In short, many would not have what it took to finish the race.

It is tragic to start out fully intending to lay hold of Christ and grow into a mature disciple—and slowly drift away, becoming cold and indifferent to Him. There is no such thing as standing still. You are either changing daily into Christ's image, or you are changing back into your old carnal ways.

For those who have determined to lay hold of Christ at all costs—who are taking up their cross, denying self, and going on with Him—Paul said, "But we all, with unveiled face, beholding as in a mirror the glory of the Lord, are being transformed into the same image from glory to glory, just as by the Spirit of the Lord" (2 Corinthians 3:18).

What a joy when we meet those who are *finishing the race*—growing in the wisdom and knowledge of Christ, becoming more distant from this world and becoming increasingly heavenly minded. The older they get, the hungrier they are for more of Christ. For them, to die is gain—with the ultimate prize to be called into His presence to sit at His side forever. It is not heaven they seek but Christ in glory!

May it be so with all who would follow Jesus—that we finish the race full of faith.

A MIRROR

But he [Stephen], being full of the Holy Spirit, gazed into heaven and saw the glory of God, and Jesus standing at the right hand of God, and said, 'Look! I see the heavens opened and the Son of Man standing on the right hand of God'" (Acts 7:55–56).

Stephen represents what a true Christian is supposed to be: one who is full of the Holy Spirit, with eyes fixed on the Man in glory. Such a person mirrors Christ's glory in a way that all who see it are amazed and filled with wonder. This Christian has his gaze fixed on the Lord, always looking to Him, fully occupied with a glorified Savior.

Consider Stephen's hopeless condition. He was surrounded by religious madness, superstition, prejudice and jealousy. The angry crowd pressed in on him, wild-eyed and bloodthirsty, and death loomed just ahead of him. What impossible circumstances!

Looking up into heaven, however, Stephen beheld his Lord in glory—and suddenly his rejection on earth meant nothing. Now he was above it all, seeing the One who is invisible.

"But we all, with unveiled face, beholding as in a mirror the glory of the Lord, are being transformed into the same image from glory to glory, just as by the Spirit of the Lord" (2 Corinthians 3:18).

How true that we become what we behold. The proper translation should read, "We all, with open face mirroring the glory, are changed!" Stephen caught the rays of His glorified Lord and reflected them to a Christ-rejecting society.

As Christians, we are like a mirror, reflecting the glory on which we gaze continuously. May we become such a mirror to the world—looking on Christ, becoming more like Him—and reflecting His glory.

A Place of No Reputation

At one time, Moses had been highly esteemed—respected in high government places, great in reputation and prestige. He moved among the wealthy and was one of the best-known men of his time.

But when God spoke to Moses out of the burning bush (see Exodus 3:5), Moses had decreased to zero point. God could not use him until He tore him away from his worldly attachments.

Who knew Moses now, hidden away, out of sight on a mountainside? Silenced and without influence, he had no outlet for his great passion and energy. But the very moment Moses' reputation was totally lost, and there was nothing left of the old, self-assured Moses, he was on holy ground.

How long did God wait by that bush, ready to break forth in a glorious new revelation? Only until that final, breaking moment when Moses truly no longer cared about his work or his reputation—when he gave up the last scraps of self-reliance—did He bring revelation.

The Lord Jesus stood on this same holy ground. The Scriptures say, "[He] made Himself of no reputation, taking the form of a bondservant" (Philippians 2:7). Shunning reputation and becoming a servant was a willful choice even for our Lord.

One great man of God wrote, "The man of God who truly preaches the Word will finally give up the idea of being known. If he preaches Christ, his reputation will constantly decrease and Christ will increase. True prophets die unknown. God gives them their dues only after they die."

I believe that if we seek a larger, more widespread reputation, something is missing in our message. Self has become too prominent. Christ should be gaining, and we should be losing recognition. May we all decrease! May He alone increase! God help us to get back to this holy ground.

I thank the Lord for all who once again are being called to such holy ground, seeking to decrease that He may increase.

Holy Ground

Moses was tending sheep when God called to him from the burning bush, commanding him: "Take your sandals off your feet, for the place where you stand is holy ground" (Exodus 3:5).

Holy ground is not a physical place, but a spiritual one. When God commanded Moses to take off his shoes because he was on holy ground, He was not referring to a two-by-four piece of real estate—He was talking about a spiritual state. A holy God must have a holy servant on holy ground. In fact, God cannot use a person until He gets him onto holy ground.

The *place* was holy! What place are we talking about? The spiritual condition that Moses had finally come to—a place in his growth where God could get through to him. Moses was finally at the place of reception, ready to listen and mature enough to be willing to respond to the dealing of God.

Do not think for a moment that Moses alone was on holy ground. So was all of Israel, even though they were at the end of their hope. I have never believed God would keep an entire nation under slavery just to give Moses time to mature into a gracious leader. Our Lord is no respecter of persons. God, in those forty trying years, was preparing Israel as well as Moses. By way of loving judgment, the Lord was driving Israel back to holy ground—back to a hunger for Jehovah.

While Moses was on the mountain being stripped of all his rights—because that is what was meant by the removal of his shoes—Israel was in the valley being stripped of all human strength. Moses would have no rights; Israel would have no strength. God could prove Himself strong on their behalf in no other way. The great I AM was being revealed!

We must go the same route to usefulness—stripped of self-pride and self-confidence.

Obedience Opens the Floodgates

It is written of Christ that He was obedient to His heavenly Father, not because of fear, but because of the joy that was set before Him. He laid aside all weights and ran the race with patience. He endured shame and never fainted or got weary in His mind, because He saw the glorious rewards of obedience.

Shouldn't we be getting weary enough of all our inner turmoil that we begin to hunger after the glorious riches promised in Christ? Fear is not the best motivator toward obedience—love is! It is sweet surrender to the will of God that opens the heavens to us. It is the yielding of every lust, every act of disobedience, that allows us the revelation of who Christ really is. The Scripture says, "Whoever sins has neither seen Him nor known Him" (1 John 3:6).

Could it be possible that by living in disobedience we become distant from Him? Could it be that we go our own way because we have never had a revelation of Christ, His hatred of sin, His glory and mercy? In plain language, "He who lives in disobedience has never truly seen Christ in reality."

Jesus said, "He who has My commandments and keeps them, it is he who loves Me. And he who loves Me will be loved by My Father, and I will love him and manifest Myself to him" (John 14:21).

What greater reward for loving obedience could we want than having Christ reveal Himself to us? "Love Me enough to obey Me—and I will love you and show you who I am!"

You can read all about Him, study His nature and historical background, but you will never get to know Him until you do the simple, basic act of obeying Him completely in all things. When we surrender, we are flooded with new light, new hope, great joy, glorious peace and abounding faith.

BE YE HOLY

Three months after Israel left Egypt, they arrived at the base of Mount Sinai and set up camp. Moses climbed that rugged mountain to commune with the Lord, and God said to him: "I am going to come to you in the form of a dark cloud so that the people themselves can hear Me when I talk to you. Then they will always believe you. Go down and get the people ready for My visit. Sanctify them."

On the morning of the third day, during an awesome thunder and lightning storm, a huge cloud came down on the mountain. Mount Sinai was completely covered with smoke because Jehovah descended upon it in the form of fire. The whole mountain shook with a violent earthquake, and as the trumpet blast grew louder, God thundered to Moses and His chosen people: "You shall be to Me a kingdom of priests and a holy nation" (Exodus 19:6). "Whose voice then shook the earth . . . saying, 'Yet once more I shake not only the earth, but also heaven'" (Hebrews 12:26).

Today, once again God is speaking from heaven with the message that He spoke in Moses' day. Our God is even now thundering this awesome command: "Be holy, for I am holy" (1 Peter 1:16).

How do we stay holy in this wicked age? Who can keep himself from being contaminated by it? No one—not in our own strength, that is. Only God has the power to keep us holy—to present us to Himself as a holy people without spot or wrinkle.

The God who gives us His holiness has the power to keep us in it. The safest place on earth is at the foot of the cross, humbled before God's throne. The more wicked the times, the more we need to stay yielded to Him.

Contentment

Contentment was a major mark of Paul's life. This is because God had said He would use Paul mightily: "He is a chosen vessel of Mine to bear My name before Gentiles, kings, and the children of Israel" (Acts 9:15). When Paul first received this commission, "Immediately he preached Christ in the synagogues, that He is the Son of God" (verse 20).

Paul was in no hurry to see everything fulfilled in his lifetime. He knew he had an ironclad promise from God, and he clung to it. For the present moment, he was content to minister wherever he was: to a jailer, to a sailor, to a few women on a riverbank. This man had a worldwide commission, yet he was faithful to testify one-on-one.

Nor was Paul jealous of younger men who seemed to pass him by. While they traveled the world winning Jews and Gentiles to Christ, Paul sat in prison. He had to listen to reports of great crowds being converted by men he had battled with over the message of grace. Yet Paul did not envy those men. He knew that a Christ-surrendered man knows how to abase as well as abound: "Now godliness with contentment is great gain. . . . And having food and clothing, with these we shall be content" (1 Timothy 6:6, 8).

The world today might say to Paul, "You are at the end of your life now. You have no savings, no investments. All you have is a change of clothes."

I know what Paul's answer would be: "Oh, but I have won Christ. I tell you, I'm the winner. I have found the pearl of great price. Jesus granted me the power to lay down everything and take it up again myself. I have only one goal in this life: to see my Jesus, face-to-face. All the sufferings of this present time cannot compare to the joy that awaits me."

THE PATH OF SURRENDER

God begins the process of surrender by knocking us off our high horse. This literally happened to Paul as he was going his self-assured way, riding toward Damascus. A blinding light came from heaven and Paul was knocked to the ground, trembling. He heard a voice from heaven, saying, "Saul, Saul, why are you persecuting Me?" (Acts 9:4).

Paul had a knowledge of God but no firsthand revelation. Now, on his knees, he heard these words from heaven: "I am Jesus whom you are persecuting" (verse 5). The words turned Paul's world upside down. Scripture says, "Trembling and astonished, [Paul] said, 'Lord, what do You want me to do?'" (verse 6).

Paul's conversion was a dramatic work of the Holy Spirit—and the Holy Spirit was leading him into the surrendered life. When Paul asked, "Lord, what would You have me to do?" his heart was crying out, "Jesus, how can I serve You? How can I know You and please You? Nothing else matters. Everything I have done in my flesh is meaningless. You are everything to me now."

Paul had no other ambition, no other driving force in his life, than this: "That I may gain [win] Christ" (Philippians 3:8). By today's standards of success, Paul was a total failure. He did not construct any buildings or organization. The methods he used were despised by other leaders. In fact, the message of the cross that Paul preached offended large numbers of his hearers.

When we stand before God at the judgment, we will not be judged by our ministries, achievements or the number of our converts. There will be but one measure of success on that day: Were our hearts fully surrendered to God? Did we succumb to peer pressure and follow the crowd, or did we seek Him alone for direction? Did we run from seminar to seminar looking for purpose in life, or did we find our fulfillment in Him? I'm talking about the path of surrender.

The Surrendered Life

Surrender—in literal terms, it means "to give up something to another person. It also means to relinquish something granted to you, which could include your possessions, power, goals, even your life."

Christians today hear much about the surrendered life—but what does that mean, exactly? The surrendered life is the act of giving back to Jesus the life He granted you. It is relinquishing control, rights, power, direction, all the things you do and say, totally giving your life over into His hands.

Jesus Himself lived a surrendered life: "I have come down from heaven, not to do My own will, but the will of Him who sent Me" (John 6:38). Christ never did anything on His own. He made no move and spoke no word without being instructed by the Father. "I do nothing of Myself; but as My Father taught Me, I speak these things. . . . For I always do those things that please Him" (8:28–29).

Jesus' full surrender to the Father is an example of how we all should live. True, Jesus was God in flesh and His life was surrendered before He even came to earth, but the surrendered life is not imposed on anyone, including Jesus.

"Therefore My Father loves Me, because I lay down My life that I may take it again. No one takes it from Me, but I lay it down of Myself. I have power to lay it down, and I have power to take it again" (10:17–18).

Jesus was telling us, "Make no mistake. I choose to lay down My life. My Father gave me the right to lay down My life, as well as the choice to pass up this cup and avoid the cross. But I choose to do it, out of love and full surrender to Him."

Our heavenly Father has given us this same right—we can have as much of Christ as we want. That means surrendering to Him as much as we will.

Holy Boldness and Spiritual Authority

The more someone is with Jesus, the more that person becomes like Christ in purity, holiness and love. His pure walk produces in him a great boldness for God. Scripture says, "The wicked flee when no one pursues, but the righteous are bold as a lion" (Proverbs 28:1). The word used for *bold* in this verse means "secure, confident." That is just the kind of boldness the synagogue rulers saw in Peter and John as they ministered (see Acts 4:1–2).

In the previous chapter, Peter and John prayed for a crippled beggar and he was instantly healed. The healing caused a great stir around the Temple, and the religious leaders arrested the disciples in an attempt to keep them from sharing their faith in Christ.

Peter and John met with the synagogue rulers, but the Bible does not go into much detail about this scene in Acts 4. Yet I can assure you, the religious leaders orchestrated it to be all pomp and ceremony. First, the dignitaries solemnly took their velvety seats. Then the high priests' relatives filed to their seats. Finally, in a moment of hushed anticipation, the robed high priests strutted in. Everyone bowed as the priests passed by, walking stiffly up the aisle toward the seat of judgment.

This was meant to intimidate Peter and John, but it did not work. The disciples had been with Jesus for too long. I imagine Peter thinking, "Come on, get this meeting started, then give me the pulpit and turn me loose. I've got a word from God for this gathering. Thank you, Jesus, for allowing me to preach Your name to these Christ-haters."

Acts 4:8 begins with: "Then Peter, filled with the Holy Spirit . . ." and this tells me it was not going to be a quiet, reserved lecture. Peter was a Jesus-possessed man, bursting with the Holy Spirit.

Likewise today, God's true servants are to stand boldly with Gospel truth. His authority gives us boldness to preach before anyone, anywhere.

Cut Them Off

Jesus tells His disciples, "And if your hand or foot causes you to sin, cut it off and cast it from you. . . . And if your eye causes you to sin, pluck it out and cast it from you" (Matthew 18:8–9).

In the King James Version, Jesus begins this sentence with the word *Wherefore,* meaning, "In the light of this." He is tying His statement into the whole context of the lesson He has been teaching about mixing works with the cross. So, when He says here, "If your hand or foot or eye offends you," He is talking about the offense that the cross brings to the flesh.

When Jesus says, "Cut it off, pluck it out," He is talking to Jewish listeners first about their confidence in their own good works. The hand, foot and the eye all represent flesh—instruments of independence by which man goes his own way, relying on self-will and human effort to rid himself of sinful bondages.

Christ is saying to such a person, "Your eye is focused on the wrong thing. You are looking at your own ability and power, your natural talents and gifts. Therefore, pluck out your eye, cut off your limb. You have to rid your body, mind and heart of all such evil thinking. Renounce it, surgically remove it—cut off all hope of offering to God anything of your own merit or goodness. Lust and offenses must be cut off—but not by your hands. It is the work of the Spirit.

"Then simply run into My arms and let Me impart My goodness and life to you. Humble yourself like a child by embracing My victory on the cross. Commit to a life of total devotion and dependence on Me. Because of My work at Calvary, you are no longer your own—I have bought you. My Spirit will fulfill My demand for holiness in you."

CROSSING THE LINE

When Jesus walked the earth, He knew all too well the fierceness of Satan's power to sift the Lord's people. I do not think any of us can comprehend how determined Satan is to destroy all believers who have fixed their hungering hearts firmly on going all the way with Christ.

Yet it is true that in our Christian walk, we cross the obedience line that sets off every alarm in hell. The moment we cross that line into a life of obedience to God's Word and dependence on Jesus alone, we become a threat to the kingdom of darkness and a prime target of demonic principalities and powers.

If you have crossed the obedience line, you are making waves in the unseen world. In Luke 22:28–34, Jesus introduces the subject of the sifting of saints. "Simon, Simon! . . . Satan has asked for you, that he may sift you as wheat" (verse 31).

In Christ's day, grain workers used a sieve just before they sacked grain. They shoveled wheat into a square box covered with netting, then turned the box upside down and shook it violently. The grit and dirt fell through the netting until only the grain kernels remained. In this verse *sift* means "to be shaken and separated—to be shocked through the agitation of sudden trials." Jesus used this analogy to say to Peter: "Satan believes you are nothing but grit and dirt. He thinks when he puts you in the sieve and shakes you, you will fall through to the ground."

I see sifting as a major, all-out satanic onslaught, usually compressed into a short but very intense period. For Peter, the sifting would only last a few days, but they became the most remorseful days of his life.

Thank God, Peter's faith did not fail—and as surely as Jesus prayed that his "faith fail not," He prays for us in the same manner. He stands with us when we choose to cross the line.

The Hour of Isolation

I know what it is like to face divine silence, not to hear God's voice for a season. I have walked through periods of total confusion with no apparent guidance, the still, small voice behind me completely silent.

There have been times when I had no friend nearby to satisfy my heart with a word of advice. All my patterns of guidance that had helped me in the past had gone awry, and I was left in total darkness. I could not see my way, and I made mistake after mistake. I wanted to say, "Oh, God, what has happened? I don't know which way to go."

Does God really hide His face from those He loves? Is it not possible that He lifts His hand for a short while to teach us trust and dependence? The Bible answers clearly: "God withdrew from him [Hezekiah], in order to test him, that He might know all that was in his heart" (2 Chronicles 32:31).

You may be going through a flood of trials right now. You know what I am talking about when I say the heavens are as brass. You know all about repeated failures. You have waited and waited for answers to prayer. You have been served a cup of affliction. But nothing and nobody can touch that need in your heart.

That is the time to take your stand! You do not have to be able to laugh or rejoice, because you may not have any happiness at the moment. In fact, you may have nothing but turmoil in your soul. But you can know God is still with you, because Scripture says, "The Lord sat enthroned at the Flood, and the Lord sits as King forever" (Psalm 29:10).

Soon you will hear His voice: "Do not get excited, do not panic. Just keep your eyes on Me. Commit all things to Me." You remain the object of His incredible love.

Something I Was Not Expecting to Hear

One night during a prayer meeting, God told me something about our church I was not expecting to hear.

The Lord whispered to me, "This church needs shock treatment. Too many have grown satisfied and complacent. You feel safe and secure from all the winds and waves of false doctrines sweeping over the land—but you are not prepared for what is coming."

Beloved, the message of having the Spirit's witness functioning in you is not a request—it is a matter of life and death! If you do not have the witness of the Holy Spirit in these last days, you are not going to make it. You will give in to the coming spirit of the Antichrist.

You need the Holy Spirit's witness every day—on your job, at home, at school. You need to rightly judge politicians and leaders so you will not suddenly be sucked into the antichrist system.

This is what Jesus was trying to tell us about the foolish virgins who ran out of oil in their lamps (see Matthew 25). They had a supply of the Holy Spirit—but they did not have His witness at the final moment.

Do not end up like a foolish virgin! If you are running out of oil—trusting your church or your pastor to keep your soul—then repent. Cry out to God to rid you of all anger and bitterness. Confess your sins and forsake them—and depend on God once again for everything.

Get the peace of God in your heart, so you can have a Holy Spirit witness. Invite Him to be your witness and guide in everything.

We face a cost of going all the way with Jesus, but we also will receive a reward: *It is simply the blessing of having Christ stand with us.* There are many other rewards as well but this one is all we will ever need.

The Witness of the Spirit

And it is the Spirit who bears witness, because the Spirit is truth" (1 John 5:6).

There are times when the Holy Spirit's inner witness will not allow me to keep quiet. The Spirit rises within me and I am compelled to speak up.

The Holy Spirit abides in us to reveal what is true and what is false. He speaks with a still, small voice, deep within the heart. Many of our holy forefathers preached much about "having the witness," but I do not hear this truth being preached anymore. In fact, the witness of the Spirit is virtually unheard of in most churches today.

Believers need the Spirit's witness as never before, and we are going to need it more as the day of the Lord draws near. Satan has come brazenly as an angel of light to deceive, if it were possible, the very elect of God. His evil seductions are going to flourish: false doctrines, false teachers, false gospels.

The Spirit's inner witness operates on the "principle of peace." The peace of God is the greatest thing you can have—so when your peace is disturbed, you can be sure the Holy Spirit is speaking to you. When there is a troubling in your spirit—a shaking and turmoil deep inside—God is telling you that something is false. You will feel His embarrassment, grief or anger.

"And let the peace of God rule in your hearts" (Colossians 3:15). Any hidden sin will rob a believer of peace. His heart will be torn by guilt, condemnation and fear—and the Spirit will only speak two words to him: "Repent! Flee!"

Yes, the Spirit will speak to you to correct you; He will deal with you about sin, righteousness and judgment. Listen to His inner witness, for it is life.

What Every Christian Should Know about Spiritual Growth

"We are bound to thank God always for you, brethren, as it is fitting, because your faith grows exceedingly, and the love of every one of you abounds toward each other" (2 Thessalonians 1:3).

What a great compliment Paul paid the Thessalonian Christians. In essence, Paul was saying, "It is incredible to see how much you have grown, both in your faith in Christ and in your love for one another. Everywhere I go, I brag to others about your spiritual growth. How I thank God for you."

In this short passage, Paul gives us an amazing picture of a body of believers who were growing in unity and love. The Greek phrase Paul uses for *grows exceedingly* means "to grow over, above and beyond that of others." Both individually and corporately, the Thessalonians' faith and love outshone that of all other churches.

Obviously, these Thessalonian Christians were not just trying to hang on to their faith till Jesus returned. They were learning, moving, growing—and their lives offered evidence to that fact. According to Paul, they were the talk of every church in Asia.

Apparently, the preaching these people heard was provoking them into an ever deeper walk with Christ. It was melting their fleshly ambitions and convicting them of un-Christlike habits. The Holy Spirit was tearing down all ethnic barriers and color lines. They were discovering how to embrace any person, whether rich or poor, educated or not. They offered great care to each other, preferring one another in love.

If you are being watered and fed by God's Word, you should experience continual spiritual growth in your life. It should be happening automatically. The anointed preaching of the pure Word of God always produces growth.

A Letter from the Devil

One of Satan's tricks is to paint a fantastic picture of what your life could be like if you make a deal with him. Scripture gives us a vivid picture of one such occasion, when Israel and their King Hezekiah were confronted by an evil messenger.

> Thus says the king of Assyria: "Make peace with me by a present and come out to me; and every one of you eat from his own vine and every one from his fig tree, and every one of you drink the waters of his own cistern; until I come and take you away to a land like your own land, a land of grain and new wine, a land of bread and vineyards, a land of olive groves and honey, that you may live and not die. But do not listen to Hezekiah, lest he persuade you, saying, 'The LORD will deliver us.'"
>
> 2 Kings 18:31–32

What a crooked salesman the devil is. Every compromise you make in your walk with Jesus is the same as "going out" to the enemy. So what do you do when you are confronted with a message from the devil?

First, you do as Hezekiah did: He spread the enemy's letter before the Lord (see 19:14–15). Then pray and seek the Lord. Do not ever reason with the devil; simply hold your peace, as the people in this passage did in the face of the taunting messenger (see 18:36).

God's response to the devil's letter is to read it and laugh (see 19:21). In other words, God takes that letter personally. He says, "Devil, you did not send that letter to My child—you sent it to Me!" For "whom have you reproached and blasphemed? Against whom have you raised your voice, and lifted up your eyes on high? Against the Holy One of Israel" (19:22).

He who touches you touches the apple of God's eye. God says His loved ones are safe and the devil cannot harm them (see 19:32, 34).

WINNING CHRIST

Yet indeed I also count all things loss for the excellence of the knowledge of Christ Jesus my Lord, for whom I have suffered the loss of all things, and count them as rubbish, that I may gain Christ" (Philippians 3:8).

Paul was completely captivated by his Lord. Why would he feel the need to "win" Christ? Christ already had revealed Himself clearly, and not just to the apostle but in his life. Yet Paul still felt compelled to win Christ's heart and affection.

Paul's entire being was focused only on pleasing his Master and Lord. All else was rubbish to him, even "good" things.

Is this scriptural, you may ask, this idea of winning the heart of Jesus? Are we not already the objects of God's love? It is true His benevolent love extends to all mankind. But there is another kind of love that few Christians ever experience. That is an affectionate love with Christ such as occurs between a husband and wife.

This love is expressed in the Song of Solomon where Solomon is portrayed as a type of Christ. In one passage the Lord speaks of His Bride this way:

"You have ravished my heart . . . my spouse; you have ravished my heart with one look of your eyes, with one link of your necklace. How fair is your love . . . my spouse! How much better than wine is your love" (Song of Solomon 4:9–10).

The Bride of Christ consists of a holy people who long to be pleasing to their Lord. They live so obediently, so separated from all other things, that Christ's heart will be ravished.

The word *ravish* in this passage means "to steal my heart." The King James Version of the above passage says that Christ's heart is ravished with just "one eye." That "one eye" is the singleness of a mind focused on Christ alone. That is how we win Him!

The Need for Endurance

To *endure* means "to carry through despite hardships; to suffer patiently without giving up." In short, it means to hold on or hold out.

I believe this word means little to the present generation. Many Christians today are quitters—they quit on their spouses, their families and their God.

Peter addresses this subject by saying, "For this is commendable, if because of conscience toward God one endures grief, suffering wrongfully" (1 Peter 2:19). Then he adds, "What credit is it if, when you are beaten for your faults, you take it patiently? But when you do good and suffer for it, if you take it patiently, this is commendable before God. For to this you were called, because Christ also suffered for us, leaving us an example, that you should follow His steps" (verses 20–21).

The apostle Paul commands, "You . . . must endure hardship as a good soldier of Jesus Christ" (2 Timothy 2:3).

What is your hardship? A marriage in turmoil? A job crisis? Conflict with a relative, a landlord, a friend?

We are to take hope. You see, just as Paul's suffering never let up, neither did his revelation, his maturity, his deep faith, his settled peace. He said, "If I am going to be a spiritual man—if I really want to please my Lord—then I cannot fight my circumstances. I will hold on and never quit. Nothing on this earth can give me what I get from God's Spirit every day in my trial."

Paul's life "breathed" with the Spirit of Christ. So it is with every truly spiritual person. The Holy Spirit pours forth out of this servant's inner being the heavenly breezes of God. This person is not downcast—he does not murmur or complain about his lot. He may be going through the trial of his life, but he is still smiling—because he knows God is at work in him, revealing His eternal glory.

HIGHER MEANING OF WALKING IN THE SPIRIT

In 1 Samuel 9 Saul's father sent him to find some runaway donkeys. Taking a servant with him, Saul searched throughout the land until he became discouraged and was ready to give up the hunt. Then his servant told him about Samuel, a seer, who might be able to tell him where the donkeys were.

Samuel is a type of the Holy Spirit, who knows the mind of God. The Spirit has more on his mind than just giving direction, because he knows God has chosen Saul to play a part in heaven's eternal purposes.

The first thing Samuel did when Saul arrived was to call for a feast (see 1 Samuel 9:19). This is exactly what the Holy Spirit desires of us: to sit at the Lord's table and minister to Him—having quality time alone, hearing His heart.

Samuel asked Saul to clear his mind so they could commune together (verses 20–25). Samuel was saying, "Don't focus on getting direction now—that's all settled. There is something more important at hand. You must get to know God's heart, His eternal purposes."

After that night of communion, Samuel asked Saul to send his servant out of the room, so they could have an intimate, face-to-face session (see verse 9:27; 10:1).

Do you see what God is saying here? "If you really want to walk in the Spirit—if you really want My anointing—you need to seek more than direction from Me. You need to come into My presence and get to know My heart, My desires. You see, I want to anoint you—to use you in My Kingdom."

Beloved, forget direction—in fact, forget everything else for now. Allow the Holy Spirit to teach you the deep hidden things of God. Stand still in His presence, and let Him show you the very heart of the Lord. That is the walk of the Spirit in the highest form!

God Loves You!

"The Father loves you." It is with this truth that multitudes of believers fail in their faith. They are willing to be convicted of sin and failure, over and over again. But they will not allow the Holy Spirit to flood them with the love of the Father.

The legalist loves to live under conviction. He has never understood the love of God or allowed the Holy Spirit to minister that love to his soul.

At Times Square Church we have taught that the righteous person, the true lover of Jesus, loves reproof. He learns to welcome having the Holy Spirit expose all his hidden areas of sin and unbelief. The more he deals with sin, the happier and freer he becomes.

The attitudes I see in response to my sermons vary. When I deliver a message that thunders with judgment, I get overwhelmingly approving responses. When I share about the sweetness and love of Jesus, I receive letters saying, "You are not preaching the truth anymore!" It is as though these people are saying, "If you are not reproving, then what you are saying cannot be the Gospel."

Such believers have never entered into the great love-mission of the Holy Spirit. This is an area where you must learn to walk in the Spirit—and not by feelings. Walking in the Spirit means allowing the Holy Spirit to do in you what He was sent to do—and that includes flooding your heart with the love of God. "Because the love of God has been poured out in our hearts by the Holy Spirit who was given to us" (Romans 5:5).

Governed by the Word of God

If Christ reigns as the supreme authority over His kingdom, and we are His subjects, then our lives must be governed by Him. What does it mean, exactly, to be governed by Jesus?

According to the dictionary, *govern* means "to guide, to direct, to control all actions and behavior of those under authority." In short, Jesus must be allowed to control all of our actions and behavior, including our every thought, word and deed.

Jesus also rules the nations of the world. The Bible tells us, "He rules by His power forever; His eyes observe the nations; do not let the rebellious exalt themselves" (Psalm 66:7). "The LORD has established His throne in heaven, and His kingdom rules over all" (103:19).

Do not be fooled—our country is not ruled by any political party or authority. It is not controlled by Wall Street or big business entities. No power, earthly or supernatural, rules America or any other nation. God alone is in control.

All across America we are seeing awful moral decay, the rise of the occult, rampant sexual deviations, raging atheism. Some Christians fear that the hordes of hell are slowly taking over our nation, establishing Satan's kingdom of darkness.

We need not worry about Satan. Isaiah assures us, "The LORD has broken the staff of the wicked, the scepter of the rulers. . . . How you are fallen from heaven, O Lucifer, son of the morning! . . . Yet you shall be brought down to Sheol [hell]. . . . Those who see you will gaze at you, and consider you, saying: 'Is this the man who made the earth tremble, who shook kingdoms?'" (Isaiah 14:5, 12, 15–16).

Beloved, God is not fretting over what we see as an evil takeover of our nation. With just one word from our Lord's mouth, Satan will be gone forever, tormented for eternity. Therefore, we are to fear no evil. If you are His, you are governed by the Word of God!

Hindrances to Growing in Grace

In Ephesians 4:31, Paul lists things we must remove from our lives if we are to grow in the grace of Christ: "Let all bitterness, wrath, anger, clamor, and evil speaking be put away from you, with all malice."

We dare not skip over these issues on Paul's list. The apostle says we absolutely must face these things if we are to grow in grace. If you ignore the heart issues Paul mentions here, you will grieve the Holy Spirit. Your growth will be stunted and you will end up a spiritual zombie.

The first three items on Paul's list—bitterness, wrath and anger—are self-explanatory. *Bitterness* is a refusal to let go of an old wound or forgive a past wrong. *Wrath* is a stronghold of resentment coupled with a hope to gain revenge. *Anger* is exasperation—either a quick explosive outburst or a slow burn of indignation toward someone.

Evil speaking is words that tear down—the opposite of edifying someone or speaking words of edification. Evil speaking is malicious, hurtful. *Clamor* is a sudden outburst over nothing—an unnecessary hubbub, a loud noise made for no purpose. We cause a clamor when we make a big issue out of something insignificant, or cause a scene rather than trying to help or heal.

The final item on Paul's list is *malice,* the desire to see someone else suffer. For many Christians malice means hoping God will punish someone who wounded them. It is a devilish spirit, and is usually hidden deep within the heart.

When Paul says, "Put away all these evils from you," he is not talking about a quick fix, but rather, a process—a matter of growth that takes time. At times, we may fail at ridding ourselves of these evils. But if we will quickly repent, and commit to making things right with the person, over time these issues will fade away.

Explosive Growth in Grace

Our growth in grace can be explosive when we attempt to edify those who try to put us down.

"Let no corrupt word proceed out of your mouth, but what is good for necessary edification, that it may impart grace to the hearers. And do not grieve the Holy Spirit of God" (Ephesians 4:29–30). The root word Paul uses for *edify* here means "house builder." That word, in turn, means "to build up." In short, everyone who edifies is building up God's house, the Church.

Paul is telling us three important things here about the words we speak:

1. We are to use our words to build up God's people.
2. We are to use our words to minister grace to others.
3. It is possible to grieve the Holy Spirit with our words.

I get deeply convicted as I read the life stories of spiritual giants of the past. These godly men and women were heavenly minded—studious in God's Word, people of prayer and concerned about growing in grace. What strikes me most about their lives is not just their devotion to Christ or the intensity of their prayers but the godly fruit produced in them.

Moreover, I discovered a common thread among these spiritual giants: Their main concern was to grow in the grace of a pure heart, out of which holy conversation would flow. "For out of the abundance of the heart the mouth speaks" (Matthew 12:34).

You grow in grace when you choose to live for others and not yourself. That growth must begin in your home by showing your spouse and your children ever-increasing Christlikeness. Your home must become a proving ground where all problems and misunderstandings are overcome by your willingness to give up your attempts to be right. Never having to be right has helped me enjoy the power of God's grace as never before.

Let us grow up—in grace.

He Wrote Your Name on His Hand

What incredible authority we have been given in prayer. When we placed our faith in Jesus, He gave us His name, enabling us to say, "I am one with Christ." Then, amazingly, Jesus took on *our* name. As our high priest, He wrote it on the palm of His hand so that our name is registered in heaven, under His glorious name.

You can see why the phrase "in Christ's name" is not just some impersonal formula. Rather, it is a literal position we have with Jesus. Jesus tells us, "In that day you will ask in My name, and I do not say to you that I shall pray the Father for you; for the Father Himself loves you, because you have loved Me, and have believed that I came forth from God" (John 16:26–27).

Jesus is telling us, in other words: "Whenever you ask in My name, your request has the same power and effect with the Father as if I were asking Him." Think of it: When we lay hands on the sick and pray, God sees us as if Jesus is laying hands on the sick to bring healing.

We are to come confidently to the throne of grace and pray boldly, "Father, I stand before You, chosen in Christ to go forth and bear fruit. Now I make my request largely, that my joy may be full."

I hear many Christians say, "I asked in Jesus' name, but my prayers were not answered." One reason may be because we have allowed sin in our lives to become roadblocks to His blessing.

Perhaps the blockage is due to lukewarmness toward the things of God. Or perhaps we are filled with doubt, which cuts us off from the power of Christ. James makes it clear: "He who wavers will not receive anything of God" (see James 1:6–7).

God knows our hearts, and He reserves the power that is in Christ for those who are wholly surrendered to Him. He has written our names on His hand!

Under the Rule of Grace

The Prodigal Son needed what the apostle Paul calls the "renewing of the mind." I love reading these words from the parable: "But the father said to his servants, 'Bring out the best robe and put it on him, and put a ring on his hand and sandals on his feet. And bring the fatted calf here and kill it, and let us eat and be merry'" (Luke 15:22–23).

The Prodigal had a mindset of condemnation, put on him by Satan. Today, the same is true of many of God's children. Our Father rejoices over us, embracing us with loving arms. To us, however, humility means telling God how bad we have been, digging up our past sins rather than trusting His expressions of love. We think guiltily, "He has to be angry with me. I have sinned worse than others."

When the father's servants brought forth the best robe in the house and put it on the son, it represented his being clothed in the righteousness of Christ. The father put a ring on the boy's finger, signifying his union with Christ. Finally, he put shoes on the boy's feet, representing being shod with the gospel of the peace of Christ.

This loving father was showing his child: "Away with those rags, those shreds of self effort to please me. Let me show you how I see you. You are coming into my house and into my presence as a new, kingly, royal child. You are coming in as my son who delights me, not as a slave. Now, enter in with boldness!"

The same is true for us today. We have to be renewed in our thinking about how God receives us into His presence. "Therefore, brethren, having boldness to enter the Holiest by the blood of Jesus, by a new and living way . . . let us draw near with a true heart in full assurance of faith" (Hebrews 10:19–20, 22).

Walk As a New Man

You know the Prodigal story. A young man took his portion of his father's inheritance and squandered it on riotous living. Ruined in health and spirit, he decided to return to his father. Scripture tells us, "And he arose and came to his father. But when he was still a great way off, his father saw him and had compassion, and ran and fell on his neck and kissed him" (Luke 15:20).

Note that nothing hindered this father's forgiveness of the young man. There was nothing this boy had to do—not even confess his sins—because the father had already made provision for reconciliation. Indeed, the father ran to his son and embraced him as soon as he saw the boy coming up the road. The truth is, forgiveness is never a problem for any loving father. Likewise, it is never a problem with our heavenly Father when we repent.

Forgiveness simply is not the issue in this parable. In fact, Jesus makes it clear that it was not enough for this Prodigal merely to be forgiven. The father did not embrace his son just to forgive him and let him go his way. No, the father yearned for more—he wanted his child's company, his presence, his communion.

Even though the Prodigal was forgiven and in favor once more, he still was not settled in his father's house. Only when the son was brought into his company would the father be satisfied. That is the issue in this parable.

Here the story gets very interesting. The son hesitated to enter the house because he was not at ease with his father's forgiveness. He thought, "If you only knew all the filthy, ungodly things I have done, sins against God and against your love and grace. I just don't deserve your love."

The father utters not a single word of reproof. In his eyes, the *old boy* was dead—his son was a new man. And so are we in our heavenly Father's eyes. Christ's gift has made us new men, new women—and we are beloved to our Father.

THE TEN COMMANDMENTS

Most of America knows that the Supreme Court of the United States has banned displaying the Ten Commandments in any government courthouse. This landmark decision has been covered exhaustively by the media. But what does the ruling mean?

A courthouse is where laws are enforced. The Ten Commandments represent God's moral law, which never shifts or changes. It is as fixed as the law of gravity. If you defy that law, it is like stepping off a high building. You can deny that the law affects you, but there are sure consequences.

Simply put, the Ten Commandments are eternal laws designed by God to keep society from destroying itself. Yet, amazingly, many sandblasting companies are at work right now grinding away those Commandments—as well as God's name—wherever they are engraved in courthouse marble or concrete.

What a telling picture of the state of our society. These unchangeable laws, originally engraved in stone by the finger of God, are being erased from stone by the law of man.

Some Christians are saying, "What's the big deal? We are not under the law." It is true that we are not under the Hebrew law, meaning the 613 additional commandments added by Jewish rabbis. Every Christian is, however, under the authority of God's moral law, summed up in the Ten Commandments.

Some believers claim, "We don't need these displays of the Commandments. They are written in our hearts." Here is what God's Word says:

"And these words which I command you today shall be in your heart . . . and [you] shall talk of them when you sit in your house, when you walk by the way, when you lie down, and when you rise up. You shall bind them as a sign on your hand, and they shall be as frontlets between your eyes. You shall write them on the doorposts of your house and on your gates" (Deuteronomy 6:6–9).

God's laws do not change. Even if they are erased from society, they are written in our hearts. May our lives be living testaments to His saving truth!

Awe and Respect

The Bible makes it clear that there is a fear of the Lord every believer is to cultivate. True fear of God includes awe and respect, but it is much more than that. David tells us, "An oracle within my heart concerning the transgression of the wicked: there is no fear of God before his eyes" (Psalm 36:1).

David is saying, "When I see somebody indulging in evil, my heart tells me such a person has no fear of God. He doesn't acknowledge the truth about sin, or about God's call to holiness."

The fact is, godly fear gives us power to maintain victory in wicked times. So how do we attain this fear? Jeremiah answers with this prophecy from God's Word: "I will give them one heart and one way, that they may fear Me forever, for the good of them and their children after them. And I will make an everlasting covenant with them, that I will not turn away from doing them good; but I will put My fear in their hearts so that they will not depart from Me" (Jeremiah 32:39–40).

This wonderful promise from the Lord assures us He will provide us with His holy fear. God does not just drop this fear into our hearts in a supernatural flash. He puts His fear in us through His Word.

God's fear is planted in our hearts when we consciously decide that we are going to obey every word we read in Scripture. We see how godly fear came upon Ezra: "Ezra had prepared his heart to seek the Law of the Lord, and to do it" (Ezra 7:10).

The fear of God is not just an Old Testament concept. We see godly fear mentioned in both Testaments. The Old tells us, "Fear the Lord and depart from evil" (Proverbs 3:7). Likewise, the New declares, "There is no fear of God before their eyes" (Romans 3:18). Let us therefore fear the Lord—with awe and respect, but also to maintain victory in wicked times.

Without Spot or Wrinkle

Christ's Church has never been approved or accepted by the world. If you live for Jesus, you will not have to separate yourself from others' company—they will do it for you. You will find yourself reproached, rejected, called evil: "Blessed are you when men hate you, and when they exclude you, and revile you, and cast out your name as evil, for the Son of Man's sake" (Luke 6:22).

Yet, Jesus adds, this is the path to true fulfillment. "For whoever desires to save his life will lose it, and whoever loses his life for My sake will find it" (Matthew 16:25). In other words: "The only way you find meaning in life is by selling out your all for Me. Then you will find true joy, peace and satisfaction."

Christ tells us, "The Church I am coming for will be without spot or wrinkle. You must therefore surrender all to Me, dying completely to self, ungodly ambition and ego. By faith you will be buried with Me, but I will raise you up into new life."

Think about what it means to be without spot or wrinkle. We know a spot is a stain. But what about a wrinkle? Have you ever heard the phrase, "a new wrinkle"? It means adding a new idea to an existing concept. A wrinkle, in that sense, applies to those who try to improve on the Gospel. It suggests an easy way to attain heaven, without full surrender to Christ.

The kind of Gospel that is being preached in many churches today is aimed only at meeting people's needs. As we read Jesus' words, we see that this kind of preaching does not accomplish the true work of the Gospel.

I am not against preaching comfort and strength to God's people—we are called to do exactly that. But Jesus' words are clear: Our needs are met not by finding some new wrinkle in Christian living or thought—but by dying to self and taking up His cross.

Drawing Our Own Circle

Are you worried about a family member or friend who does not seem to be maturing in Christ? As you size up that person, have you drawn your own circle of what it means to be a true follower of Christ?

Is it possible that you are limited in your view of what Christ is doing with that person? Is your Jesus so small that you cannot believe His Spirit may be doing a deep, hidden work? Do you condemn this person for not measuring up to your imprint?

About 35 years ago a desperate woman walked into Teen Challenge in Brooklyn. She was New York's most notorious madam, running a prostitution ring that catered to some of the nation's most famous men. She had grown up in a Pentecostal home and her praying grandmother had prophesied over her, "You are going to be an evangelist." This woman rejected her church upbringing, however, and turned to prostitution.

As her prostitution ring grew, she became addicted to drugs. All during that time, a battle was going on in her heart. Night after night, she prayed, "God, please let me live just one more day." Eventually she was arrested and the news made national headlines. At one point her brother wrote to her, "You have so shamed our family, you are beyond redemption."

But Jesus never forsook her. One day in her loneliest hour, this woman prayed—and the change in her was immediate. Everyone who had seen her life from the outside thought she was utterly hopeless—but they had a limited view of Christ. While the people in her life had seen her only as common and unclean, the Lord had seen in her an evangelist.

We took her in at Teen Challenge just before she was sentenced. As she served time in prison, she became the evangelist God had called her to be. She led many souls to Jesus while in jail—and after she was released, she became a powerful street preacher.

Let us never draw our own circle of limits on how Jesus sees people. Rather, let us ask Him to give us His eyes to see others.

LIMITING THE HOLY ONE OF ISRAEL

They] limited the Holy One of Israel" (Psalm 78:41). The word for *limited* here comes from two root words, meaning "grieving God by scratching out an imprint." In short, limiting God means drawing a line, or making a circle, and stating, "God is in here, and He goes no farther."

This describes the thinking of many believers. We have a very small concept of Christ's magnitude.

The early Church in Jerusalem limited Christ to a small circle, confining Him to the Jewish population. But Jesus cannot be confined. He is constantly breaking out of our little circles and extending His reach to the uttermost, in ways far beyond what we imagine.

God's Spirit bursts through everyone's drawn circles. The Holy Spirit falls on believers in all different denominations. A classic book entitled *They Speak with Other Tongues* by John and Elizabeth Sherrill was written about this move of the Spirit.

The Lord also used my book *The Cross and the Switchblade,* especially in Catholic circles. Yet, like Peter and the early Church, I had to allow God to work in my heart before I could accept what was going on. I had been raised Pentecostal, and for the first time in my life I saw priests weeping with conviction, crying out to Jesus.

Evangelical preachers contended with me, demanding, "What about those Catholics' Maryology? How can you minister to people who believe in that?" I answered the same way Peter did: "I don't know anything about Maryology, but there are hungry people in the Catholic Church. And there are true Jesus worshipers among the priests. God is filling these people with His Spirit."

God has His people everywhere—and we are to obey Him in reaching out to them.

On Our Feet and Ready

Saul was afraid of David, because the Lord was with him" (1 Samuel 18:12).

Satan most envies and fears those who have been with God in prayer and are determined to stand up and fight in faith. Satan fears even a small army of those who are girded up in faith for a fight. He cowers before those who are up on their feet and ready to resist. He also fears you, and because of this his design is to neutralize your fighting spirit.

The devil does this by trying to flood your mind with defeating, distracting, hellish thoughts that breed mistrust and questions about God's power. He will whisper into your mind and spirit, "It is no use fighting. You are too weak from your personal struggles, so you might as well relax. The powers of hell are just too big to overcome. You don't need to be so intense about the battle anymore."

That is a distraction! Satan's entire strategy is to get you to take your eyes off the victory of the cross. He wants to turn your focus onto your weaknesses, your sins, your shortcomings—and that's why he turns up the heat of your present problems and sufferings. He wants to make you believe you are not strong enough to go on. But *your* strength is not the point—Jesus' strength is!

We all are going to be in a fight until we either go home to be with the Lord or Jesus comes back. We may be given seasons of calm, times of reprieve, but as long as we are on this earth, we are engaged in spiritual warfare. That is why Paul says Jesus has given us weapons that are mighty to the pulling down of strongholds. We have been equipped with every weapon needed, which Satan cannot withstand: prayer, fasting and faith.

A Pleasing Walk

The apostle Paul taught the Colossian church: "Walk worthy of the Lord, fully pleasing Him, being fruitful in every good work and increasing in the knowledge of God" (Colossians 1:10).

What is required for a pleasing walk? Paul says: "Put on therefore, as the chosen of God, holy and beloved, a heart of compassion, kindness, humility, gentleness and patience; bearing with one another, and forgiving one another, whoever has a complaint against another; just as the Lord forgave you, so also should you" (3:12–13, my paraphrase).

Paul is telling us: "Here is my word to you in these critical times. In light of the hard times you know are coming, you are to measure your walk with the Lord."

We must therefore ask ourselves: "Am I becoming more like Christ? Am I growing more patient, or more quick-tempered? Kinder and gentler, or meaner and more argumentative? More tender and forgiving or less, holding on to grudges? Do I put up with the weaknesses and faults of those near to me, or do I always have to be right? Do I criticize or offer encouragement?"

According to Paul, in light of the coming hard days it does not matter what works you accomplish or what charitable deeds you do. No matter how generous you are to strangers, no matter how many souls you bring to Christ, this question remains: Are you becoming more loving, patient, forgiving, forbearing?

Examining your walk with Christ means looking not so much at what you are doing, as at who you are becoming. Such a walk will not come about by self-determination, merely saying, "I am going to become that kind of believer." Rather, it happens by the work of the Holy Spirit—through faith in His Word.

HE HOLDS ALL THE KEYS

Throughout Scripture, the greatest revelations of God's goodness came to people in their times of trouble, calamity, isolation and hardship. We find an example of this in the life of John.

For three years, this disciple was "in Jesus' bosom." It was a time of utter rest, peace and joy, with no troubles or trials. During that time, John received little revelation. He knew Jesus only as the Son of man. So, when did he receive his revelation of Christ's Second Coming in all His glory?

It happened only after John was dragged from Ephesus in chains. He was exiled to the Isle of Patmos, where he was sentenced to hard labor. He was isolated, with no fellowship, no family or friends to comfort him. It was a time of utter despair, the lowest point in his life.

That is when John's revelation of his Lord came: the Book of Revelation. In the midst of that dark hour, the light of the Holy Spirit came to John and he saw Jesus as never before. He literally saw Christ as the Son of God.

John did not receive this revelation while he was with the other apostles or even during Jesus' days on earth. In his darkest hour, all alone, John saw Christ in all His glory, declaring, "I am He who lives, and was dead, and behold, I am alive forevermore. Amen. And I have the keys of Hades and of Death" (Revelation 1:18).

This incredible revelation put John on his face. But Jesus lifted him up and showed him the set of keys He held in His hand. And He reassured John, "Do not be afraid" (verse 17).

I believe this revelation comes to every praying, hurting servant in his or her time of need. The Holy Spirit says, "Jesus holds all the keys to life and death, so everyone's departure rests in His hands."

May His revelation to us bring peace to our hearts!

Conquering the Darkness

Only one thing conquers and dispels darkness, and that is light. Isaiah declared, "The people who walked in darkness have seen a great light" (Isaiah 9:2). Likewise, John stated, "The light shines in the darkness, and the darkness did not comprehend it" (John 1:5).

Light represents understanding. When we say, "I see the light," we are saying, "Now I understand." Do you see what Scripture is saying? The Lord is about to open our eyes, not to see a victorious devil but to receive new revelation. Our God has sent us His Holy Spirit, whose power is greater than all the powers of hell: "He who is in you is greater than he who is in the world" (1 John 4:4).

In Revelation we read of hell spewing forth locusts and scorpions that have great power. We read of a dragon, beasts, horned creatures, as well as a coming Antichrist. Yet we do not know the meaning of all these creatures—and we do not need to. Paul declares that the power of the Holy Spirit is alive in us, working in us at this very moment.

So, how does the Spirit work in us in the midst of hard times? His power is released *only as we receive Him as our burden bearer.* The Holy Spirit was given to us for this very reason—to bear our cares and worries. How can we say we have received Him if we have not turned over our burdens to Him?

The Holy Spirit is abiding in us, waiting anxiously to take control of every situation in our lives. If we continue in fear, we have not received Him as our comforter, helper, guide, rescuer and strength. Our witness to the lost world is, first, to cast our every burden on the Holy Spirit. Have you done this?

THE PROMISED LAND

I believe that Psalm 46 is a picture of the New Testament "Promised Land." Indeed, it reflects the divine rest referred to in Hebrews: "There remains therefore a rest for the people of God" (Hebrews 4:9).

This psalm speaks of God's ever-present strength, His help in time of trouble, His peace in the midst of chaos. God's presence is with us at all times, and His help always arrives on time. Israel rejected this rest, however: "They despised the pleasant land; they did not believe His word" (Psalm 106:24).

Sadly, the Church today is much like Israel. In spite of God's great promises to us—His assurance of peace, help and full supply—we do not trust Him fully. Instead, we often complain, "Where is God in my trial? Is He with me or not? Why does He keep letting these hardships pile up on me?"

Today, I hear the Lord asking His Church, "Do you believe I still speak to My people? Do you believe I desire to give you My help and guidance? Do you truly believe I want to speak to you daily, hourly, moment by moment?" Our response must be like David's. That godly man shook all hell when he made this statement about the Lord: "He spoke, and it was done; He commanded, and it stood fast" (Psalm 33:9).

Here is God's promise to every generation that believes His Word: "The counsel of the LORD stands forever, the plans of His heart to all generations" (verse 11). Think of it! Our God spoke to His people in the past, He is speaking now, and He will continue to speak till the end of time.

More to the point, God wants to speak to you about your problem today. He may do it through His Word, through a godly friend, or through the Spirit's still, small voice, whispering, "This is the way; walk in it."

Bound to the Living Word

The Lord rules over all of creation with majesty and power. His laws govern the whole universe—all of nature, every nation and all the affairs of men. He rules over the seas, the planets, the heavenly bodies and all their movements.

"He rules by His power forever; His eyes observe the nations" (Psalm 66:7). "The Lord reigns, He is clothed with majesty; the Lord is clothed . . . with strength. . . . Your throne is established from of old; You are from everlasting. . . . Your testimonies are very sure" (93:1–2, 5).

These psalms were written by David, who testifies, in essence: "Lord, Your testimonies—Your laws, decrees and words—are irrevocable. They are utterly reliable." The author of Hebrews echoes this, declaring that God's living Word is eternal and unchangeable: "the same yesterday, today, and forever" (Hebrews 13:8).

There are laws operating in the universe that govern how things work, without exception. Consider the laws that rule the movements of the sun, moon, stars and earth. These heavenly bodies were all put into place when God spoke a word, and since that time they have been ruled by laws that God also spoke into being.

We are told throughout the New Testament that this great God is our Father and that He takes pity on His children. Hebrews tells us the Lord hears our every cry and bottles every tear. Yet we also are told that He is the righteous King who judges by His law. Everything in existence is judged by His immutable Word.

Simply put, we can hold the Bible in our hands and know, "This Book tells me who God is. It describes His attributes, nature, promises and judgments. It is His rule of law, from His own mouth, by which He reigns. And it is a Word to which He has bound Himself. It is a Word, therefore, that I can stand on daily, firm and sure."

Be Ready

In Matthew 24 Jesus uses a parable to teach about being ready for His return:

> Therefore you also be ready, for the Son of Man is coming at an hour when you do not expect. Who then is a faithful and wise servant, whom his master made ruler over his household, to give them food in due season? Blessed is that servant. . . . Assuredly, I say to you that he will make him ruler over all his goods.
>
> But if that evil servant says in his heart, "My master is delaying his coming," and begins to beat his fellow servants, and to eat and drink with the drunkards, the master of that servant will come on a day when he is not looking for him . . . and will cut him in two and appoint him his portion with the hypocrites. There shall be weeping and gnashing of teeth.
>
> 24:44–51

Jesus is speaking about servants here, meaning believers. One servant is described as faithful and the other evil. What makes the latter evil in God's eyes? According to Jesus, it is something he "says in his heart" (verse 48).

This servant does not voice such a thought or preach it, but he entertains this demonic lie: "The Master delays His coming." Notice he does not say, "The Master *is not* coming," but "He *delays* His coming." In other words, "Jesus will not return in my generation."

This "evil servant" is clearly a type of believer, perhaps even one in ministry. He was commanded to watch and be ready, "for the Son of Man is coming at an hour when you do not expect" (verse 44). Yet this man eases his conscience by accepting Satan's lie.

The fruit of this kind of thinking is that a servant sees no need for right living. Living in two worlds, he indulges in evil living while believing he is safe from righteous judgment.

May every servant remain faithful to our Master, continuing to watch and be ready.

Enlargement of Heart

The evangelists George Whitefield and John Wesley were two of the greatest preachers in history. These men preached to thousands on the streets and in parks and prisons, and through their ministries many were brought to Christ.

At one point a doctrinal dispute arose between the two men, however, over how a person is sanctified. Both doctrinal camps defended their positions strongly, and some vicious words were exchanged, with the followers of both men arguing in unseemly fashion.

A follower of Whitefield came to him one day and asked, "Will we see John Wesley in heaven?" He was asking, in effect, "How can Wesley be saved if he is preaching such error?"

Whitefield answered, "No, we probably will not see John Wesley in heaven. He will be so high up near Christ's throne, so close to the Lord, that we will not be *able* to see him."

Paul called this kind of spirit "enlargement of heart." He had it himself as he wrote to the Corinthians, a church in which some had accused him of hardness and who had sneered at his preaching. Paul assured them, "O Corinthians! We have spoken openly to you, our heart is wide open [enlarged]" (2 Corinthians 6:11).

When God enlarges your heart, suddenly so many limits and barriers are removed. You do not see through a narrow lens anymore. Instead, you find yourself with compassion, being directed by the Holy Spirit to those who are hurting, and being drawn by His magnetic pull.

So, do you have a gentleness of heart when you see hurting people? When you see a brother who has stumbled in sin or may be having problems, are you tempted to tell him what is wrong in his life? Paul says the hurting ones around us need to be restored in a spirit of meekness and gentleness.

May all hurting people encounter in us the spirit that Jesus demonstrated—and may our compassion continually increase for them. That is enlargement of heart!

Despite False Teaching

The true Church of Jesus Christ is the apple of God's eye. Yet, from the beginning, His Church has experienced apostasies and false teachers.

The earliest churches—those apostolic bodies founded by Paul and the apostles—had the full counsel of God taught to them. Nothing "profitable to growth and steadfastness" was withheld from Christ's followers. They were given truth, not only in word but in demonstration and power of the Holy Spirit.

Paul warned Timothy that a time was coming when some of God's people "will not endure sound doctrine, but according to their own desires, because they have itching ears, they will heap up for themselves teachers; and they will turn their ears away from the truth, and be turned aside to fables [so-called mystical truths]" (2 Timothy 4:3–4).

History records that this happened just as Paul had predicted. After the apostles died—and the generation that had sat under their teaching had passed away—a conspiracy of wicked error flooded the Church. Believers were seduced by strange doctrines, and science and philosophy eroded the truth of Christ's Gospel.

Consider what Paul said of the purity of Christ's Church: "Christ . . . loved the church and gave Himself for it, that He might sanctify and cleanse her with the washing of water by the word, that He might present her to Himself a glorious church, not having spot or wrinkle . . . holy and without blemish" (Ephesians 5:25–27).

God's great concern is not about the apostate Church. Even apostasies will not be able to kill or destroy the Church of Jesus Christ. In spite of problems, God has everything under control, and His mystical, invisible, overcoming Church is not dying. Rather, the river of the Holy Spirit is flowing into the "dead sea" of apostate churches, exposing iniquity and lukewarmness and causing new life to spring up.

God still loves His Church—blemishes and all—and His Spirit is still at work!

Holding Fast the Word of Life

Paul writes, "Holding fast the word of life, so that I may rejoice in the day of Christ that I have not run in vain or labored in vain" (Philippians 2:16). Paul was picturing a day when he would stand in Christ's presence and the secrets of redemption would be unveiled.

Scripture says that on that day our eyes will be opened, and we will behold the Lord's glory without rebuke from Him. Our hearts will be set on fire as He opens all the mysteries of the universe and shows us His power behind it. Suddenly, we will see the reality of all that had been available to us in our earthly trials: the power and resources of heaven, the protective angels, the abiding presence of the Holy Spirit.

As we behold the awesomeness of these things, the Lord will say to us, "All along, my warriors were camped about you, an army of protectors; you were never in any danger from Satan. You never had any reason to fear your tomorrows."

Then Christ will show us the Father—and what an overwhelming moment that will be. As we behold the majesty of our heavenly Father, we will fully realize His love and care for us. Suddenly the truth will come to us in full force: "This was, and is, and forever will be *our Father,* truly the great I AM."

Paul says he "held fast" his word about God's faithfulness because he did not want to stand in the Lord's presence, thinking, "How could I have been so blind?"

The apostle is exhorting us: "I want to rejoice on that day, when my eyes are fully opened. I want to be able to enjoy every revelation knowing I trusted in His promises. I want to know that I held fast the Word of life in all my reactions to my sufferings, that I fought a good fight, that I proved my Lord faithful." May it be so for you!

Give Me All Your Tomorrows

The Lord appeared to Abraham one day and gave him an incredible command: "Get out of your country, from your family and from your father's house, to a land that I will show you" (Genesis 12:1).

I have preached on this amazing event. Suddenly, God picked out a man and told him, "I want you to get up and go, leaving everything behind: your home, your relatives, even your country. I want to send you someplace, and I will direct you how to get there along the way."

How did Abraham respond to this incredible word from the Lord? "By faith Abraham obeyed when he was called to go out to the place which he would receive as an inheritance. And he went out, not knowing where he was going" (Hebrews 11:8).

What was God up to? Why would He search the nations for one man and then call him to forsake everything and go on a journey with no map, no preconceived direction, no known destination?

Think about what God was asking of Abraham. He never showed him how he would feed or support his family or how far to go or when he would arrive. He only told him two things in the beginning: "Go," and, "I will show you the way."

In essence, God told Abraham, "From this day on, I want you to give me all your tomorrows. You are to live the rest of your life putting your future into My hands, one day at a time. If you will commit your life to this promise that I am making to you, Abraham, I will bless you, guide you and lead you to a place you never imagined."

Abraham is what Bible scholars call a "pattern man," someone who serves as an example of how to walk before the Lord. Abraham's example shows us all what is required if we would seek to please God in our walk.

The Lies of the Enemy

In our times of trial, Satan comes to us bringing lies: "You're surrounded with no way out. Greater servants than you have quit in circumstances no worse than this. Now it's your turn to go down. You're a failure, otherwise you wouldn't be going through this. There is something wrong with you and God is greatly displeased."

In the midst of his trial, King Hezekiah acknowledged his helplessness. The king realized he had no strength to stop the voices raging at him—voices of discouragement, threats and lies. He also knew he could not deliver himself, so he sought the Lord for help.

God answered by sending the prophet Isaiah to Hezekiah with this message: "The Lord has heard your cry. Now tell the Satan standing at your gate, 'You are the one who is going down! You are going to turn around and go back the very way you came.'"

Hezekiah had very nearly fallen for the enemy's trick. The same is true for multitudes of Christians under attack today. If we do not stand up to Satan's lies—if, in our hour of crisis, we do not turn to faith and prayer and draw strength from God's promises of deliverance—the devil will zero in on our wavering faith and intensify his attacks.

Hezekiah gained courage from the word he received, and he was able to say in no uncertain terms: "Devil, you did not blaspheme *me*. You lied to God Himself. My Lord is going to deliver me—and because you blasphemed Him, you will face His wrath!"

The Bible tells us that God supernaturally delivered Hezekiah and Judah on that very night: "It came to pass on a certain night that the angel of the LORD went out, and killed in the camp of the Assyrians one hundred and eighty-five thousand" (2 Kings 19:35).

Through the shed blood of Jesus Christ, we already have victory over every sin, temptation and battle—and over the enemy's lies.

Neglect Cripples Spiritual Growth

If you neglect plants or animals, depriving them of water and nutrients, death begins to set in. Drive through many suburban neighborhoods and you will see beautifully landscaped yards, green grass and colorful flowers—the result of careful tending. Occasionally, however, you may come to a house that breaks up the beautiful scenery. You see overgrown grass and tall weeds sprouting everywhere. The whole scene screams, "Neglect, laziness!"

Solomon describes such a picture: "I went by the field of the lazy man, and by the vineyard of the man devoid of understanding; and there it was, all overgrown with thorns; its surface was covered with nettles; its stone wall was broken down. . . . I looked on it and received instruction: A little sleep, a little slumber, a little folding of the hands to rest; so shall your poverty come like a prowler, and your need like an armed man" (Proverbs 24:30–34).

Solomon is telling us, "Everything had wasted away from neglect. I saw the results of being slothful, and I took it to heart."

This lesson applies equally to neglecting God's Word and time alone with Him in prayer. Paul instructs young Timothy, "Till I come, give attention to reading, to exhortation, to doctrine. Do not neglect the gift that is in you. . . . Take heed to yourself and to the doctrine. Continue in them" (1 Timothy 4:13–16). Paul is speaking here, of course, about reading God's Word.

I once planted a tree in the shade and it began to slump. I replanted it in the sun, making sure to water it every day with a mixture of water and plant food. Whenever I missed a day of watering, the tree's leaves began to droop, but a little watering perked it right up.

Dearly beloved, tend your soul regularly with the "miracle food" of His Word—and you will always be full of strength and life.

MIDDLE GROUNDERS

There is a "middle ground" in the Christian life—and those who choose to live on it share certain characteristics. One of these is a refusal to die to the things of this world.

The names of the tribes of Reuben, Gad and half of Manasseh expose this characteristic in them. Reuben means "a son who sees." Reuben was Jacob's firstborn, but he lost his birthright because he was driven by lust. Jacob described this son as "unstable as water, you shall not excel" (Genesis 49:4).

Reuben had eyes only for this world—its lusts, its things, its pleasures. He was unstable because his heart was always divided, and this spirit was passed on to his posterity.

Gad means "fortune or troop." Simply put, this suggests soldiers of fortune or mercenaries. Moses said of Gad, "He provided the first part for himself" (Deuteronomy 33:21). In other words, Gad's tribe was outwardly obedient, but inwardly they were consumed with their own problems and the need to "make it" in the world.

Gad's philosophy was, "I will fight with the Lord's army and do everything God expects of me—but first I must get myself and my family set up. Then I'll be free to do more for the Lord."

Manasseh means "to forget, to neglect." This was Joseph's firstborn son, and he should have received the birthright. But even in Manasseh's childhood Jacob saw a sad trait developing. Manasseh would one day forget the ways of his father Joseph and neglect the commandment of the Lord.

Consider these combined traits of middle-ground Christians: unstable as water in spiritual convictions; never excelling in the things of God; lukewarm, weak with lust; ruled by selfish needs; neglecting the Word; not taking the Lord's commandments seriously; making their own choices instead of trusting God; forgetting past blessings and dealings; unwilling to let go of certain idols; justifying their own decisions; not willing to die to all that would seduce them back to middle ground.

The Lord's fullness requires following Him "with all the heart, all the strength." May the names of these tribes be lessons to all who would follow Jesus to higher ground.

God Said, "Cross Over!"

"Be sure your sin will find you out!" This is one of the most misunderstood statements in all of God's Word. The truth is that many sins go unexposed here on earth but will be revealed at the Judgment.

God commanded Israel: "You will cross over the Jordan and go in to possess the land which the LORD your God is giving you, and you will possess it and dwell in it" (Deuteronomy 11:31). Their inheritance was on the other side of Jordan where God would choose to set up His tabernacle. The Ark of the Covenant, a symbol of the Lord's presence among them, also would be there.

Two crossings were necessary for Israel. Crossing the Red Sea was a type of leaving the world and all its idols and lust behind—a clear type of conversion. The second crossing was the Jordan, which represents dying to self and going on into the fullness of Christ. It represents death to all that is unlike Christ—all ambition, idolatry, self.

Between the two crossings was the territory of Gilead and Jazer, which bordered the Jordan and the Land of Promise. This middle ground, a place of half surrender, was totally indefensible. It was a most dangerous place to live, as it was surrounded by heathen enemies. It speaks of falling short of God's ultimate place and purpose.

Of course, two-and-a-half tribes—Reuben, Gad and half of Manasseh—felt most comfortable with this middle ground and stopped there. They said, "This is as far as we go. This suits our lifestyle just fine."

"For we will not inherit with them on the other side of the Jordan and beyond, because our inheritance has fallen to us this eastern side of the Jordan" (Numbers 32:19). These tribes were eventually overcome by the enemy. They returned to idolatry and ended up more wicked than when they were in Egypt.

Their tragic story, an example of the compromise of the Church today, shows us the terrible consequences of partial obedience. May we all obey God's command to "cross over."

Forbearing One Another

"*Forbearing* one another, and *forgiving* one another, if any man have a quarrel against any: even as Christ forgave you, so also do ye" (Colossians 3:13, KJV, emphasis mine).

Forbearing and forgiving are two different issues. *Forbearing* means "ceasing from all acts and thoughts of revenge." In other words, "Don't take matters into your own hands. Instead, endure the hurt. Lay the matter down and leave it alone."

Yet forbearing is not just a New Testament concept. Proverbs tells us, "Do not say, 'I will do to him just as he has done to me; I will render to the man according to his work'" (Proverbs 24:29).

A powerful example of this admonition is David's life. He was in a vengeful rage toward a wicked man named Nabal, because Nabal refused to help him when he needed it. David swore revenge but ended up obeying God's counsel, "Do not avenge yourself. . . . Let the Lord fight your battle." That situation was resolved in a timely manner, and David praised God for His intervention (see 1 Samuel 25).

Another opportunity for easy revenge came when David found his pursuer, Saul, asleep in a cave. David's men urged him, "God has delivered Saul into your hands. Kill him now, and avenge yourself." But David forbore, instead cutting off a piece of Saul's garment he could use later as proof.

Such wise actions are God's ways of putting our enemies to shame, and that was the case when David showed Saul the garment (see 24:17).

Forgiving encompasses two other commandments: (1) loving your enemies and (2) praying for them. "Love your enemies, bless those who curse you, do good to those who hate you, and pray for those who spitefully use you and persecute you" (Matthew 5:44).

One wise old preacher said, "If you can pray for your enemies, you can do all the rest." I have found this to be true in my own life.

Trusting God's Mysterious Workings

Stop trying to figure out how and why you got hurt. Your situation is not unique. Whether you were right or wrong means absolutely nothing at this point. All that matters is your willingness to move on in God and trust His mysterious workings in your life.

"Do not think it strange concerning the fiery trial which is to try you, as though some strange thing happened to you; but rejoice to the extent that you partake of Christ's sufferings, that when His glory is revealed, you may also be glad with exceeding joy" (1 Peter 4:12–13).

Most likely you did what you had to do. You moved in the will of God, honestly following your heart, willing to give of yourself. Love was your motivation. You did not abort the will of God—someone else did. If that were not true, you would not be the one who is hurting so. You are hurt because you tried to be honest.

You cannot understand why things blew up in your face, when God seemed to be leading all along. Your heart asks, "Why did God allow me to get into this in the first place if He knew it would never work out right?"

Even Judas was called by the Lord. He was handpicked by the Savior to be a man of God, but he aborted God's plan and broke the heart of Jesus. What started out as a plan of God ended in disaster because Judas chose to go his own way.

Lay off all your guilt trips. Stop condemning yourself and trying to figure out what you did wrong. It is what you are thinking right now that really counts with God. You did not make a mistake. More than likely, you simply gave too much. Like Paul, you have to say, "The more I loved, the less I was loved" (see 2 Corinthians 12:15).

So, you see, you are in godly company. It is a special company of believers who are bound to trust God's mysterious workings—because they chose to follow Him with all their heart.

The Least Amount Will Do

If you have not been faithful in what is another man's, who will give you what is your own?" (Luke 16:12). Jesus is saying, "You say you want a revelation, something to enable you to do greater things. Yet how can you be entrusted with that kind of faith if you are not reliable with the things others have given you?"

Jesus' words must have left His disciples scratching their heads in confusion. Their Master knew they did not own anything, much less something that another person had given them. They had forsaken all to be His disciples and had followed Him to the best of their ability. His words here simply did not seem to apply to them.

What does Jesus mean by the words "what is another man's"? He is speaking of our bodies and souls, which He purchased with His own blood. "For you were bought at a price; therefore glorify God in your body and in your spirit, which are God's" (1 Corinthians 6:20).

Jesus is telling us, "Your body does not belong to you anymore. If you will not allow Me to look inside you, deal with your sin and sanctify you, how can you expect Me to entrust you with something greater?"

The disciples had requested an increase of faith. Jesus had a ready answer for them: "If you have faith as a mustard seed, you can say to this mulberry tree, 'Be pulled up by the roots and be planted in the sea,' and it would obey you" (Luke 17:6).

Jesus is speaking of the hidden things we must deal with as His followers. He is saying, "Before you can believe God to move mountains, you must remove the roots of sin. Examine your heart and remove everything that is unlike Me."

We do not need great apostolic faith to do this. The very least amount of faith will do.

Pride and the Voice of the Spirit

Let me distinguish clearly between pride and humility, because often among Christians there is confusion on these issues.

A humble person is not one who thinks little of himself, hangs his head and says, "I am nothing." Rather, he is someone who depends wholly on the Lord for everything, in every circumstance. He knows the Lord has to direct him, empower him and quicken him—and that he is dead, ineffective and useless without that direction.

A proud person, on the other hand, is one who may love God in a fashion, but he acts and thinks on his own. At its root, pride is simply independence from God. The proud person makes decisions based on his own reasoning, skill and abilities. He says, "God gave me a good mind and lots of talent, and He expects me to use it. It is silly to ask Him for direction in every detail of life."

This person is unteachable because he already "knows it all." He might listen to someone who is higher in authority or better known than himself, but not to someone he thinks is inferior.

Nothing a proud person says is of God. It is impossible for him to judge righteous judgment—impossible to speak God's mind—because the Holy Spirit is not present in him to bear witness to truth. "There is a way that seems right to a man, but its end is the way of death" (Proverbs 14:12).

Pride is independence—humility is dependency. The humble Christian is one who makes no move, no decision, without seeking counsel from the Lord. The Bible says the steps of a righteous man are ordered by the Lord, but He cannot order the steps of an independent spirit. What I am saying to you is that God wants full control—so let us give it to Him.

"God resists the proud, but gives grace to the humble" (James 4:6).

Enemies within the Church

How are we to react to Christians who have made themselves our enemies? Jesus commands us, "Love your enemies, bless those who curse you, do good to those who hate you, and pray for those who spitefully use you and persecute you" (Matthew 5:44).

Let us review our lives in light of these three things, to see if we are being obedient to Christ.

1. "Bless those who curse you." What exactly does it mean to bless? The Greek word for *bless* here implies "speaking only what is good and edifying, out loud, with the mouth." We are not just to think good things about our enemies, but we must speak them openly.
2. "Do good to those who hate you." What does it mean to do *good* to those who oppose us? The Greek meaning here implies "honesty plus recovery." Jesus is saying, "Do everything in your power to seek your enemy's healing and recovery from Satan's snare. Your focus is not to be on your own hurt, but on the deception of your enemy's soul." Christ's command here is simple: "Make the first move. Do not wait—do not miss the opportunity. You be the first to seek reconciliation."
3. "Pray for those who spitefully use you." We see this command illustrated in the duties of the high priest. First, the law required the priest to slay the sacrifice and place it on the altar, to deal with the people's sin. Second, the priest was to pray for the congregation, to act as an intercessor on their behalf.

Right now, Christ is interceding for your enemies. "If anyone sins, we have an Advocate with the Father, Jesus Christ the righteous" (1 John 2:1). Jesus is an advocate even for those who have used and persecuted you. If He is interceding for their souls, how can you remain an enemy to them? It is simply impossible!

Committed—Live or Die!

King Nebuchadnezzar spoke to the three Hebrew men, saying, "If you do not worship, you shall be cast immediately into the midst of a burning fiery furnace. And who is the god who will deliver you from my hands?" (Daniel 3:15).

Daniel's friends were facing the worst possible crisis. If God did not come and deliver them by a miracle, they were dead.

What will bring Christ into your crisis? He comes when you make the same commitment the three Hebrew men made: "[They] said to the king, 'O Nebuchadnezzar, we have no need to answer you in this matter. If that is the case, our God whom we serve is able to deliver us from the burning fiery furnace, and He will deliver us from your hand, O king. But if not, let it be known to you, O king, that we do not serve your gods, nor will we worship the gold image which you have set up'" (verses 16–18).

In other words: "It looks hopeless. Yet our God is able to deliver us from this fiery crisis. Even if He doesn't, we still will not quit on Him. Live or die, we will trust our Lord."

Beloved, this is the kind of faith that causes angels to rejoice and blesses the very heart of God. It is a faith that says, "Lord, I am fully persuaded You are able to deliver me with a mere word. But if for some reason you keep me here, I am not going to run. I will remain faithful and true. Your ways are higher than mine, Lord—and my life is in Your hands. Though You slay me, yet will I trust You."

This is what brings Christ into our crises—the full confidence that He is able to rescue and deliver us out of any crisis. It is a confidence that, no matter what comes, we are in His hands.

How Important Is It to Forgive and Bless Our Enemies?

Paul writes, "Give place to wrath" (Romans 12:19). He is saying, "Put up with the wrong. Lay it down and move on. Get a life in the Spirit!" If we refuse to forgive the hurts done to us, however, we face these consequences:

1. We will become guiltier than the person who did us wrong or inflicted our wound.
2. God's mercy and grace toward us will be shut off. Then, as things begin to go wrong in our lives, we will not understand them, because we will be in confusion from our disobedience.
3. Our persecutor's vexations against us will continue to rob us of peace. He will become the victor, succeeding in giving us a permanent wound.
4. Because Satan succeeds in driving us to thoughts of revenge, he will be able to lead us into deadlier sins. We will end up committing transgressions far worse than these.

The writer of Proverbs advises, "The discretion of a man makes him slow to anger, and his glory is to overlook a transgression" (Proverbs 19:11). In other words, we are to do nothing until our anger has subsided. We are never to make a decision or follow through with any action while we are still angry.

We bring glory to our heavenly Father whenever we overlook hurts and forgive the sins done to us. To do so builds character in us. When we forgive as God forgives, He brings us into a revelation of favor and blessing we have never known.

Jesus commands us to love those who have made themselves our enemies by doing three things: bless them, do good to them and pray for them.

Matthew 5:44 sums it up for us: "Love your enemies, bless those who curse you, do good to those who hate you, and pray for those who spitefully use you and persecute you."

Obedience Is Better than Blessing

Then Samuel said: 'Has the LORD as great delight in burnt offerings and sacrifices, as in obeying the voice of the LORD ? Behold, *to obey is better than sacrifice*, and to heed than the fat of rams'" (1 Samuel 15:22, emphasis mine).

It is written, "To obey is better than sacrifice." I say to obey is also better than blessing.

This is the deepest meaning in the story of Abram offering Isaac on the altar. God said, "Go and do this," and Abram obeyed. At the last minute an angel of the Lord stayed Abram's hand from sacrificing his son.

So, did Abram leave that altar saying, "God changed His mind"? I think not. God wanted only obedience—and Abram must have known it.

I have experienced this. God told me to negotiate for a certain thing and gave me every indication that I should claim it. I obeyed and did all in my power to obtain it—but I did not get it.

What did this mean? Should I have questioned God? Should I have doubted He spoke to me? Should I have believed Satan hindered me?

No, I would believe none of these things. I sought the Lord diligently, He instructed, "Do this," and I did it. I will rest in the peace of obedience. *That makes it better than blessing!*

God shows us only one side of the coin—obedience. The servant must obey without questioning the master. So it is in matters of faith: "When a master commands his servant to go, he goes; to come, and he comes" (see Matthew 8:9).

Can a Christian purpose in his heart to trust God when it appears all his leadings have "blown up" in his face? The giants of faith, like Abram, did. The deeper in God we go, the more peculiar will be our testing.

We cannot be led to think that afflictions are necessarily proof you are displeasing Him. After all, miracles are produced only amidst impossibilities. So you desire to be a child of faith? Then ready yourself for a life of most peculiar testings!

A Fountain of Life

I have seen men who were mightily used of the Spirit later be put on the shelf by God. The Lord told them, "I am sorry, son—I love you, I forgive you, and my mercy will come through for you. But I cannot use you."

To me, this is one of the most dreadful things that could ever happen. Yet it happened to Israel's own king, Saul. "Samuel said to Saul, 'You have done foolishly. You have not kept the commandment of the LORD your God. . . . For now the LORD would have established your kingdom over Israel forever. But now your kingdom shall not continue'" (1 Samuel 13:13–14).

What sad words! God told the king, "Saul, you could have had my blessing in your life continually. I had great plans for you, but you would not deal with your sin. You became bitter and hardhearted." From that moment on, Saul was no longer of use to the Kingdom. It all ends this way when we continue in sin: We become absolutely barren and fruitless.

The Word declares that the fear of God is a fountain of life (see Proverbs 14:27). In the same verse we read that this fear helps us avoid the snares of death. Proverbs 3:7 tells us, "Fear the Lord and depart from evil." And Hebrews 12:28 instructs us to "Serve God acceptably with reverence and godly fear." Those who desire to walk in the fear of God will soon be led into the full revelation of the promises and provisions that God has made available for us.

Perhaps God is dealing with you about your sin right now. He has shot His arrows of conviction into your heart, and you are feeling a sense of guilt. Do not panic! That is the gift of God. He is planting His divine power in you, teaching you, "Only through My holy fear will you depart from your sin."

Come Do Your Work in Me

I believe if a Christian has an intensity for a holy life—if he desires to give his all to the Lord—there can be only one reason why he fails to enjoy the blessing and freedom promised by the indwelling of the Holy Spirit. That reason is *unbelief.* As surely as Jesus could not perform His works wherever there was unbelief, so His Spirit cannot do anything in our lives when we harbor unbelief.

It is vital for every follower of Jesus not to judge God's promises according to past experiences. If we cast ourselves fully on His promises—believing them with all our being, trusting Him for a supply of faith, holding the Spirit to His own word—we can know that all the results are God's responsibility. Moreover, we will be able to stand on Judgment Day, having been faithful. We simply cannot give up our desire to enter into His promised blessings.

I once put out this challenge to Almighty God: "Lord, I believe You have given me Your Holy Spirit and He will convict me, lead me and empower me to overcome. I believe He causes me to obey Your Word, and He will never depart from me, nor will He let me depart from You."

The Lord told Ezekiel, "Prophesy to these bones, and say to them, 'O dry bones, hear the word of the Lord'" (Ezekiel 37:4). In all we face, we are to do what the Lord told Ezekiel to do—pray the Word of God. We are to remind the Holy Spirit of God's promises to us.

Pray with me now: "Holy Spirit, the heavenly Father promised me He would put You in my heart—and I have committed myself to that promise. You said You will cause me to walk in His ways and obey His every word. I do not know how You plan to do that—but You cannot lie. So, come, do Your work in me."

Handcuffed to Jesus

Paul often refers to himself as "the prisoner of Christ Jesus" (Ephesians 3:1). In Ephesians 4:1, he says being a prisoner of the Lord is actually his calling! He considered this God's gift of grace to him (see 4:7).

Paul wrote to Timothy: "Therefore do not be ashamed of the testimony of our Lord, nor of me His prisoner" (2 Timothy 1:8). Even into his old age the apostle rejoiced in having been apprehended by the Lord and taken captive to God's will: "Being such a one as Paul, the aged, and now [or still] also a prisoner of Jesus Christ" (Philemon 9).

Paul could tell you the very hour that the Lord handcuffed him and took him captive. He was on the road to Damascus, with letters in hand from the high priest, bound and determined to bring back Christians to Jerusalem. He was "breathing threats and murder against the disciples of the Lord" (Acts 9:1)—full of hatred, bitterness and anger in his misguided zeal for God.

As Paul approached the city of Damascus, "Suddenly a light shone around him from heaven" (9:3). He was struck completely blind by that light—Christ!

Paul testified again and again how he had to be taken by the hand and led into Damascus, a helpless prisoner. He spent three days in an isolated room without sight and without eating anything. He had been taken captive totally—in spirit, soul, mind and body.

What happened in that room for three days? The Lord was handcuffing Saul and making him into Paul, the prisoner of Jesus Christ. You can almost hear his agonizing prayer: "Oh, Lord, I thought I was doing Your will. How could I have been so blind? I have been doing whatever I thought was right, but I can't trust my own thoughts!"

Let our prayer be like Paul's: "Jesus, take me prisoner—take my thoughts, my heart, my will. Lead me wherever you want me to go."

Just a Voice

John the Baptist's definition of his ministry was blunt and simple: "I am the voice of one crying in the wilderness" (John 1:23). This servant of the Most High, who according to the Scripture was the greatest "among them that are born of women," was the most blessed of all the prophets and a revered preacher of righteousness.

The crowds flocked to hear John's scorching messages. Many were baptized and became his disciples, and even royalty came under his mighty influence. Some thought he was Christ, while others considered him to be Elijah raised from the dead.

John refused to be exalted or promoted. He was emptied of self-serving and he continually withdrew from center stage. In his own eyes, this greatest of all prophets was not even worthy to be called a man of God—but only a wilderness voice. Modest, retiring and unconcerned about honor, he did not care about having a ministry or being "mightily used of God." In fact, John considered himself unworthy to even touch his Master's shoes. His entire life was devoted to "the Lamb of God who takes away the sin of the world" (verse 29).

What a powerful rebuke to us in this age of self-preoccupation, promotion of personalities, influence-grabbing, ego-tripping and seeking of honors. John could have had it all, but he cried out, "He must increase, but I must decrease" (3:30). To reach that goal, John kept reminding all who heard him, "I am just a voice."

The secret of John's happiness was that his joy was not in his ministry or in his work, nor in his personal usefulness or widespread influence. His pure joy was to stand in the presence of the Bridegroom and watching as others, including his own disciples, flocked to Jesus.

John's life is an example to all. The greatest fulfillment a child of God can know is to simply rejoice in being a son or daughter living in the presence of Jesus.

PART 7

Sharing God's Burden

He Delights in Our Service

Total Surrender

But now the righteousness of God apart from the law is revealed . . . even the righteousness of God, through faith in Jesus Christ, to all and on all who believe. For there is no difference . . . being justified freely by His grace through the redemption that is in Christ Jesus" (Romans 3:21–24).

God has revealed to us a sure way to become absolutely holy and perfect in His sight. It is a way to know He looks on us as holy and pure. Best of all, this is a free gift.

His gift of holiness can never be a reward for anything we have done. It is an unearned, undeserved favor—an outright gift. "For what does the Scripture say? '*Abraham believed God, and it was accounted to him for righteousness.*' Now to him who works, the wages are not counted as grace but as debt. But to him who does not work but believes on Him who justifies the ungodly, his faith is accounted for righteousness" (4:3–5, emphasis mine).

Submission is the only way into God's holiness. It is to submit to the righteousness of Christ through faith. To *submit* means to "surrender the power of your will." With God there is no such thing as willpower—all power is His.

God demands absolute holiness so that we will be humbled by this demand and repent. The kind of repentance He is looking for is confessing the weakness of our futile efforts and denying we have any power at all in ourselves.

You can never be clothed in Christ's holiness until you fall on your face before God's throne—naked, poor, wretched, weak and totally helpless. You must once and for all admit you have no power to resist sin and that you cannot be holy, even with others' help. You must be given holiness as a gift. The greatest gift you can give to God is your surrender—and your belief that He will give you His holiness!

The Word Will Prevail

For as the rain comes down, and the snow from heaven, and do not return there, but water the earth, and make it bring forth and bud, that it may give seed to the sower and bread to the eater, so shall My word be that goes forth from My mouth; it shall not return to Me void, but it shall accomplish what I please, and it shall prosper in the thing for which I sent it.

Isaiah 55:10–11

The "Word" Isaiah refers to here is Jesus Christ. The apostle John describes Jesus in similar terms: "In the beginning was the Word, and the Word was with God, and the Word was God" (John 1:1).

Why is Jesus called the Word? It is because the Father spoke Him into being. From God's very mouth, His Son was sent forth. Isaiah is prophesying what Jesus would accomplish while on earth—in short: "Christ will not return to the Father without fulfilling His mission." Jesus was not going to leave this world empty-handed!

The Father sent His Son to redeem humankind, to break the chains of darkness, to set captives free. Indeed, Christ—God's living, breathing, active Word—would accomplish all He was sent to do. When He returned to the Father, He would leave with victory assured. According to Isaiah, all of nature would rejoice: "For you shall go out with joy, and be led out with peace; the mountains and the hills shall break forth into singing before you, and all the trees of the field shall clap their hands" (Isaiah 55:12).

Christ's victory would be total. He would return to the Father a conquering captain. When He said from the cross, "It is finished," He was stating, "I have accomplished My Father's will. The Word He spoke will not return to Him void. When I ascend to Him, I will be able to say, 'My mission is accomplished.'"

Thank God, His Word prevails!

He Calls Us to Fight

What king, going to make war against another king, does not sit down first and consider whether he is able with ten thousand to meet him who comes against him with twenty thousand? Or else, while the other is still a great way off, he sends a delegation and asks conditions of peace. So likewise, whoever of you does not forsake all that he has cannot be My disciple.

Luke 14:31–33

Enoch once prophesied, "Behold, the Lord comes with ten thousands of His saints" (Jude 14). Scripture says we are kings and priests unto the Lord, and we represent these tens of thousands going out to battle Satan's army. Satan wars against us because he hates us greatly (see Revelation 12:17).

We must be prepared for what is coming, ready to spend our days in spiritual warfare. Indeed, we have to know that a flood of iniquity is aimed against the people of God. Moreover, we must realize we are invincible in Christ. It is written, "He who is in you is greater than he who is in the world" (1 John 4:4). God says we are guaranteed victory over all the power of the enemy—for we have all the hosts of heaven fighting for us.

May God give us more Holy Ghost fight so that each of us can shout to the world and all the hordes of hell, "Who shall separate us from the love of Christ? . . . Yet in all these things we are more than conquerors through Him who loved us. For I am persuaded that neither death nor life, nor angels nor principalities nor powers, nor things present nor things to come, nor height nor depth, nor any other created thing, shall be able to separate us from the love of God" (Romans 8:35, 37–39).

These words from Paul are the battle cry of all who hunger for Jesus. Satan cannot keep down any believer who puts his trust in the Lord.

Put Your Heart Into It!

God does not accept grudging service from anyone. "And whatever you do, do it heartily, as to the Lord and not to men" (Colossians 3:23). *Heartily* means "with all your heart, all your strength, all that is within you."

Paul writes, "So let each one give as he purposes in his heart, not grudgingly or of necessity [unwillingly] . . ." (2 Corinthians 9:7). The apostle makes a dual application of this matter of giving: our financial offerings—and the giving of our very lives to God's work.

Paul wrote that the church in Macedonia literally begged him to let them take up a collection for the poor saints in Jerusalem. These Macedonians were so wholly given to the Lord they gave generously out of their own poverty. How could this be?

"But [they] first gave themselves to the Lord, and then to us by the will of God" (8:5). Paul says the Macedonians gave much more than money. They spared nothing in serving both the Lord and their brethren. "Beyond their ability, they were freely willing" (8:3). They gave beyond their human ability, with much prayer.

If you give only because you believe it is commanded—or wonder, "Is tithing a New Testament concept or just Old Testament?"—your heart attitude is all wrong. If you tithe because the pastor asks it of you, that is wrong also. None of this gets to the issue, the very heart of what it means to give.

If you are going to give yourself wholly to the Lord and His service, you must do it cheerfully: "For God loves a cheerful giver" (9:7).

The word for *cheerful* in Greek means "hilarious, glad." God is saying, "Whatever you do in your labors for Me—interceding, worshiping in My house, or seeking Me in your secret closet—do it cheerfully."

Do not complain about your burdens. Instead, serve the Lord cheerfully in all ways, even in the midst of your need. He loves a cheerful giver—and He will meet you!

Get God's Power—and then Go!

As soon as the disciples heard about receiving a baptism of power, they asked, "Lord, will You at this time restore the kingdom to Israel?" (Act 1:6). Jesus answered in no uncertain terms: "It is not for you to know times or seasons which the Father has put in His own authority" (verse 7).

Stop and think about what the disciples' question implied: "Lord, do you mean that beginning in that room, with just us, You will restore the Kingdom to Israel? Are we to be the ones to cleanse the land, set up the Kingdom and bring You back?"

We know that Jesus had to deal with these men's lust for leadership and authority. Yet I sense something else in their question here, something beyond a thirst for place and power. It speaks of a human need to be involved in some great, final destiny. It was a need to be special—to be the right people at the right time.

In their hearts the disciples may have been saying, "Lord, where are we in Your prophetic schedule? What a great spiritual incentive to know we are at the end of a dispensation, that a new day is about to dawn. How excited we would be if You would let us know we are living and ministering in a day of destiny—that You are using us to wrap up all things."

This same need to be people of destiny is in all of us to some degree. Jesus' response to this was blunt: "It is not for you to know the times." He is saying, "The issue is not that some future destiny is appointed to you. The issue is that you are My witnesses in this present generation."

Yes, we are to preach about His coming and warn of His judgments. But first and foremost, we must be filled with the Holy Spirit and be His witnesses.

God Uses People to Proclaim His Word

I think the majority of Christians would like to escape to some safe, quiet hideaway in the mountains to keep from being tainted by all the iniquity surrounding them. Many despair, saying, "What can one Christian do about all this moral degradation? What can one church do in such a huge, wild and wicked city? It is enough for me just to stay close to Jesus, so that I don't get carried away with the flood."

Others think, "Is there really anything I can do—an insignificant Christian like me? I have no money, no training, no influence, only love for Jesus."

We often expect God to move in one of two ways: by sending a supernatural outpouring of His Holy Spirit to sweep multitudes into His Kingdom, or by sending judgment to bring people to their knees.

Beloved, that is not God's method of changing things in an evil day. His way of rebuilding ruins has always been to use ordinary men and women whom He has touched. He does this by filling them with His Holy Spirit—and sending them into warfare with great faith and power.

God is today raising up a holy ministry consisting of people totally given to the Word and prayer. They do not lord it over anyone. They are caring men and women with hearts that are stirred and no plan but to seek, hear and obey God.

The Lord is also calling you into immediate service. He needs the common man and woman, the layperson. He uses people whom the high priests would call "uneducated and untrained" (Acts 4:13).

The Bible says that in the Upper Room at Pentecost, "They were *all* filled with the Holy Spirit" (2:4, emphasis mine). *All* became mighty in boldness, powerful witnesses for Jesus. These Spirit-filled believers included not just Peter, James, John and other well-known disciples, but also the widows, the young, the servants and the handmaidens.

Take heart, and give ear: You are being called into service!

Forcible Fortitude to the End

Caleb, whose name means "forcible, fortitude," is a type of those who cling to the Lord. Caleb was inseparable from Joshua, representing one who continually walks with the Lord through all the distractions of life.

Caleb had accompanied the spies over Jordan, where the Holy Spirit drew him to Hebron—"the place of death." Abraham and Sarah were buried there, as were Isaac and Jacob and the patriarchs (and years later David's kingdom would begin there). With awe Caleb climbed that hallowed mountain, and faith flooded his soul. He prized this sanctified place, and from that time onward he wanted Hebron for his possession.

It was said of Caleb that he "has followed Me fully" (Numbers 14:24). He never wavered to the very end, and at 85 years old he could testify, "As yet I am as strong this day as I was on the day that Moses sent me; just as my strength was then, so now is my strength for war, both for going out and for coming in" (Joshua 14:11).

It was in his old age that Caleb waged his greatest battle. "'Now therefore give me this mountain [Hebron]. . . .' And Joshua blessed him, and gave Hebron to Caleb . . . as an inheritance. Hebron therefore became the inheritance of Caleb . . . because he wholly followed the Lord God of Israel" (verses 12–14).

Here is the glorious message of Caleb's life: It is not enough to have died to sin or to have entered into fullness sometime in the past. The need is to grow in the Lord *to the very end*—to keep your spiritual power and strength without wavering, to "wholly follow the Lord"—even in your old age.

A Place Where Leprosy Is Exposed

Moses truly was a man touched by God, supernaturally called and full of revelation about who God was. He was humble, pious and burdened for the honor of God. He was also given guidance as few others have known, as he loved God and grieved over the sins of the people.

In spite of all this, Moses did not know of the leprosy in his own bosom: "Furthermore the Lord said to him, 'Now put your hand in your bosom.' And he put his hand in his bosom, and when he took it out, behold, his hand was leprous, like snow" (Exodus 4:6).

What terror—to reach into your own bosom and touch leprosy. What an object lesson on the utter depravity of the flesh. Was God indulging in a little magic with Moses? No, this was a powerful lesson the man of God had to learn. It was God's way of saying, "When self is in control, you end up hurting people and bringing reproach on My work. When you attempt to do My work in fleshly ways, you minister death, not life."

God was declaring, "I cannot use that old nature from Egypt. It cannot be transformed, but will always be leprous. There must be a *new* man, one caught up in the glory and power of the I am."

Moses then was commanded to put his leprous hand back into his bosom, where "it was restored like his other flesh" (verse 7).

What happens when a man of God gets on holy ground? His inner soul is exposed. Stretching forth the hand represents ministry. Thank God for that second, sanctifying touch! It is a cleansing moment, when by faith the old flesh is crucified and the hand of ministry is purified—when we are once again clothed in the proper flesh: *His* flesh.

Thank God we can rejoice in the cleansing, by the precious, healing blood of Christ.

The New Temple Priesthood

In Ezekiel 44:15–16, the prophet refers to a righteous, faithful man named Zadok. The Hebrew name *Zadok* means "right" or "righteous." Ezekiel here is referring to a man who served as a priest during David's reign.

Zakok always remained loyal to David because he knew the king was the Lord's anointed. Indeed, Zadok was a prime example of a true minister of God—separated from this world, shut in with the Lord, consistently hearing from heaven. Such a minister recognizes his main work as prayer: seeking God daily, constantly communing with the Holy Spirit and ministering to Jesus.

Today's "new temple priests" are faithful to stand before the Lord before they ever stand before the congregation. They spend precious hours in the Lord's presence, until they are saturated with a message that has been burned into their souls. When they emerge from God's presence, they are able to speak straight to the people's hearts. Their message gets down to where the sheep live, because it has come directly from God's throne.

The Lord says of the Zadok priesthood, "These ministers will enter My sanctuary and stand before Me. They shall come near to My table and minister to Me and then I will lead and direct them and give them My word for My people" (see verse 16).

We see the "priesthood of believers" echoed throughout the books of the New Testament. John tells us, "[He] has made us kings and priests to His God and Father" (Revelation 1:6). Peter writes, "You also, as living stones, are . . . a holy priesthood . . . acceptable to God through Jesus Christ" (1 Peter 2:5).

You may not have ministerial credentials, but you are just as called and ordained to serve in the Zadok priesthood as the most well-known preacher or evangelist. You do it by ministering primarily unto the Lord—offering up sacrifices of praise and service to Him. You are part of His royal priesthood!

The Bountiful Servant

Recently I went to the Lord in prayer very heavyhearted and began to plead my case. "Oh, Lord," I cried, "I've never been so weary in all my life. I can hardly go on." I was so exhausted the tears literally burst out of me. As I lay crying, I thought, "Surely my tears will move the Lord's heart. He will feel for me."

I wanted sympathy and understanding. The Holy Spirit did come and minister to me—but not in the way I thought He would! Rather, He gently instructed me to go to 2 Corinthians 9:6–10:

"But this I say, He who sows sparingly will also reap sparingly, and he who sows bountifully will also reap bountifully. So let each one give as he purposes in his heart, not grudgingly or of necessity; for God loves a cheerful giver. And God is able to make all grace abound toward you, that you, always having all sufficiency in all things, have an abundance for every good work. . . . Now may He who supplies seed to the sower, and bread for food, supply and multiply the seed you have sown and increase the fruits of your righteousness."

I read this passage and reread it—but I got nothing. Finally, I closed my Bible and prayed, "Lord, I'm confused. I see nothing here to help or encourage me."

Finally, the Spirit spoke forcefully but lovingly to my inner man: "David, this has everything to do with what you are going through. Lately you have been serving Me without a cheerful spirit. My Word isn't talking only about giving money to help the poor. It is speaking of ministry to Me and to My Body.

"I have called you to New York City, but I did not send you without abundant resources. All you need is available—strength, rest, power, ability, joy and cheer. Do not be downhearted, because you have access to all My resources."

May we all be ever mindful: "He who sows sparingly will also reap sparingly, and he who sows bountifully will also reap bountifully. So let each one give as he purposes in his heart, not grudgingly or of necessity; for God loves a cheerful giver."

Proving Us

"God withdrew from him, in order to test him" (2 Chronicles 32:31).

We have become so preoccupied in proving God that we have not prepared our hearts for the great tests of life whereby God proves us. Could it be that the great trial you are now facing is actually God at work proving you?

"God tested Abraham, and said to him . . . 'Take now your son . . . and offer him there as a burnt offering'" (Genesis 22:1–2). God proved an entire nation to find out what was really in its heart. "The Lord your God led you all the way these forty years in the wilderness, to humble you and test you, to know what was in your heart, whether you would keep His commandments or not" (Deuteronomy 8:2).

We see something amazing in 2 Chronicles 32:31. God was silent toward a great king for a season to prove him: "God withdrew from him, in order to test him, that He might know all that was in his heart."

Often, while in the righteous pursuit of God's work, the steward of the Lord finds himself apparently forsaken. He feels tried to the limits of endurance and left all alone to battle the forces of hell. Every man or woman whom God has ever blessed has been proved in the same manner.

Do you fight a losing battle with an unpredictable enemy? Victory is always desired, but should you fail, remember: It is what remains in your heart that God is interested in. Your devotion to Him in spite of failure is His desire.

Jesus has promised never to leave us, but the record of Scripture reveals there are seasons when the Father withdraws His presence to prove us. Even Christ experienced that lonely moment on the cross. It is in these times that our blessed Savior is most touched by the feeling of our infirmity—and He whispers, "I have prayed for you, that your faith should not fail" (Luke 22:32).

Let this Mind Be in You

"Let this mind be in you which was also in Christ Jesus" (Philippians 2:5).

In this exhortation the apostle Paul is telling the people of God, "Let the mind that is in Christ—the very thinking of Jesus—be your thinking also. His mindset is the one we all are to seek."

What does it mean to have the mind of Christ? Simply put, it means thinking and acting as Jesus did. It means making Christlike decisions that determine how we are to live.

Every time we look into the mirror of God's Word, we are to ask ourselves: "Does what I see about myself reflect the nature and thinking of Christ? Am I being conformed to Jesus' very likeness by every experience that God brings into my life?"

According to Paul, here is the mindset of Christ: "[He] made Himself of no reputation, taking the form of a bondservant, and coming in the likeness of men" (verse 7).

Jesus made a decision while He was still in heaven—an agreement with the Father—to lay down His heavenly glory and come to earth as a man. He would descend to the world as a humble servant and seek to minister rather than be ministered to.

For Christ, this meant saying, "I go to do Your will, Father." Indeed, Jesus determined ahead of time, "I am laying down My will in order to do Yours, Father. Everything I say and do has to come from You."

In turn, the Father's agreement with the Son was to reveal His will to Him. God said to Him, "My will won't ever be hidden from You. You will always know what I am doing, and You will have My mind."

Paul states boldly, "I have the mind of Christ," and asserts that the same can hold true for every believer: "We [all can] have the mind of Christ" (1 Corinthians 2:16).

Pray the Lord of the Harvest

As Jesus looked down from His own time on earth to the end of the age, He pointed out a terrible problem. He told His disciples, "The harvest truly is plentiful, but the laborers are few" (Matthew 9:37).

As I read these words, I wonder, "What is the solution? How can more laborers be raised up to go to the nations?" Jesus gave the answer in the very next verse: "Therefore pray the Lord of the harvest to send out laborers into His harvest" (verse 38).

You may think, "Doors are closing to the Gospel all over the world." That may be true, but it does not matter how closed some nations may look to our eyes. If God can tear down the Iron Curtain in Europe and the Bamboo Curtain in Asia, nothing can stop Him from working wherever He will.

In the 1980s, when our ministry was headquartered in Texas, I spent a year praying that God would send someone to New York City to raise up a church in Times Square. I pledged to help whomever God chose: to raise money, to hold meetings, to build up support. Yet while I was praying for God to send a laborer into this specific harvest, the Lord put the burden on my own heart.

The apostle Paul was sent forth as a missionary through the power of prayer. It happened in Antioch, where leaders of the church were praying over the harvest (see Acts 13:2–6). Paul's first missionary journey was the direct result of the prayers of these godly men beseeching God to send laborers into the harvest.

The same is true today. We are to be about the work of praying for the harvest, just as those godly men in Antioch did. The fact is, while we are praying, the Holy Spirit is searching the earth, putting an urgency into the hearts of those who desire to be used. The Lord of the harvest makes a way!

HE DOES IT THROUGH LIFE

Let me tell you how God brings people into His house, how He speaks to them, and how He saves them. *He does it through life.* The Lord builds His Church through the testimonies of light shining forth from those who love Him.

Christ's life produces light in homes, neighborhoods, workplaces and cities. How is this life obtained? It comes down to every saint living as an example of God's mercy and grace, those who lead an honest, selfless life wholly devoted to Jesus.

Paul speaks of servants who "know His will, and approve the things that are excellent, being instructed out of the law, and are confident that you yourself are a guide to the blind, a light to those who are in darkness" (Romans 2: 18–19). Such saints are to be commended.

The CEO of a large company in New York called our office and told one of our pastors about two women from our church who work for him. He said they were not like the others in his office. These two women were always courteous, smiling, helpful to others, never complaining or backbiting. "There is something different about them," he said. "I would like to meet with you to find out what the difference is."

These women were heavenly candlesticks, placed in their jobs by Jesus. The light they shone lit up their workplace because they had the life of Christ in them! Their boss recognized it as something beyond what this world has to offer.

That CEO was Jewish. Do you think he would have responded to an invitation to a revival meeting? Would he have read a packet of materials produced by a church? No, he would have tossed it all out. But he responded to true light—the life of Christ being lived out daily by two godly, humble women.

God help us to remember that the light shines through in the little things of life.

A Light Not Meant to Be Hidden

Jesus tells us, "You are the light of the world" (Matthew 5:14). This statement is about much more than just doing ministry. It extends beyond teaching, preaching or passing out tracts. Christ is plainly saying, "You are not just a reflection of the light, a mere conduit. You *are* the light itself. The intensity of your light depends on the intensity of your walk with Me."

The world recognizes those who walk closely with Him. Your neighbors or co-workers may not know about your daily communion with Christ, your faith in Him, your utter dependence on Him. But they see the light that shines from you because of the life you have with Him. As long as nothing hinders that life, your light will continue to shine in the darkness.

"You are the light of the world. A city that is set on a hill cannot be hidden" (same verse). Jesus is saying, "I have put you on exhibition to the world. You are a light that is not meant to be hidden."

Who exactly are His lights set on a hill, and where do we see them? They are not usually found in the limelight. In fact, many of them are the faithful who give of themselves sacrificially, seeking no recognition.

Through the years I have seen many believers who appear godly but in truth are spiritually lazy. They tell others about their failings and weaknesses, thinking this makes them humble. Yet at the same time they are quick to judge others.

They do not possess the true, giving, loving servant-like spirit of Christ. On the contrary, the "light" they have is actually darkness. Jesus says, "If therefore the light that is in you is darkness, how great is that darkness!" (6:23).

Where there is no life of Christ, there can be no light for others. We must always let our light shine forth in order that God may receive glory.

The Life Behind the Light

Then Jesus spoke to them again, saying, 'I am the light of the world. He who follows Me shall not walk in darkness, but have the light of life'" (John 8:12).

Jesus was, and still is, the light of the world. "In Him was life, and the life was the light of men" (John 1:4). Simply put, the life that Christ possessed was His source of light to the world. He said that all who believe "shall have the light of life" (same verse). What is the "life behind the light" that Scripture speaks of?

When John uses the word *life*, he is speaking of the whole biography of Jesus' existence. Jesus tells us that we are to live as He did. For us to be as Christ was in the world, His life has to be something we can know and experience for ourselves.

I relate to the life that is in Christ by rejoicing in the kind, little things that He did and said. His everyday deeds, words and walk with the Father are meant to define the meaning of the Christ-life to us.

I think of Jesus' friendship with Lazarus; of His retreat from the multitudes after a long period of ministry; of His enjoyment of time spent in the home of Mary, Martha and Lazarus. I think of His taking the little children into His arms and blessing them; of His obedience to His mother, even as a grown man; of turning the water into wine at the wedding feast. I think of Jesus' love and care for the scorned, the unlovely, the poor; of His compassion for the woman caught in adultery; of His honoring the widow who had only two mites to give.

I doubt there would be enough books to record all the loving things Jesus did while on earth. In these passages, we find the ways we are to relate our lives to His and comprehend *the life that is the light*.

People Grace

God uses angels to minister to people, but more often He uses His own caring people to dispense His grace. One reason we are made partakers of His grace is that we become channels of it and dispense it to others. I call this "people grace."

"But to every one of us grace was given according to the measure of Christ's gift" (Ephesians 4:7). Because of the comfort we are given through God's grace, it is impossible for any of us to continue grieving our whole lifetime. At some point, we are being healed and we begin to build up a reservoir of God's grace.

I believe this is what Paul meant when he wrote, "I became a minister according to the gift of the grace of God given to me . . . that I should preach among the Gentiles the unsearchable riches of Christ" (3:7–8). "You all are partakers with me of grace" (Philippians 1:7).

The apostle is making a profound statement here. He is saying, "When I go to God's throne to obtain grace, it is for your sake. I want to be a merciful shepherd to you, not a judgmental one. I want to be able to dispense grace to you in your time of need." God's grace made Paul a compassionate shepherd, able to weep with those who grieved.

Peter writes, "As each one has received a gift, minister it to one another, as good stewards of the manifold grace of God" (1 Peter 4:10). What does it mean to be a good steward, or dispenser, of God's grace? Am I such a person? Or do I spend my time praying only for my own pain, grief and struggles?

Our present sufferings are producing something precious in our lives. They are forming in us a cry for the gift of grace to offer to others who are hurting. Our sufferings make us want to be grace-givers.

I Have Need of You

Some Christians do not want to be connected to other members of the Body of Christ. They commune with Jesus, but they deliberately isolate themselves from other believers. They want to be connected to the head only—yet a body cannot be comprised of just a single member. Can you picture a head with only an arm growing out of it? Christ's Body consists of many members. We simply cannot be one with Christ without being with His Body also.

Our need is not just for the Head but for the whole Body. We are knit together not only by our need for Jesus, but by our need for each other. Paul states, "The eye cannot say to the hand, 'I have no need of you'; nor again the head to the feet, 'I have no need of you'" (1 Corinthians 12:21).

Note the second half of this verse. Even the head cannot say to another member, "I do not need you." Paul is telling us, "Christ will never say to any member that He has no need of him." We all are important, even necessary, to the functioning of His Body.

This is especially true of members who may be bruised and hurting. Paul emphasizes, "No, much rather, those members of the body which seem to be weaker are necessary" (verse 22). The apostle then adds, "And those members of the body which we think to be less honorable, on these we bestow greater honor; and our unpresentable parts have greater modesty" (verse 23). He is speaking of those who are unseen, hidden, unknown. In God's eyes, these members have great honor.

As important members of the Body of Christ, all believers are to rise up and take serious action against Satan's attacks on fellow believers. You may think that you are not measuring up, but the Lord Himself says, "I need you. You are vital and necessary for the body to function."

The Body of Christ

The apostle Paul instructs us, "You are the body of Christ, and members individually" (1 Corinthians 12:27). He says even more specifically, "For as the body is one and has many members, but all the members of that one body, being many, are one body, so also is Christ" (verse 12).

Paul is telling us, "Take a look at your own body. You have hands, feet, eyes, ears. You are not just an isolated brain, unattached to the other members. Well, it is the same way with Christ. He has a Body, and we comprise its members."

The apostle then points out, "We, being many, are one body in Christ, and individually members of one another" (Romans 12:5). In other words, we are not just connected to Jesus but are joined to each other. The truth is we cannot be connected to Him without also being joined to our brothers and sisters in Christ.

Paul drives this point home, saying, "The bread which we break, is it not the communion of the body of Christ? For we, though many, are one bread and one body; for we all partake of that one bread" (1 Corinthians 10:16–17). Simply put, we are all fed by the same food: Christ, the manna from heaven. "The bread of God is He who comes down from heaven and gives life to the world" (John 6:33).

Jesus declared, "I am the bread of life. . . . I am the living bread which came down from heaven. . . . He who feeds on Me will live because of Me" (John 6:35, 51, 57). The image of bread here is important. Our Lord is telling us, "If you come to Me, you will be nourished—you will be attached to Me. Therefore, you will receive strength from the life-flow that is in Me."

Indeed, every member of His Body draws strength from a single source: Christ, the Head. Everything we need to lead an overcoming life flows to us from Him.

A Friend of Sinners

In Luke 7 we read the story of Simon, a Pharisee who invited Jesus to his house to have a meal. I am not sure why any Pharisee would invite Jesus for dinner, let alone bring in other strict religious men to eat with Him. A likely reason for the invitation was that Simon and his friends wanted to determine whether Jesus was a prophet or, really, to discount Him as one. The passage makes clear, however, that Simon knew of Jesus' reputation as a prophet (Luke 7:39).

Scripture does not tell us what this group discussed around that supper table, but we can assume it had to do with theology. The Pharisees specialized in the subject, and they had tried to trick Jesus on other occasions with fanciful questions. Christ knew, however, what was in these men's hearts.

The next thing we read is that a woman of the streets "who was a sinner" crashed the scene. Scripture tells us, "Then He turned to the woman" (verse 44). Here I see Jesus showing us where our focus must be: not on false religion, not on false teachers, but on sinners.

Looking away from Simon and his guests, Jesus turned to the woman and then addressed the men, "Her sins, which are many, are forgiven, for she loved much. . . . Then He said to the woman, 'Your faith has saved you. Go in peace'" (verses 47, 50). Jesus was revealing here why He came: to befriend and restore the fallen, those overtaken by sin. He is saying to us today, "This is what My ministry is all about."

Our focus must be love, as our Savior's is. We are not to judge the fallen, but to seek to restore them.

What is the law of Christ? It is love: "A new commandment I give to you, that you love one another; as I have loved you, that you also love one another" (John 13:34).

God Uses People

God uses people to refresh other people. He so loves this kind of ministry that He moved the prophet Malachi to speak of it as a most-needed work in the last days. Malachi described how, in his day, God's people built each other up through one-on-one edification: "Those who feared the LORD spoke to one another" (Malachi 3:16).

Malachi's words came during a time of rampant ungodliness, when the "devourer" had destroyed much fruit in the land. God's people had grown weary and started to doubt that walking with the Lord was worth it. They thought, "We're told it pays to serve the Lord, obey His Word and carry His burdens. Yet as we look around at the proud and the compromisers, they are the ones who seem happy, enjoying prosperity, living carelessly in pleasure."

The Holy Spirit began to move in Israel. Soon the fear of the Lord came and everyone opened up to one another. They edified each other and comforted the hurting around them.

I am convinced Malachi's word about this ministry is a mirror image of the present day. He has given us a picture of an outpouring of the Holy Spirit in the last days, as God's people stop gossiping and complaining and instead minister refreshing.

This ministry is happening by phone, by letter, by e-mail, and face-to-face. God is so pleased with this ministry, with every kind word spoken, every call made, every letter written, every effort to comfort the downcast. It is all recorded in His "book of remembrance."

These ministering saints are precious to Him: "'They shall be Mine,' says the LORD of hosts, on the day that I make them My jewels'" (verse 17).

You have been given the power to refresh a hurting believer. Call that someone today and say, "Brother, sister, I want to pray for you and encourage you. I have a good word for you."

Heavenly Preview

Thanks be to God, who gives us the victory through our Lord Jesus Christ" (1 Corinthians 15:57). Many believers quote this verse daily, applying it to their trials and tribulations. Yet, the context in which Paul speaks it suggests a deeper meaning. Just two verses earlier, Paul states, "Death is swallowed up in victory. O Death, where is your sting? O Hades, where is your victory?" (verses 54–55).

Paul was speaking eloquently about his longing for heaven. He wrote, "We have a building from God, a house not made with hands, eternal in the heavens. For in this we groan, earnestly desiring to be clothed with our habitation which is from heaven" (2 Corinthians 5:1–2). The apostle then adds, "We are confident, yes, well pleased rather to be absent from the body and to be present with the Lord" (verse 8).

According to Paul, heaven—being in the Lord's presence for all eternity—is something we are to desire with all our hearts.

As I ponder these things, a glorious picture begins to emerge. First, I imagine Jesus' description of a huge gathering, when the angels "will gather together His elect from the four winds, from one end of heaven to the other" (Matthew 24:31). When all these throngs have been gathered, I picture millions of glorified children singing hosannas to the Lord. Then come all the martyrs, crying, "Holy, holy, holy!" Finally, there is a mighty roar from the Church of Jesus Christ, with multitudes from all nations and tribes praising their God.

This may sound farfetched to you, but Paul himself testified about it. When the faithful apostle was caught up into heaven, he "heard inexpressible words, which it is not lawful for a man to utter" (2 Corinthians 12:4). I believe he was given a preview of the singing and praising of God by those who will be rejoicing in His presence. It was a sound so glorious that Paul could hear it but not repeat it.

That is our preview—let us desire its fullness.

Revealed in Our Difficulties

Paul's closing words to the Philippians were, "Rejoice in the Lord always. Again I will say, rejoice" (Philippians 4:4). He was not saying, "I am in prison, and these chains are a blessing. I am so happy for this pain." No, I am convinced Paul prayed daily for his release and at times cried out for strength to endure.

Even Jesus, in His hour of trial and pain, cried to the Father, "Why have You forsaken me?" If we are honest, we will acknowledge that our first impulse in our afflictions is to cry out, "Why?" The Lord wants us to know He is patient with that cry.

Yet God has also made provision so that our "what ifs" and "whys" can be answered by His Word. Paul writes, "Knowing that I am appointed for the defense of the gospel. . . . Christ is preached; and in this I rejoice, yes, and will rejoice" (1:17–18).

The apostle is telling us, "I am determined that God's Word will be validated by my reaction to this affliction. The fact is, Christ is being preached by my calm countenance, by my rest in the midst of all this. Everyone who sees me knows that the Gospel I preach takes me through these hard times. It proves that the Lord can take anybody through any situation, and His Gospel will be preached through the experience."

An elder in our church named Sam once told me, "Pastor David, the way you respond to hard times is a testimony to me." What Sam did not realize is that his life is a sermon to me. He lives with chronic pain that allows him to sleep no more than a few hours each night. Despite his constant, raging pain, his devotion to the Lord is a testimony to all of us.

Here is the message I hear through Paul: *We do not have to do something great for the Lord. We only have to trust Him. Christ will be revealed in us in our difficult circumstances.*

THROUGH IT ALL

As Paul faced his court trial in Rome, he was held under horrible conditions. Imagine the indignities he suffered (see Philippians 1:13–14). Guarded around the clock, his feet chained to a soldier on either side, he had no time alone, not a single moment of freedom. It would have been so easy for this godly man's dignity to be totally stripped away under that kind of treatment.

Paul had been very active, loving to travel the open road and high seas to meet and fellowship with God's people. He drew his greatest joy from visiting the churches he had established throughout that region of the world. Now he was chained down, however, literally bound to the hardest, most profane men alive, with no possible way out.

Paul had two options in his situation. He could spin out into a sour mood, asking the same self-centered question over and over: "Why me?" He could crawl into a pit of despair, completely consumed with the thought, "Here I am bound up, with my ministry shut down, while others out there enjoy a harvest of souls. Why?"

Instead, Paul chose to ask, "How is my present situation going to bring glory to Christ? How can great good come out of my trial?" This servant of God made up his mind: "I cannot change my condition, and I could very well die in this state. Yet I know my steps are ordered by the Lord and He is faithful. I will magnify Christ, therefore, and be a testimony to the world while in these chains."

Paul's attitude demonstrates the only way we can be emancipated from our dark pit of unhappiness and worry. "Now also Christ will be magnified in my body, whether by life or by death" (verse 20).

Be Steadfast and Immovable

We have learned from Isaiah 49 that the Lord knows your battle. He has fought it before you. It is no sin to endure thoughts that your labor has been in vain, or to be cast down with a sense of failure over shattered expectations. Jesus Himself experienced this and was without sin.

It is very dangerous, however, to allow these hellish lies to fester and inflame your soul. Jesus showed us the way out of such despondency with this statement: "I have labored in vain . . . yet surely my just reward is with the Lord, and my work with my God" (Isaiah 49:4). The Hebrew word for "just reward" here is *verdict*. Christ is saying, in effect, "The final verdict is with My Father. He alone passes judgment on all that I have done and how effective I have been."

God is urging us through this verse: "Stop passing a verdict over your work for Me. You have no business judging how effective you have been. You also have no right to call yourself a failure. You simply do not have the vision to know the blessings that are coming to you." Indeed, we will not know many such things until we stand before Him in eternity.

While the devil is lying to you, saying that all you have done is in vain, God in His glory is preparing a greater blessing. He has better things in store, beyond anything you could think or ask.

We are not to listen to the enemy's lies any longer. Instead, we are to rest in the Holy Spirit, believing that He will fulfill the work of making us more like Christ. We are to rise up from our despair and stand on this word: "Be steadfast, immovable, always abounding in the work of the Lord, knowing that your labor is not in vain in the Lord" (1 Corinthians 15:58).

I Have Labored in Vain

Would it shock you to know that Jesus experienced the feeling of having accomplished little?

In Isaiah 49:4 we read these words: "Then I said, 'I have labored in vain, I have spent my strength for nothing and in vain.'" These are not the words of Isaiah himself, who was called by God at a mature age. No, they are Christ's own words, spoken by One called "from the womb; from the [body] of My mother. . . . The Lord . . . formed Me from the womb to be His Servant, to bring Jacob back to Him" (verses 1, 5).

When I came upon this passage, one I had read many times before, my heart was in wonder. I could hardly believe what I was reading. Jesus' words about "laboring in vain" were a response to the Father who had just declared, "You are My servant . . . in whom I will be glorified" (verse 3). We read Jesus' surprising response in the next verse: "I have labored in vain, I have spent my strength for nothing" (verse 4).

After reading this, I stood to my feet in my study and said, "How amazing! I can hardly believe that Christ was this vulnerable. In His humanity, He tasted the same discouragement that we do. He was having the same thoughts I have had about my own life at times."

Reading those words made me love Jesus all the more. I realized that Hebrews 4:15 is not a cliché. Our Savior truly is touched with the feelings of our infirmities, and was tempted as we are, yet was without sin. He heard the same accusation that Satan whispers to us: "Your mission is not accomplished. There is nothing to show for Your labors."

Why would Jesus, or any man or woman of God, think such despairing thoughts? It is all the result of measuring little results against high expectations. God tells us differently: "You are My servant . . . in whom I will be glorified."

Feed My Sheep

When I asked the Holy Spirit to show me how to guard against neglect, He led me to consider Peter's drifting and his eventual renewal. The once bold disciple denied Christ, lying to his accuser, "I don't know this man."

What had brought Peter to this point? It was pride, the result of self-righteous boasting. He had said to himself and others, "I could never grow cold toward Jesus. Others may drift, but I will die for my Lord."

Yet Peter was the first among the disciples to give up the struggle. He forsook his calling and returned to his old career, telling the others, "I am going fishing" (see John 21:2–3). He really was saying, "I cannot handle this. I just cannot face the struggle anymore."

Peter had repented of his denial of Jesus and had been restored in Jesus' love. Yet, he was still a frayed man inside because an issue remained unsettled in his life. It was not enough that he was restored, secure in his salvation. No, the issue that Christ needed to address in Peter's life was neglect in another form. Let me explain.

As the disciples sat around the fire on shore, eating and fellowshiping, Jesus asked Peter three times, "Do you love Me more than these others?" Each time Peter answered, "Yes, Lord, you know I do"—and each time Christ responded in turn, "Feed my sheep."

Note that Jesus did not remind Peter to watch and pray, or to be diligent in reading God's Word. Christ presumed those things had already been well taught. No, the instruction He gave Peter was, "Feed my sheep" (see verses 16–17).

I believe that in that simple phrase, Jesus was instructing Peter—and us today—on how to guard against neglect. He was saying, "You are restored. Now it is time to get your focus off your failures and problems. The way to do that is by not neglecting My people. As the Father has sent Me, so I send you." Amen!

LOVING OTHERS

To be Christlike is to acknowledge Jesus in others. In my travels I meet many precious men and women whom I know are given wholly to the Lord. The moment I meet them, my heart leaps. Even though we have never met, I have a witness from the Holy Spirit that they are full of Christ.

I can still see some of their faces: pastors, bishops, poor street evangelists. The moment I meet them, I realize without a word being spoken, "This man has been with Jesus. This woman is satisfied in Christ." In greeting them, I always say the one thing I would want others to say of me: "Brother, sister, I see Jesus in you."

Christlikeness has to do with how I treat those outside my family, loving others as He loves us. It also means loving our enemies—those who hate us, who seem incapable of loving us. We are to do this expecting nothing in return. Loving this way is impossible, in human terms—yet we are commanded to do it.

How do I love the Muslim who spit in my face a block from our church? How do I love those who run Internet websites calling me a false prophet? How do I truly love them in Christ?

I cannot even love all Christians in my own ability. It has to be the work of the Holy Spirit. Jesus prayed to the Father, "That the love with which You loved Me may be in them, and I in them" (John 17:26).

Christ asks the Father to put His love in us. He promises that the Holy Spirit will show us how to live out that love. "You know Him, for He dwells with you and will be in you . . . He will teach you all things" (14:17, 26).

CHOSEN TO BEAR FRUIT

"You did not choose Me, but I chose you and appointed you that you should go and bear fruit" (John 15:16).

Many sincere Christians think bearing fruit means simply bringing souls to Christ. Bearing fruit means something much larger even than soul-winning.

The fruit Jesus is talking about is Christlikeness. Simply put, bearing fruit means reflecting the likeness of Jesus. Likewise, the phrase *much fruit* means "the ever-increasing likeness of Christ."

Growing more and more into Jesus' likeness is our purpose in life. It has to be central to all our activities, our lifestyle, our relationships. Indeed, all our gifts and callings—our work, ministry and witness—must flow out of this core purpose.

If I am not Christlike at heart—if I am not becoming noticeably more like Him—I have missed God's purpose in my life.

You see, God's purpose for me cannot be fulfilled by what I do for Christ. It cannot be measured by anything I achieve, even if I heal the sick or cast out demons. No, God's purpose is fulfilled in me only by how I am being transformed into His likeness.

Go into a Christian bookstore and you will find mostly self-help books—how to overcome loneliness, survive depression, find fulfillment. But we have it all wrong! We are not called to be successes—to be free of all trouble, to be special, to "make it." Many are missing the one focus that is meant to be central to their lives: to become fruitful in the likeness of Christ.

Jesus was totally given to the Father and that was everything to Him. He stated, "I do not do or say anything except what my Father tells Me."

Do you want to bear the "much fruit" that springs forth from becoming more like Christ? Increase in your love for others—that is how to grow more Christlike. Bearing fruit comes down to how we treat people.

ARE YOU AMONG THE SEVEN THOUSAND?

All through the Bible the number seven is equated with God's eternal purpose. I believe, therefore, that the number seven thousand that God quoted to Elijah in 1 Kings 19:18 simply denoted everyone who made up His remnant. In truth the people He sets aside for Himself could number seventy or seven million. What matters is that they are wholly given to Him.

What are the characteristics of the remnant? Here are three defining marks:

1. *An unchangeable commitment to cling to the Lord.* Every remnant believer has made a single-minded choice to swim against the tide of evil. At some point, we have to make a commitment, declaring, "I do not care what others say or do. I am the Lord's, and I will not give in to the wicked spirit of this age."
2. *A willingness to identify with the poor.* While society's trend is to associate with the rich and successful, we align ourselves with the suffering class. Obadiah was a godly man serving in Jezebel's house, someone determined to fear God and no one else. He proved that his heart was right and was with the poor by taking care of one hundred ragged, suffering prophets (see 1 Kings 18:4).
3. *A reliance on hope.* The seven thousand in Elijah's time endured because of their hope in a coming day of deliverance. Likewise today, the Church's blessed hope is the soon return of Jesus. With one trumpet blast, all wickedness will end. Our Lord will do away with all killing of babies, all blatant perversions, all ethnic genocide.

Do these three marks characterize you as a part of God's holy remnant? If so, God boasts of you, "This one has given his heart to Me. He is focused on Me—and he is wholly Mine!"

We are to evangelize, minister to the poor, and work while it is still day, living in the hope that King Jesus is coming to rule!

Safeguards against Satan's Lies about Grace

Thank God, Jude has given us three safeguards against the seductions of Satan's lies concerning grace. Jude writes, "But you, beloved, building yourselves up on your most holy faith, praying in the Holy Spirit, keep yourselves in the love of God, looking for the mercy of our Lord Jesus Christ unto eternal life" (Jude 20–21).

Let us note three things in this verse:

1. *We are to build up our faith*. How do we do this? By diligently studying God's Word. However, faith comes not just by reading the Bible, but by hearing—or doing—what we read. We are to read God's Word, apply it to our hearts and accept its reproof. That will produce in us a spiritual soberness. Then, no matter what kind of message we hear preached, we will not be carried away by the lies or the lightness of any man.
2. *We are to pray in the Holy Spirit*. This means we do not just pray in church, but we shut ourselves in with the Lord in private. We are to ask God's Spirit to shine His light on our hearts and receive His correction, so we can obtain grace for any lack.
3. *We are to be anxious for nothing, and instead be looking for our Lord's coming.* If we are studying God's Word and praying in the Spirit, then we cannot help but look for Jesus' sudden appearing. We will know this world is not our home, and we will expect our Lord to come for us at any moment.

If you are applying these three safeguards, then you will understand true grace. You will not be seduced into lasciviousness by any perverted message of true grace. If we do these things, Jude declares, we will reap the benefits of this prayer: "Now to Him who is able to keep you from stumbling, and to present you faultless before the presence of His glory with exceeding joy" (Jude 24).

Are You Growing in Grace?

One question has been at the forefront of my mind in recent weeks. It is a question I believe every sincere believer must ask himself: Am I growing in grace?

To me, grace is Holy Spirit empowerment to become more like Jesus. Therefore, to grow in grace means to increase in Christlikeness through the unmerited power of God's Spirit. Now let me rephrase my question in these terms: "Am I relying on the Holy Spirit to make me more like Jesus—in my home, my ministry, my relationships?"

This question applies especially to mature Christians—people who have built a spiritual foundation over the years through regular Bible study, a consistent prayer life and godly instruction. If this describes you, let me ask: After all of your studying, praying and learning, are you still becoming more like Jesus? Are you more compassionate, meek, merciful and forgiving than you were at this time last year? Or has your growth been stunted? Have you settled onto a plateau of zero growth?

Here is one way to tell if you are growing in grace: God has been merciful to you—so, have you in turn been merciful to others? If you are not sure, ask yourself how you respond to the hurts others cause you. Are you kind and gentle? Or do you grow angry and bitter? Are you patient and understanding, or irritable and argumentative?

Take an honest look at your life over the last year. Have you learned through your trials to be more kind, patient, gentle and soft-spoken? Or do you have to admit, as I do, that you have reacted with flashes of anger, harsh words and self-pity?

We should all ask, "Have I reacted to my critics and enemies with compassion, love, mercy and forgiveness? Or have I reacted with anger, indignation and self-righteousness?"

"But grow in the grace and knowledge of our Lord and Savior Jesus Christ" (2 Peter 3:18).

Our Ministry: Transformation

"But we all, with unveiled face, beholding as in a mirror the glory of the Lord" (2 Corinthians 3:18). What does it mean to behold the Lord's glory? Paul is speaking here of devoted, focused worship. It is time that is given to God simply to behold Him.

The apostle then quickly adds, "Therefore, since we have this ministry" (4:1). Paul makes it clear that beholding the face of Christ is a ministry we all must devote ourselves to.

The Greek word for *beholding* in this verse is a very strong expression that indicates not just "taking a look" but "fixing the gaze." It means deciding, "I will not move from this position. Before I try to accomplish a single thing, I must be in God's presence."

Many Christians misinterpret the phrase "beholding as in a mirror" (3:18). They think of a mirror with Jesus' face being reflected back to them. That is not Paul's meaning here. He is speaking of an intensely focused gaze, as if peering at something earnestly through a glass, trying to see it more clearly. We are to "fix our eyes" this way, determined to see God's glory in the face of Christ. We are to shut ourselves in the holy of holies with but one obsession: to gaze so intently, and to commune with such devotion, that we are changed.

The Greek word for *changed* here is "metamorphosed," meaning "transformed, transfigured." Everyone who goes often into the holy of holies and fixes his gaze intently on Christ is being metamorphosed. A transfiguration is taking place. That person is continually being changed into the likeness and character of Jesus.

Do you see what Paul is saying here? He is telling us, "When you spend time beholding the face of Christ, there is freedom to be changed." This act of submission says, "Lord, my will is Yours. Whatever it takes, transform me into the image of Jesus."

PLANT A TREE

God has not promised to keep His children from suffering. He has not promised to keep us from facing an hour of need. We have no promise of world peace, tranquility, security or continuous financial well-being. We are promised, however, peace and security of soul and mind. We are pledged supernatural provision for every true need and assurance that we would never have to beg for bread. God would rather we come to the place Paul came to when he said, "Having food and clothing, with these we shall be content" (1 Timothy 6:8).

Globally, the future looks evil and foreboding. But David speaks for God's people in Psalm 23:4: "I will fear no evil." This is the message for believers today. The future is always under God's control, so we need not fear. The Lord has it all preprogrammed. He knows the exact moment Christ will return. The Creator God who controls all of heaven and earth said, "The nations are as a drop in a bucket, and are counted as the small dust on the scales. . . . All nations before Him are as nothing . . . less than nothing" (Isaiah 40:15, 17).

God wants us to keep working in His Spirit until the return of Christ. That means simply that we are to work as though the end will never come, and live as though it were coming tomorrow. A renowned preacher was asked, "What would you do today if you knew Jesus Christ was coming tomorrow?" His answer came, "I would plant a tree."

So let it be with us today! Let the true Christian go about planting and sowing God's seed and keeping busy doing God's work. When He returns, let Him find us "doing His will."

Detailed Directions and Unclouded Decisions

God's purpose for every one of His children is to surrender to the reign and rulership of the Holy Spirit: "If we live in the Spirit, let us also walk in the Spirit" (Galatians 5:25). In other words: "If He lives in you, let Him direct you."

I have not yet fully arrived in this glorious walk—but I am gaining ground daily. I believe Acts 16 gives us one of the best examples of what it means to walk in the Holy Spirit. "They [Paul and Timothy] were forbidden by the Holy Spirit to preach the word in Asia. . . . They tried to go into Bithynia, but the Spirit did not permit them" (Acts 16:6–7).

The Holy Spirit provides clear, detailed instructions to those who walk in Him. If you walk in the Spirit, then you do not walk in confusion—your decisions are not clouded ones.

The early Christians did not walk in confusion. It was because they were led by the Spirit in every decision, every move, every action. The Spirit talked to them and directed them in their every waking hour. No decision was made without consulting Him. The Church's motto throughout the New Testament was: "He who has ears to hear, let him hear what the Spirit has to say!"

I began ministering in New York City because the Holy Spirit told me very clearly: "Go to New York City and raise up a church." He also told me when to come. No devil or demon could move me from this—because the Spirit gave detailed instructions.

I remember standing between Broadway and Seventh Avenue, weeping and raising my hands. The Holy Spirit said, "In this very area I am going to raise up a church. Obey me, David. Start a church in New York City!"

Times Square Church is not an accident. It is the result of clear, detailed instructions from the Holy Spirit!

POSSESSING YOUR PROMISED LAND

Multitudes from all nations have possessed Christ as their all-in-all. Yet the majority of these people, including many in ministry, have forsaken Jesus as their source. Why? They know how costly it would be to give up relying on their own flesh.

You see, something happens when we cross the line into the holy of holies. The moment we enter our Lord's presence, we realize all flesh must die. This includes all desire for spiritual excitement, all talk of great revivals, all focus on deliverance, all seeking out some new work or movement.

Jesus—and Jesus alone—has to become your everything. He alone is to be your source of excitement, your constant revival. He is to be your continual word of direction, your new grace every morning. Once you cross the border, you can no longer rely on gifted teachers, anointed preachers, powerful evangelists. If you still seek out men instead of Christ—rushing from meeting to meeting, looking for some person to bless you—then you are not satisfied with Jesus. Moreover, your works will be in vain.

Abraham was called "the friend of God" (see James 2:23) because of his intimate relationship with the Lord. A friend is someone who freely gives his heart to another. Clearly the Lord shared his heart with Abraham. God Himself testified, "Shall I hide from Abraham what I am doing?" (Genesis 18:17).

Paul declares, "And the Scripture . . . preached the gospel to Abraham beforehand" (Galatians 3:8). In other words, the Lord showed Abraham great things to come. Abraham knew Jesus was our promised possession. He saw a victorious Jesus bringing down all principalities and power. He saw the victory of the cross and many nations streaming into the Promised Land, possessing their promise: Christ Himself.

These people were possessing their promise by faith, trusting God's Word to them. Have you possessed your Promised Land? I urge you, make Jesus your everything. Enter into the peace and rest of your everlasting possession, Jesus Christ.

PART 8

Help Is on the Way

He Delights in Helping Us

Hope in the Coming Storm

David gives us a clear picture of Jesus' attitude in the face of the coming storm. He speaks prophetically of Christ, saying, "I foresaw the Lord always before my face, for He is at my right hand, that I may not be shaken" (Acts 2:25).

The literal meaning here is, "I was always in His presence, beholding His face." David quoted Jesus as saying, "Therefore my heart rejoiced, and my tongue was glad; moreover my flesh also will rest in hope" (verse 26).

Here is the secret: Jesus kept the Father always before His face. He met Him in secret places, and only after being in God's presence did Christ come forth to minister. Jesus was saying, "None of these evils or coming events can cast Me down or shake My confidence. My Father is always with Me—and He is in complete control."

If we are going to face the coming storm, we must be prepared so nothing disturbs our spirit. The only way to do that is to spend time in the Father's presence beholding His face. We have to be shut in with Him—on our knees, practicing His presence, seeking Him—until we are thoroughly persuaded He is at our right hand.

God is clearly telling us, "Do not be moved or agitated by anything you see. Keep your eyes focused on Me and you will retain your joy." According to David, Jesus testified, "You will make me full of joy in Your presence" (verse 28).

It is as if Christ is telling us, "I faced everything you are going to face in the closing days of time. I had the same feelings of foreboding, but I ran quickly to be with My Father. In His presence I found all the joy, hope and rest I would ever need. I have peace and joy because I have been with Him."

"My flesh also will rest in hope" (verse 26).

Wholly Dependent on Him

God has always wanted a people who would walk totally reliant on Him before the eyes of the world. That is why He took the insignificant little nation of Israel and isolated the people in a wilderness.

He was placing Israel in a school of testing, to produce a people who would trust in Him no matter what their circumstance. He wanted Israel to testify, "I can go through any test, any difficulty, even those beyond my abilities. I know this because I know my God is with me in every trial. He will always bring me through."

Consider Moses' statement to Israel: "[God] allowed you to hunger" (Deuteronomy 8:3). The Lord was telling them, "It was I who orchestrated your trial, not the devil. I possessed all the bread and meat you needed, and I was ready to drop it out of the sky at any minute. It was all stored up, waiting for you to receive it.

"I withheld it for a while, however, as a brief season of testing. I was waiting for you to come to the end of all your self-reliance. I wanted to bring you to a point of crisis, where only I could deliver you. I allowed you to experience a helplessness that would require a miracle of deliverance from Me."

Today, the Lord is still looking for a people who will rely totally on Him. He wants a Church that will testify to His power both in words and actions—all so that an unsaved world will see He works mightily for those who love Him.

Job suffered overwhelming tragedies in a short span of time: loss of all his children, loss of wealth, loss of health. Yet he made an incredible statement, especially considering the context in which he spoke it: "He knows the way that I take; when He has tested me, I shall come forth as gold" (Job 23:10).

God performed a miracle of restoration and deliverance for Job. Trust Him for yours.

Favorite Bible Promises

Here are several of my favorite Bible verses—promises that I have marked in my Bible over the years. Read them over and over and trust them. They are yours:

- "Do not fear, for you will not be ashamed; neither be disgraced, for you will not be put to shame; for you will forget the shame of your youth" (Isaiah 54:4).
- "'For the mountains shall depart and the hills be removed, but My kindness shall not depart from you, nor shall My covenant of peace be removed,' says the Lord, who has mercy on you" (verse 10).
- "'No weapon formed against you shall prosper, and every tongue which rises against you in judgment you shall condemn. This is the heritage of the servants of the Lord, and their righteousness is from Me,' says the Lord" (verse 17).
- "Oh, how great is Your goodness, which You have laid up for those who fear You, which You have prepared for those who trust in You in the presence of the sons of men! You shall hide them in the secret place of Your presence from the plots of man; You shall keep them secretly in a pavilion from the strife of tongues" (Psalm 31:19–20).
- "You are my hiding place; You shall preserve me from trouble; You shall surround me with songs of deliverance. I will instruct you and teach you in the way you should go; I will guide you with My eye" (32:7–8).
- "Delight yourself also in the Lord, and He shall give you the desires of your heart. Commit your way to the Lord, trust also in Him, and He shall bring it to pass" (37:4–5).
- "You, who have shown me great and severe troubles, shall revive me again, and bring me up again from the depths of the earth. You shall increase my greatness, and comfort me on every side" (71:20–21).

Faith Reactions

God has given us an ironclad promise for life on this earth. He says that when our enemy attempts to walk over us, "My people shall know My name; therefore they shall know in that day that I am He who speaks: 'Behold, it is I'" (Isaiah 52:6).

God says, in other words, "When you are in your darkest trial, I will come and speak a word to you. You will hear Me say, 'It is I, your Lord. Do not be afraid.'"

In Matthew 14, the disciples were on a boat in an awful storm, being tossed about by torrents of waves and fierce winds. Suddenly, the men saw Jesus walking toward them on the water. Scripture says, "When the disciples saw Him walking on the sea, they were troubled, saying, 'It is a ghost!' And they cried out for fear" (Matthew 14:26).

What did Jesus do in that fearful moment? "But immediately Jesus spoke to them, saying, 'Be of good cheer! It is I; do not be afraid'" (verse 27).

I have often wondered why Jesus used these particular words, "Be of good cheer." Why would He say this to men who thought they were very close to dying?

The word *cheer* means "to be relieved, happy, released from fear." Here, in the disciples' time of distress, Jesus tied the word to His identity.

Remember, the disciples knew Him personally and He expected them to act on His word by faith. He was saying, "The Father has promised I will come to you in your storm. It is written, 'They shall know in that day that I am He who speaks' [Isaiah 52:6] and brings peace. Now I have come to you in your storm. Look at Me. It is Jesus, here with you in the midst of it all. Cheer up!"

Let us give our Savior the same faith reaction in our distressing times.

A Den of Religious Thieves

At Passover, Jesus went up to Jerusalem and entered the Temple (see John 2:13–17). He was appalled to see that merchants had taken over God's house. He came seeking a house of prayer, but what He found was a preoccupation with the promotion, display and sale of religious merchandise.

Tables had been set up everywhere in God's house. It was all to promote and sell sheep, oxen, doves, incense and other merchandise for religious purposes. The loudest noise in the house was the sound of money changing hands—money that was being made on God and religion.

Meanwhile, the religious leaders were counting their profits. What busyness! Men of God had become hucksters of religious merchandise, running about promoting their goods.

Suddenly, with whip in hand, our Lord stormed through the Temple and began flailing in all directions. He overturned tables piled high with merchandise, scattering the promoters, pitchmen, hawkers and peddlers.

Christ's voice thundered, "Out of My Father's house! You have desecrated this holy place, turning a house of prayer into a commercial market."

It was one of the most painful experiences in all His ministry. Yet Jesus could not stand by and permit His Father's house to become a den for religious thieves.

Are we willing to fellowship with Christ in this aspect of His sufferings today? Do we share His hurt at seeing God's house once again being turned over to merchandisers? Will we be outraged by the horrible commercialism of the Gospel? Will we feel His rage against spiritual hucksterism enough to withdraw from all such activities? Do we feel His hurt enough to renounce ministries that grind out merchandise just for the sake of making money?

Can we share His suffering enough to stand against those who would turn God's house into a theater or entertainment center for promoters? Can we grieve over the profiteering on the name of Jesus? Can we get our eyes off the cash and back on the cross?

When Those He Loves Doubt Him

Jesus loved Lazarus and He also dearly loved his two sisters, Mary and Martha. Their home was an oasis for the Master, and He visited them often. We know Lazarus and his family loved Jesus, but the Scripture is most emphatic in pointing out Christ's love for them: "He whom You love is sick" (John 11:3).

When Jesus heard that, He sent them a message: "This sickness is not unto death, but for the glory of God, that the Son of God may be glorified through it" (verse 4).

Jesus knew that His Father intended for this miracle to give Him glory—and also to give these beloved ones confidence and faith. Yet what an experience of deep suffering it turned out to be for Jesus. The disciples doubted Him, Mary and Martha doubted Him, and so did the weeping friends of Lazarus.

Did Mary know how deeply she hurt Him when she accused Him of being preoccupied and disinterested? "Lord, if You had just been here on time—but it's too late now, the damage is done" (see verse 21).

Did Martha know how it hurt her Master when she questioned His resurrection power? He had plainly told her, "Your brother will rise again"—but His word was not enough. She answered, in essence, "Oh, yes, on resurrection day he will arise but that doesn't help us today" (see verse 24).

How painful it must have been for Christ to have His dearest friends doubt that He had all the power they needed. "Do you not know who I am yet?" is what the Lord seemed to say. "I am the resurrection, and the life. Believe in Me. I have the power, the life" (see verse 25).

It is the doubting of His power that causes such pain and distress to our Lord. What truly satisfies His heart is the child of His who rests completely in His love and tender care.

Tested by Falls and Failings

When I speak of tests and failings, I'm not talking about Christians who fall back into old sins and turn back to the world. Those aren't tested believers—they are believers who face a shipwreck of faith.

Peter warned, "Beware lest you also fall from your own steadfastness, being led away with the error of the wicked" (2 Peter 3:17). Peter is warning believers who are set on following the Lord and are growing in holiness.

Maybe you have fallen in spite of all the progress you have made with the Lord. If I asked you what caused your fall, you might answer, "I was provoked by my own family and I blew up. I can't understand it. I thought I was becoming a little sweeter, a little more like Jesus. But somebody just pushed the wrong button and I lost it." If I asked why, you might try to explain, "I'm only human. How much am I supposed to take?"

It does not matter that you were provoked or even that you were in the right. The provoking simply proved you need deliverance. Scripture says, "Let all bitterness, wrath, anger, clamor [fighting], and evil speaking be put away from you, with all malice [grudges]" (Ephesians 4:31).

God is going to keep testing you until you say, "I have a spirit that has to go." You will see no growth in Christ, no peace at home or on the job, until you can say, "You're right, Lord—take it out!"

If you are being tested in this area, or any other area, you may also be feeling unworthy, thinking, "How much ground have I lost? Does the Lord still love me?"

Dearly beloved, if you have truly repented, you have not lost any ground whatsoever. God puts His loving arms around you and says, "I allowed that to happen so you would see what is in your heart. You are making progress—and that pleases Me."

Nothing but Christ

What is it that our Lord wants most from those who claim to be devoted to Him? Shall we build Him more churches? More Bible schools? More homes and institutions for hurting people?

These are all worthwhile and needed, but He who dwells not in buildings made by hands wants much more than this. Solomon thought he had built an everlasting temple for God, but within years it was in decay. In less than four hundred years, it was completely destroyed.

The one thing our Lord seeks above all else from His people, ministers, and shepherds is *communion at His table*. He seeks oneness around His heavenly table, a place and time of intimacy, a continual coming to Him for food, strength, wisdom and fellowship.

This present generation has a limited revelation of the Lord Jesus because so many are missing from the feast. Few know the grandeur and majesty of the high calling in Christ Jesus to have communion alone with the Lord.

We mistakenly get our spiritual joy out of service rather than communion. We are doing more and more for a Lord we know less and less! We run ourselves ragged, burn out, go anywhere on this earth and give our bodies to His work—but we seldom keep the feast of communing with Him. We are too casual about the Lord's table, not serious enough about taking our place to learn of Him.

Paul speaks of three separate years in the desert of Arabia. They were three glorious years, sitting in the heavenlies at the table of the Lord. It was there that Christ taught Paul all he knew—and the wisdom of God was made manifest in him.

Something in Paul's soul cried out, "Oh, that I might know Him!" Conversion was not enough for Paul. A one-time miraculous hearing of His voice from heaven was not sufficient. He had caught a fleeting vision of the Lord—and he wanted more! May the same be said of us.

Tempting Christ

"Nor let us tempt Christ, as some of them also tempted, and were destroyed by serpents." (1 Corinthians 10:9).

What does Paul mean here when he speaks of "tempting Christ"? Simply put, this means putting Him to a test, such as when we ask, "Just how merciful will God be to me if I move forward into this sin? How long can I indulge my sin before His anger is stirred? How could He possibly judge me when I am His child?"

Multitudes of Christians casually ask the same question today as they toy with temptation. They want to see how close they can get to the edge without facing the consequences of their sin. In short, they are tempting Christ, while casting off conviction from God's Word.

Any time we go against truth that God's Spirit has made clear to us, we are casting off Paul's warning: "Nor let us commit sexual immorality, as some of them did, and in one day twenty-three thousand fell. . . . Let him who thinks he stands take heed lest he fall" (verses 8, 12).

Ask yourself if you are testing the limits of God's precious gift of grace. Perhaps you have convinced yourself, "I am a New Testament believer, covered with His blood—therefore God will not judge me."

By continuing in your sin, you are treating Jesus' great sacrifice for you with utter disregard. You are putting Him to open shame, not just in the world's eyes, but before all of heaven and hell (see Hebrews 6:6).

In 1 Corinthians 10:13 Paul describes a way of escape from all temptation: "God is faithful, who will not allow you to be tempted beyond what you are able, but with the temptation will also make the way of escape, that you may be able to bear it."

He has given us a means of escape—through a growing knowledge and experience of the holy fear of God. Commune with Him and acknowledge His love—and you will never want to tempt Him.

The Blink Generation

Many Christians read the Bible regularly, believing it is God's living, revealed Word for their lives. Over and over in the pages of Scripture, they read that God spoke to His people again and again, with this phrase repeated time after time: "And God said . . ."

Yet many of these same Christians live as though God does not speak to His people today. Indeed, an entire generation of believers has come to make decisions without praying or consulting God's Word. Many simply decide what they want to do, then ask God to validate it.

We are living in a time referred to as the "blink generation." People are making major decisions in the blink of an eye. A bestselling book was written on this concept, entitled *Blink: The Power of Thinking Without Thinking* by Malcolm Gladwell. The theory is, "Trust your instincts. Blink-of-the-eye decisions prove to be the best."

Think about the hurried-up "blink language" we hear every day: "Make a bundle overnight! This is an offer of the century, but you have only a short window of opportunity!" The driving spirit behind it is, "Blink! Blink!"

Such thinking has begun to infect the Church, affecting the decisions made not just by "blink Christians" but by "blink ministers." Scores of bewildered parishioners have written to us telling the same story: "Our pastor came back from a church-growth conference and immediately announced, 'As of today, everything changes.' He decided we would become one of the popular trend churches overnight. He didn't even ask us to pray about it."

Just a few years ago, the watchword among Christians was, "Did you pray about it? Have you sought godly counsel?" How many important decisions have you made "in the blink of an eye" recently? The reason God wants full control of our lives is to save us from disasters—which is exactly where most of our "blink decisions" take us.

Where Are the Timothys?

It was to the Philippian Christians that Paul first introduced the truth, "Let the mind of Christ be in you" (see Philippians 2:5). Paul wrote this message to them while he was imprisoned in Rome.

From his cell Paul declared that he had the mind of Christ, casting aside his reputation to become a servant of Jesus. He wrote, "I trust in the Lord Jesus to send Timothy to you shortly, that I also may be encouraged when I know your state" (verse 19).

This is the outworking of the mind of Christ. Think about it: Here was a pastor sitting in jail, yet he was not thinking of his own hard situation. He was concerned only about the spiritual and physical condition of his people: "My comfort will come only when I know you are doing well, in spirit and body. I am sending Timothy, therefore, to check up on you for me."

Paul then makes an alarming statement: "For I have no one like-minded, who will sincerely care for your state" (verse 20). What a sad statement! As Paul wrote this, the church around him in Rome was growing and being blessed. Clearly, there were godly leaders in the Roman church, but according to Paul, "I have no man who shares with me the mind of Christ." Why was this?

"For all seek their own, not the things which are of Christ Jesus" (verse 21). Evidently, there was no leader in Rome with a servant's heart—no one who had become a living sacrifice. Instead, everyone was set on pursuing his own interests. None had the mind of Christ. Paul could trust no one to go to Philippi to be a true servant to that body of believers.

Our prayer should be: "Lord, I don't want to be focused only on myself in a world that is spinning out of control. Give me Your mind, Your thinking, Your concerns. I want to have Your servant's heart."

MEN OF ANOTHER SORT

When I read about the exploits of godly men in the Old Testament, my heart burns. These servants were so burdened for the cause of God, they did powerful works that baffle the minds of most Christians today.

These saints of old were rocklike in their refusal to go forward without a word from God. They wept and mourned for days at a time over the backslidden condition of His house, refusing to eat, drink or even wash their bodies. They tore out clumps of hair from their scalp and beard. The prophet Ezekiel even lay on his side in the streets of Jerusalem for 390 days, continuously warning of God's coming judgment (see Ezekiel 4).

I wonder, where did these saints get the spiritual authority and stamina to do all they did? They were men of a different sort, servants of a totally different type from those we see in the Church today. I simply cannot relate to them and their walk. I know I am not totally of their kind, and I do not know a single Christian who is.

Something about this troubles me. The Bible says these men's exploits were recorded as lessons for us: "All these things happened to them as examples" (1 Corinthians 10:11). Their stories are meant to show us how to move God's heart, or how to bring a corrupt people to repentance.

Were they supermen, with a predetermined destiny, endowed with supernatural powers unknown to our generation? Not at all. The Bible states emphatically that our godly forefathers were people just like you and me, subject to the same passions of the flesh (see James 5:17).

The fact is, their examples reveal a pattern for us to follow. These men possessed something in their hearts and character that caused God to choose them to accomplish His purposes. He is urging us to seek that same character quality today.

Daniel—A Man of Another Sort

Daniel was also "a man of another sort" who speaks of being broken: "I set my face toward the Lord God to make my request by prayer and supplications, with fasting, and sackcloth, and ashes. And I prayed to the LORD my God, and made confession" (Daniel 9:3–4).

In his brokenness, Daniel was able to discern the times because he knew God's heart: "I, Daniel, understood by the books the number of the years specified by the word of the Lord, given through Jeremiah" (verse 2).

How did Daniel come to this path of brokenness, knowledge and discernment? It began when he allowed the Scriptures to lay hold of him fully. He quoted them often and at length, because he had hidden them away in his heart.

In chapter 10, this godly prophet was given a vision of Christ: "I lifted my eyes . . . and behold, a certain man clothed in linen, whose waist was girded with gold of Uphaz! . . . His face like the appearance of lightning, his eyes like torches of fire . . . and the sound of his words like the voice of a multitude" (10:5–6).

I urge you, do as Daniel did and set your heart today to seek God with all diligence and determination. Go to His Word with ever-increasing love and desire. Pray with fasting for brokenness, to receive His burden. Finally, confess and forsake everything that hinders the Holy Spirit from opening heaven's blessings to you.

Such a walk brings the touch of God. Daniel testified, "Suddenly, a hand touched me, which made me tremble on my knees and on the palms of my hands" (verse 10). The word for *touched* here means "to violently seize upon." Daniel was saying, "When God placed His hand upon me, it put me on my face. His touch gave me an urgency to seek Him with all that is in me."

The path of "men of another sort" is open to everyone. Will you walk in it?

PREPARING THE BRIDE

The Holy Spirit does not perform His work in us in some disjointed, haphazard way. He does not exist to simply help us cope with life, to get us through crises and to see us through lonely nights. He is not there just to pick us up and pump in a little more strength before putting us back into the race.

Everything the Holy Spirit does is related to His reason for coming—to bring us home as a prepared bride. He acts only in keeping with that mission. Yes, He is our Guide, our Comforter, our Strength in time of need. But He uses every act of deliverance, every manifestation of Himself in us, to make us more suitable as a bride.

Neither is the Holy Spirit here to just give gifts to the world. His every gift has a purpose behind it. The Holy Spirit has only one message; everything He teaches leads to one central truth. He may shine in us like a many-splendored jewel, but every ray of truth is meant to bring us to one truth, and it is this:

"You are not your own—you have been bought with a price. You have been chosen to be espoused to Christ—and the Spirit of God has been sent to reveal to you the truth that will set you free from all other loves. Truth will break every bondage to sin and deal with all unbelief. For you are not of this world—you are headed for a glorious meeting with your Espoused, and you are being readied for His marriage supper. All things are now ready—and I come to prepare you! I want to present you spotless, with a passionate love in your heart for Him."

That is the work of the Holy Spirit—to manifest Jesus to the Church, so that we will fall in love with Him.

Never Being Intimidated

If you walk in the Spirit, you will constantly be harassed by demonic powers—but you do not have to be intimidated anytime or anywhere.

Paul was continually harassed by demonic powers: "A false prophet, a Jew whose name was Bar-Jesus . . . withstood them, seeking to turn the proconsul away from the faith" (Acts 13:6–8).

Bar-Jesus means "son of Jesus" or "angel of light." This was the devil standing up against Paul. But the Holy Spirit welled up inside of the apostle: "Then Saul . . . filled with the Holy Spirit . . . said, 'O full of all deceit . . . you son of the devil, you enemy of all righteousness, will you not cease perverting the straight ways of the Lord?' And now, indeed, the hand of the Lord is upon you, and you shall be blind. . . . And immediately a dark mist fell on him. . . . Then the proconsul believed . . . being astonished at the teaching of the Lord" (verses 9–12).

Can you believe it? Paul, "filled with the Holy Spirit," brought down all the powers of darkness!

In Acts 16, Paul was grieved, meaning "disturbed, troubled." God allowed it for many days, but the Holy Spirit welled up in Paul and he cried out, "That's it—enough! In the name of Jesus, be gone" (see 16:16–18).

Beloved, we take too much from the devil. There comes a time when we, too, must stand up in the power of the Holy Spirit and say, "Enough—that's it! I command you in Jesus' name to go!"

When you take authority and command devils to flee, Satan will come back at you saying, "So you think you've won the victory?" He does not seem to know that the more you attack a Spirit-filled servant, the more praise you whip up in him. Throw a saint a crisis and he will sing, shout and worship Jesus.

Are you ready to say, "Enough"?

TAKING SPOILS

While David and his army were away at war, the Amalekites raided his village of Ziklag. These marauders burned down the whole town and took all the women and children captive. When David returned, he "was greatly distressed, for the people spoke of stoning him . . . but David strengthened himself in the LORD his God" (1 Samuel 30:6).

Talk about spiritual warfare—this was not just an attack against David. It was an all-out assault against God's eternal purposes.

The focus of all spiritual warfare has always been the destruction of the seed of Christ—and that has not changed even now, two thousand years after the cross. Satan is still attacking us, the seed of Christ.

David heard the grumbling of his men, but he knew his heart was right with God. Scripture says he encouraged himself in the Lord and was strengthened. Immediately David took off in pursuit and overtook the Amalekites. He rescued every person and possession that had been stolen (see verses 19–20), not just from Ziklag but also everything the Amalekites had plundered from other conquests.

What did David do with all these spoils of war? He used them for the purposes of God. This is another example of God's purpose in our spiritual warfare. We are to take spoils from battle not just for ourselves, but to bless the body of Christ.

Are you getting the picture? Are you beginning to understand the reason for your present battle? Those who put their trust in the Lord are promised glorious victory over all power of the enemy.

The Lord turned David's whole situation around, and He wants you to know, "Yes, you will come through victorious. But I am going to make you more than an overcomer. I am working out an even greater purpose in you for My Kingdom. You will come out of this battle with more spoils than you can handle."

More Precious than Gold

The story of Queen Esther is one of intense warfare. Here is one of the greatest spiritual battles in all of Scripture, with the devil trying to destroy God's purpose on earth. This time he used the evil Haman, a wealthy, influential man. Haman persuaded the king of Persia to declare an edict calling for the death of every Jew under his rule, from India to Ethiopia.

The first Jew in Haman's sights was righteous Mordecai, the uncle of Queen Esther. Haman had a gallows built especially for Mordecai, but Esther intervened. She called God's people to prayer and laid her life on the line to countermand Haman's order. God exposed the wicked scheme, and Haman ended up hanging on his own gallows. The king not only reversed the death order, but he gave Haman's house to Esther, an estate worth millions by today's standards.

Haman's mansion and possessions were not the only spoils taken in this story of victory. Scripture tells us, "The Jews had light and gladness, joy and honor" (Esther 8:16). These were the true spoils gained in battle with the enemy—and the same holds true today.

You see, our trials not only gain us spiritual riches, but keep us strong, pure, under continual maintenance. As we put our trust in the Lord, He causes our trials to produce in us a faith more precious than gold. "That the genuineness of your faith, being much more precious than gold that perishes, though it is tested by fire, may be found to praise, honor, and glory at the revelation of Jesus Christ" (1 Peter 1:7).

Jesus plundered the devil at Calvary, stripping him of all power and authority. When Christ rose victorious from the grave, He led an innumerable host of redeemed captives out of Satan's grasp. That blood-bought procession is still marching on today. Remember, there is value in your battle—and you can be confident that God's spoils will come out of it.

True Spirituality Cannot Be Duplicated

Here on the streets of New York City, you can buy a Rolex watch for fifteen dollars. As every New Yorker knows, these watches are not authentic Rolexes. They are simply "knock-offs"—cheap copies of the original.

There seems to be a duplicate for just about everything today. There is one thing, however, that cannot be duplicated and that is true spirituality. Nothing truly spiritual can be copied. The Lord recognizes the work of His own hands—and He will not accept a man-made duplication of any of His divine workings. Why?

It is impossible for man to duplicate what is truly spiritual. That is the work of the Holy Spirit alone. He is constantly at work doing something new in His people, and there is no possible way for us to reproduce that work.

Very little of the work God's Spirit does in us can be seen. Paul says, "We do not look at the things which are seen, but at the things which are not seen" (2 Corinthians 4:18). In the context of this passage, Paul is speaking of sufferings and afflictions. He is saying, "No one knows all the things we face, except the Holy Spirit. Here is where true spirituality is manifested—in the crucible of suffering."

Those who submit to the leading of God's Spirit—who face their afflictions confident the Lord is producing something in them—emerge from their crucible with strong faith. They testify that the Spirit taught them more during their suffering than when all was well in their lives.

In all my years of walking with the Lord, I have rarely seen an increase in my spirituality during good times. Rather, any such increase usually took place as I endured hard places, agonies, testings—all of which the Holy Spirit allowed. As we endure afflictions, we can know God is producing in us a revelation of His glory that will last forever.

Satan Uses Subtle Devices

"Then the king of Assyria sent . . . Rabshakeh . . . with a great army against Jerusalem, to King Hezekiah" (2 Kings 18:17). The Assyrians represent today's "guides to prosperity." The devil will parade his army around your walls—people who are powerful, beautiful and seemingly successful in all they undertake. When you see them, you will feel walled in like a prisoner.

The first trick of the enemy's emissary is to question a believer's commitment to trust the Lord fully. Rabshakeh, whose name means "drunken envoy," was the king's ambassador. He mocked the godly with a taunt (see verses 19–20): "God is not going to get you out of this mess. You are going down! You are in real trouble, and your faith is not going to work."

Satan then adds another twist by telling you that God is the one behind all your troubles. Assyria's messenger claimed, "The Lord said to me, 'Go up against this land, and destroy it'" (verse 25). Satan will try to convince you that God is mad at you—his slickest lie! He will tell you that all your problems are the result of God's punishment for your past sins. Do not believe it. It is Satan who is out to destroy you.

Our Lord is a deliverer, a fortress. Isaiah said he comes "to console those who mourn in Zion, to give them beauty for ashes, the oil of joy for mourning, the garment of praise for the spirit of heaviness; that they may be called trees of righteousness, the planting of the Lord, that He may be glorified" (Isaiah 61:3).

No, dearly beloved, you are not going down. You are simply under attack, being barraged by the enemy's lies—because you have set your heart truly to trust in the Lord. Satan is trying to destroy your faith in God. Do not fall prey to his subtle devices.

KEEP YOURSELF IN THE LOVE OF GOD

Years ago, God put it on my heart to start a boys' home on Long Island. I truly sensed the Lord was behind this work. Yet after just eighteen months, state officials imposed such stringent regulations on the operation of the home that we had no option but to close it down.

We had taken in four boys during the brief time we were open. Sadly, after we closed down, I lost touch with them. I have always thought that venture was one of the greatest failures of all time. For more than three decades, I wondered why God ever allowed us to move forward with it in the first place.

Recently I received a letter from a man named Clifford. He told the following story:

"Brother David, I was one of the four boys sent to the home on Long Island. Your houseparents were so loving and kind. They taught us the Bible and took us to church.

"One day they took us to a church that was holding a tent revival. I was so bitter and despondent that I resisted going with them. But it was there, under the tent, that the Holy Spirit began tugging at my heart. I heard the preacher say, 'Jesus loves you.'

"All the years of pain, confusion and hopelessness came to the surface. I got on my knees and prayed. That was 35 years ago. Now God has called me to preach, and He is moving me into full-time ministry.

"This 'thank you' has been brewing in me all this time. I just want to thank you for caring. I know what the love of God is."

This man's letter proves to me that nothing we do for Christ is in vain. No matter what Satan tried to tell me, I know that boys' home was not a failure—because one lost, confused Jewish boy discovered the meaning of God's love.

Where You Stand

In Exodus 33, Moses did not know it, but God was about to bring him into a greater revelation of His glory and nature. This revelation would go far beyond friendship, far beyond intimacy. It is a revelation God still wants all His hurting people to know.

The Lord told Moses He was going to show him His glory: "I will make all My goodness pass before you, and I will proclaim the name of the Lord before you" (Exodus 33:19). Then He said, "You cannot see My face; for no man shall see Me, and live. . . . [But] here is a place by Me, and you shall stand on the rock. So it shall be, while My glory passes by, that I will put you in the cleft of the rock, and will cover you with My hand while I pass by" (verses 20–22).

The Hebrew word for *glory* in this passage means "My own self." God was telling Moses, "I Myself will pass by near you."

This is what the apostle Paul means when he says that we are "hid in Christ." When we fail God, we are not to linger in our fallen condition. Instead, we are to run to Jesus quickly, to be hidden in the Rock. Paul writes, "Our fathers . . . all drank the same spiritual drink. For they drank of that spiritual Rock that followed them, and that Rock was Christ" (1 Corinthians 10:1, 4).

The Lord instructed Moses, "Come up to this rock in the morning and I will give you a hope that will keep you. I will show you My heart as you have never seen it before. You will receive a greater revelation of who I am."

Christ is the full expression of His glory. Indeed, all that is in the Father is embodied in the Son. Even when we are hurting, we are hidden in Him—and we are near to His glory.

Knowing God as He Desires to Be Known

Jesus said, "He who has seen Me has seen the Father" (John 14:9). We must see Jesus not as man teaches, but as the Spirit reveals Him to us—that is, as God wants us to know and see Him. We are to get God's vision and testimony of Christ. Then we will know God as He desires to be known.

Here is how I believe God wants us to see His Son: "Every good gift and every perfect gift is from above, and comes down from the Father of lights, with whom there is no variation or shadow of turning. Of His own will He brought us forth" (James 1:17–18).

Jesus was a gift. God wrapped all His resources up in the Son—"For God so loved the world that He gave His only begotten Son, that whoever believes in Him should not perish but have everlasting life" (John 3:16).

Christ is God's good and perfect gift to us, come down from the Father. Do you see Jesus as God's perfect gift to you? Do you see Him as all you need to live joyfully, victoriously, righteously, full of peace and rest?

Ages ago, before you were created, God saw what your hurts and needs would be. He knew ahead of time what you would need to solve all your problems. He did not wrap up His answers and send them to you as a rule book or an army of "answer men." No, He gave us all one solution to all our crises and needs—one Man, one Way, one Answer to everything we need: Jesus Christ.

I Have Already Given You a Word

We are living in a time of the greatest Gospel revelation in history. There are more preachers, more books and more Gospel-media saturation than ever. Yet there has never been more distress and affliction among God's people, and their minds are troubled. Pastors today design their sermons just to pick people up and help them deal with despair.

There is nothing wrong with this. I preach these truths myself. Yet I believe there is still one reason why we see so little victory and deliverance: unbelief. The fact is, God has spoken with great clarity in these last days, telling us, "I have already given you a Word. It is finished and complete. Now, stand on it!"

Let no one tell you we are experiencing a famine of God's Word. The truth is we are experiencing a famine of *hearing* God's Word, and of obeying it. Why? Faith is so unreasonable—it never comes to us by logic or reason. Paul states plainly, "Faith comes by hearing, and hearing by the word of God" (Romans 10:17). This is the only way true faith will ever rise up in any believer's heart. It comes by hearing—that is, believing, trusting and acting on—God's Word.

"The eyes of the Lord are on the righteous, and His ears are open to their cry. . . . The righteous cry out, and the Lord hears, and delivers them out of all their troubles. The Lord is near to those who have a broken heart. . . . Many are the afflictions of the righteous. . . . The Lord redeems the soul of His servants, and none of those who trust in Him shall be condemned" (Psalm 34:15, 17–19, 22).

In just these few passages from Psalms, we are given enough of God's Word to drive out all unbelief. I urge you now to hear it, trust it, obey it. Finally, rest in it.

UNDEFILED IN THE MIDST OF WICKEDNESS

"But Daniel purposed in his heart that he would not defile himself with the portion of the king's delicacies, nor with the wine which he drank: therefore he requested of the chief of the eunuchs that he might not defile himself" (Daniel 1:8).

The word *defile* here suggests "freeing through repudiation." Daniel was saying, "Any compromise of my standards will rob me of my freedom." So he committed to eat only beans and drink only water for ten days.

When the chief of the eunuchs learned this, he told Daniel, "You are going to cost me my life! You will look sickly at the end of ten days. Your cheeks will be sunken, and the king will surely notice. Here, eat just a little meat. You need the protein. Drink the wine to build up your blood. Eat some of these sweets to give you energy!"

I believe Daniel and the three Hebrew men had something more in mind than avoiding being ceremonially unclean. They had been taken captive along with thousands of their countrymen. What they saw when they first arrived in Babylon must have shocked them beyond belief. It was a society so loose, immoral and full of wickedness, these four men's spiritual sensibilities were assailed.

They made a commitment with each other: "We dare not compromise. We will be separate from society and disciplined in our walk of faith." They did not go about preaching their way of life to others. It was strictly a matter between them and God.

When you are in a crisis, do you cry out in unbelief and frustration? What if the Lord should answer, "I need strong voices in these sinful times through whom I can speak. Where are you when I need a voice? You say you want Me to come to your crisis—yet you remain a part of the wicked, worldly system. Tell Me—are you committed to My purposes?"

Daniel and his friends' witness was a testimony that turned all the people's heads around. They were delivered from the lions' den and the fiery furnace—and the whole society knew it was God who did it.

Going through a Dry Spell

Even though I preach to thousands, there are times I feel dry, far away from the warm presence of God. When I am dry and empty, I have no great yearning to read the Word and little compulsion to pray. I know my faith is intact and my love for Jesus is strong, and I have no desire to taste the things of this world. Still, I cannot seem to touch God for days, even weeks.

Have you ever watched other Christians get blessed while you feel nothing? They testify of God's answers to their prayers and shed tears of joy. They seem to live on a mountaintop of happy experiences while you just plod along, loving Jesus but not setting the world on fire.

Jesus felt His own isolation when He cried aloud, "Father, why have You forsaken me?"

The truth is, without the nearness of God there can be no peace. Deep down we know our dryness can be stopped only with the dew of His glory. Our despair can be dispelled only by the assurance that God is answering.

There are times I feel unworthy, like the worst kind of sinner—yet in spite of it all, I know He is not far off. Somehow I hear a distinct, small voice calling, "Come, My child. I am aware of all you are experiencing. I still love you and I will never leave you nor forsake you because I am still your Father and you are My child."

"For the LORD's portion is His people" (Deuteronomy 32:9).

"Behold, I will do a new thing, now it shall spring forth . . . I will even make a road in the wilderness and rivers in the desert. The beast of the field will honor Me . . . because I give waters in the wilderness and rivers in the desert, to give drink to My people, My chosen" (Isaiah 43:19–20).

Hang on. He will meet you in your wilderness with His living waters.

Don't Be Afraid of a Little Suffering

Christ's resurrection was preceded by a short period of suffering among His followers. The simple truth is there is pain and sorrow in everyone's life.

We do not want to suffer or be hurt—we want painless deliverance, supernatural intervention. "Intervene and deliver me, God," we pray, "because I am weak and always will be. I will go my way in the meantime, waiting for Your supernatural deliverance."

We may blame our troubles on demons. We may seek out a man of God hoping he can cast out the spirit so that we can go on our way with no pain or suffering. We want someone to lay hands on us and drive away all the dryness. "There, all done!" we tell ourselves afterward. "Now I can breeze right through to a peaceful life of victory."

But victory is not always without suffering and pain. We have to look at our sin, face it and suffer it through. You see, we are to enter into Christ's suffering, for even He was not immune. Suffering endures for a night, but joy always follows in the morning.

God's love demands a choice. If God supernaturally lifted us out of every battle without pain or suffering, it would abort all trials and all temptation. There would be no testing and purifying as by fire. Instead, it would just be a matter of God superimposing His will on us. His way is to meet us in our dryness—to show us how it can become a way into a new life of faith.

It is often the will of God that we suffer dryness and even pain. "Therefore let those who suffer according to the will of God commit their souls to Him in doing good, as to a faithful Creator" (1 Peter 4:19).

Thank God our suffering is always followed by final victory. "But may the God of all grace, who called us to His eternal glory by Christ Jesus, after you have suffered a while, perfect, establish, strengthen, and settle you" (5:10).

The Danger of Unbelief

God has embedded in me a dread of unbelief. This dread comes from searching the Scriptures for examples of the dire consequences of doubting and lack of faith.

I thank God with all my heart for revealing to me the harm and ruin caused by unbelief. We believers have taken this matter too lightly, supposing God overlooks the doubting of those facing great affliction and hard times.

I once thought the Lord ought to give some slack to those facing seemingly hopeless situations. I thought, for example, of the disciples as their ship began sinking in a raging storm. My thinking was, "Lord, they were just human. They were overwhelmed by it all. It was just a human response." Yet Jesus reprimanded their little faith.

Yes, there is a time to weep—when Jesus whispers lovingly, "Go ahead, cry. I bottle every tear." There are times when we are overwhelmed and we cry, "Where are You in this, Lord?" There are eclipses of faith when fears overwhelm us.

Yet we dare not linger on these fears and passing doubts. Instead, we must rise up and "trust in the shadow of His wings." God has no pity for unbelief, and the whole of Scripture bears this out. It may sound harsh, but He will not accept any excuses. He grants no other option but faith.

Unbelief is mostly caused by neglect of God's Word. Faith is impossible without a constant input of Scripture and a clinging to the promises. God has told me, "Stop looking at circumstances. Feed daily on My Word. Memorize My promises. Pray with confidence. Your weeping will endure for a night, but joy will come in the morning."

Whatever you are going through—even walking through the valley and shadow of death—God promises to be with you. Today, take a stand and start trusting. Your unbelief changes nothing—but faith opens the door to deliverance. Choose to trust God.

GET INTO THE ARK

John Owen, the great Puritan preacher, spoke the following message to his congregation on April 9, 1680:

"You know that for many years, without failing, I have been warning you continually of an approaching calamitous time, and considering the sins that have been the causes of it. . . . I have told you that judgment will begin in the house of God; that God seems to have hardened our hearts from His fear . . . and that none knows what the power of His wrath will be. In all these things I have foretold you of perilous, distressing, calamitous times. . . . These all now lie at the door, and are entering in upon us."

God did send His awful judgments on that society. John Owen lived to weep over a flaming holocaust that engulfed London.

Before he saw a single one of these calamities take place, however, Owen faithfully cried out from his pulpit: "I am going to show you how we ought to comport ourselves in and under the distressing calamities that are coming upon us."

Beloved, we are living in just such a time as Owen's. In times like these, there is only one response to the coming storm: "The just shall live by faith."

Owen admonished his people with tears, "Prepare an ark for the safety of you and your families." He then added, "The ark is Jesus Christ. There is no other way."

We may see dangers on all sides, but we have a fiery guard of angels surrounding us and a God who will carry us through any disaster we may face.

Do you want to face the coming storm with quiet confidence and peace of mind? Then die today to all your own ways and commit the keeping of your life wholly to God's care. He is your good, loving Shepherd—and He is faithful to see you through.

PART 9

God Has Everything Under Control

He Delights in Planning Our Future

LOOKING UNTO JESUS

Looking unto Jesus, the author and finisher of our faith" (Hebrews 12:2).

If you should ask me what is happening in the world right now, I would answer, "Everything Jesus warned us would happen in the last days! He warned of men's hearts failing them with fear from beholding the things happening on earth. He warned of earthquakes in various places, nations rising against nations, ethnic group against ethnic group, riots and unrest."

We have lived to see the beginning of all the end-time prophecies being fulfilled before our very eyes. Consider Luke 21:11, "great earthquakes in various places."

What did Jesus tell us to do when we see all these things coming to pass? He said, "Look up and lift up your heads [eyes], because your redemption draws near" (verse 28).

Tensions with Israel are once again on the rise in the Middle East. We are beholding the fulfillment of prophecies we have preached about for many years, with events approaching Armageddon.

Yes, we tremble when we first see and hear such dire news—but this is the time to look unto Jesus. He brought us this far—He is the author of our faith—and He will bring us to the finish line with hope and peace, no matter what happens.

Those who know the Scriptures have a Holy Spirit inner sense of the Lord's return, compelling us to cry, "Even so, Lord Jesus, come." Jesus said: "Watch therefore, for you do not know what hour your Lord is coming" (Matthew 24:42). "Be ready, for the Son of Man is coming at an hour you do not expect " (verse 44). "Blessed is that servant whom his master, when he comes, will find so doing" (verse 46).

Dearly beloved, if you love Jesus you should not be surprised or fearful. God has everything under control. Look up—our redemption is drawing near!

FEAR THAT LEADS TO LIFE

The prophets warn us that when we see God shaking the nations and perilous times come, our natural man will fear. Ezekiel asked, "Can your heart endure, or can your hands remain strong, in the days when I shall deal with you?" (Ezekiel 22:14).

When God warned Noah of His coming judgments and told him to build an ark, Noah was "moved with godly fear" (Hebrews 11:7). Even bold, courageous David said, "My flesh trembles for fear of You, and I am afraid of Your judgments" (Psalm 119:120). When the prophet Habakkuk saw disastrous days ahead, he cried out, "When I heard, my body trembled; my lips quivered at the voice; rottenness entered my bones; and I trembled in myself, that I might rest in the day of trouble" (Habakkuk 3:16).

As you read these passages, note that the fear coming upon these godly men was not a fleshly fear, but a reverential awe of the Lord. They were not afraid of the enemy of their souls—but they did fear God's righteous judgments. You see, they understood the awesome power behind the approaching calamities. They did not fear the outcome of the storm, but rather God's holiness. Likewise today, any fear we experience must come from a holy reverence for the Lord, and never from a fleshly anxiety about our fate.

God despises all sinful fear in us—the fear of losing material things and wealth, a change in our standard of living. All over the world, people are filled with this kind of fear as they see economies deteriorating. They are afraid of losing everything they have labored for.

If you are a child of God, your heavenly Father will not endure such unbelief in you. It is because He has a higher purpose for you: "The Lord of hosts, Him you shall hallow [honor]; let Him be your fear, and let Him be your dread [awe]" (Isaiah 8:13).

Let God be your fear and awe. That kind of fear leads not to death, but to life!

OUR FOCUS

As Christians in Paul's day sensed the destruction of Jerusalem drawing near, they wanted to know more about prophetic events. They were fearful over rumors about the ruthlessness of invading armies and perilous times that were close at hand. So they asked Paul to tell them more about what was to come: "Write to us about how to read the times."

Paul responded with these words of assurance: "But concerning the times and the seasons, brethren, you have no need that I should write to you. For you yourselves know perfectly that the day of the Lord so comes as a thief in the night" (1 Thessalonians 5:1–2).

Paul described to them what would take place when Christ returned: "The Lord Himself will descend from heaven with a shout, with the voice of an archangel, and with the trumpet of God. And the dead in Christ will rise first. Then we who are alive and remain shall be caught up together with them in the clouds to meet the Lord in the air" (4:16–17).

Paul's exhortation was meant to be encouraging. In short: "There is no need for you to fret about those things coming on the earth. You know this is signaling the coming of Jesus to take away His people."

We can be sure that the swift current of unfolding events today is carrying us toward God's eternal purpose. The world is not adrift. God has simply picked up the pace toward the "one divine event" ahead: the re-creation of a new heaven and earth, where Christ will reign supreme for all eternity.

As followers of Christ, our focus is not to be on daily news reports. We are not to dwell on wars, calamities, the possibility of a nuclear accident, nor other things that are coming on the earth. When Jesus said, "[In that day] look up" (see Luke 21:28), He was talking about where our focus should be.

SOMETHING NEW AND GLORIOUS

But I acted for My name's sake, that it should not be profaned before the Gentiles [heathen]" (Ezekiel 20:14).

God is about to do something new and glorious. This will be beyond an awakening. It will be a work He alone initiates when He can no longer endure the polluting of His holy name. There comes a time when God determines that His Word has been so trampled into the mire, that abominations have so defiled what is called "the Church," He must rise up and defend His name before a lost world.

"For His own name's sake" God is going to do two mighty works. First, He is going to purge the nations and His Church with awesome redemptive judgments. He is going to stop the invasion of His house by charlatans and the flesh—and He is going to purify and cleanse the ministry and raise up shepherds after His own heart.

Second, God is going to glorify His holy name with a great intervention of mercy. In the throes of judgments being fulfilled, God is going to save the day by a supernatural "turning" of a remnant back to Himself. What He did for Israel when they were being judged, He will do again in the days ahead.

You can read it all in Ezekiel 36:21–38. Summed up, this is what is prophesied: "I will have pity for My holy name which has been profaned among the heathen. I will do it not for your sakes but for My own name's sake. The heathen shall know that I am God. I will sprinkle clean water upon you, and you shall be clean of all filthiness. I will give you a new heart and a new spirit. I will cause you to walk in my ways. I will save you from all your uncleanness. Not for your sakes will I do all of this, but for my own name's sake."

"Then you shall know that I am the LORD " (Ezekiel 20:44).

One Minute Before Midnight

In 1 Samuel 13, we see Saul facing a crucial moment that every believer must eventually confront. It is a time of crisis, when we are forced to decide whether we will wait on God by faith, or get impatient and take matters into our own hands.

Saul's pivotal moment came when ominous clouds of war were gathering over Israel. The Philistines had amassed a huge army of horsemen, iron chariots and legions of soldiers brandishing the latest weapons. By contrast, the Israelites had only two swords in their entire army—one for Saul and one for his son Jonathan. Everyone else had to use makeshift weapons such as wooden spears or crude farm tools.

A week earlier, the prophet Samuel—God's spokesman to Israel—had warned Saul to wait for him at Gilgal before going into battle. Samuel had said he would arrive after seven days to make the proper sacrifices to the Lord.

When the seventh day came and Samuel had not arrived, Saul's soldiers began to scatter. Worse, the king did not have God's direction for battle.

Did Saul stand firm and declare that he was going to stand on God's Word and wait for Samuel, even if Samuel arrived on day eight? No—Saul panicked. He allowed himself to be overwhelmed by his circumstances and ended up manipulating his way around God's Word.

Beloved, God is never too late! All along, the Lord knew each step Samuel was taking and that he would be there by day seven, even if it was one minute before midnight.

God has not changed throughout the ages. He is still concerned about whether His people obey this command: "Obey the voice of the Lord, and [do not] rebel against the commandment of the Lord" (1 Samuel 12:15, paraphrased).

It does not matter if things look hopeless. We are to walk in total confidence in the Lord—waiting patiently on Him to deliver us, as His Word promises.

To Die Is Gain

Paul said, "To die is gain" (Philippians 1:21). That kind of talk is absolutely foreign to our modern spiritual vocabularies. We have very little desire to depart to be with the Lord.

Paul said, "I am hard pressed between the two, having a desire to depart and be with Christ, which is far better" (verse 23). Yet, for the sake of edifying the converts, Paul thought it best to "remain in the flesh."

Did Paul show a lack of respect for the life God had given him? Absolutely not! To him, life was a gift, and he had used it to fight a good fight. He could say, "It is better to die and be with the Lord than to stay in the flesh."

Those who die in the Lord are the winners; we who remain are the losers. Death is not the ultimate healing—resurrection is! Death is the passage, and sometimes that passage can be painful—but it is not even worth comparing to the unspeakable glory that awaits those who endure the passage.

Any message about death bothers us. We try to ignore even thinking about it. Occasionally, we discuss what heaven must be like, but most of the time the subject of death is taboo.

How different the first Christians were! Paul spoke much about death. In fact, our resurrection is referred to in the New Testament as our "blessed hope."

Nowadays, however, the world has trapped us with materialism: "I don't want to leave my beautiful home, my cars, my gorgeous jewelry." We are bombarded with messages on how to use our faith to acquire more things, even though our lives are already cluttered with possessions.

Christ calls us to come and die—without building memorials to ourselves or worrying about our legacy. Jesus left no autobiography, no headquarters complex, no university or Bible college. He left nothing to perpetuate His memory but the bread and the wine.

Our "gain" is Christ Himself. May we forsake all to cling to Him continually!

The Day of Christ Is at Hand

Paul wrote, "Now, brethren, concerning the coming of our Lord Jesus Christ and our gathering together to Him, we ask you, not to be soon shaken in mind or troubled, either by spirit or by word or by letter, as if from us, as though the day of Christ had come" (2 Thessalonians 2:1–2).

Scoffers point out, "See, someone in the early Church shook up believers with the message that Christ was about to come. But Paul told them, 'Don't worry about it.'"

That is not what the original Greek reveals. The root word is "[be not shaken] . . . that the day of the Lord *has* come." What disturbed the Thessalonians was the thought that Christ had already come, and they had missed it.

Paul reassures them in the next verse: "Let no one deceive you by any means; for that Day will not come unless the falling away comes first, and the man of sin is revealed, the son of perdition" (verse 3). Paul was only addressing their fears when he said, "Do not be worried. Two things have to happen first."

Skeptics may say, "Christ cannot return for a while. First, a great apostasy has to take place. Second, the Antichrist has to rise up and proclaim himself God."

You have to be willfully blind not to see a raging apostasy gripping the whole world. Unbelief is sweeping through nations, with believers falling away from faith on all sides. The apostasy Paul refers to has arrived.

Some may say, "Paul clearly says Jesus cannot come until the Antichrist is in power." According to John, anyone who denies the Father and the Son is antichrist (see 1 John 2:22). Moreover, he says, the increase of such antichrists is proof we are living in the last days.

In short, nothing is holding back Christ's return! "The Lord is at hand" (Philippians 4:5).

GOD IS ABLE TO SEE YOU THROUGH

The most important question facing God's people in these last days is this: "Do you believe God is able to see you through? Do you believe He can do all that is necessary to answer your prayers and meet your needs?"

This is the same question our Lord asked the two blind men who begged Him for mercy and healing. "And Jesus said to them, 'Do you believe I am able to do this?' They said to Him, 'Yes, Lord'" (Matthew 9:28). Jesus then touched their eyes and immediately they were opened (see verses 29–30).

The Lord asks all of us, "Do you believe I am able to guide you and perform My perfect will in your life? Or do you harbor secret thoughts that I have forsaken you and let you down?" He says to us the same thing He said to Mary and Martha, "Did I not say to you that if you would believe you would see the glory of God?" (John 11:40).

God is not primarily interested in our doing some great work for Him. Rather, He desperately wants us simply to trust Him. God does not want anything you possess—He wants your trust! He wants you to be firmly established in your confidence in Him.

An American soldier in Germany wrote offering me his coin collection, which he called an idol. I wrote back, "God wants more than your coin collection—He wants your trust!"

We want to do things—to give up things, to sacrifice, work, suffer. All the while, what God desires most is our obedience and trust. He will be pleased with nothing short of our faith.

"But without faith it is impossible to please Him, for he that comes to God must believe that He is, and that He is a rewarder of those who diligently seek Him" (Hebrews 11:6).

While the Foundations Are Shaking

The foundations of the world are shaking and Satan roars like an enraged lion. Yet those who trust in the Lord and place their confidence in Him will see His salvation. They will have hearts and minds at peace. Amid confusion, violence and uncertainty, God's children can enjoy rest and sleep sweetly, unafraid of conditions around them.

Here are some glorious promises of God for all who trust in Him in these perilous times.

- "As for God, His way is perfect; the word of the Lord is proven; He is a shield to all who trust in Him" (2 Samuel 22:31).
- "Oh, how great is Your goodness, which You have laid up for those who fear You, which You have prepared for those who trust in You in the presence of the sons of men!" (Psalm 31:19).
- "You shall hide them in the secret of Your presence from the plots of man; You shall keep them secretly in a pavilion from the strife of tongues" (verse 20).
- "Be of good courage, and He shall strengthen your heart, all you who hope in the Lord" (Psalm verse 24).
- "Commit your way to the Lord, trust also in Him, and He shall bring it to pass" (37:5).
- "In God I have put my trust; I will not fear. What can flesh do to me?" (56:4).
- "Trust in Him at all times, you people; pour out your heart before Him; God is a refuge for us" (62:8).
- "Whoever trusts in the Lord shall be safe" (Proverbs 29:25).
- "Those who trust in the Lord are like Mount Zion, which cannot be moved, but abides forever" (Psalm 125:1).

God's Word is still all powerful, and the devil still trembles when we stand firm with this Sword in hand. The only safeguard against Satan's deceit and evil devices is to face him boldly with the promises of God.

Today—now—take your stand.

The Noise of a Great Army

The Syrian army besieged the city of Samaria during a famine. The Syrians were not in a hurry—they simply camped outside the city, waiting for the Samaritans to starve.

Conditions got so bad within the city walls, a donkey's head sold for eighty pieces of silver. Things grew so desperate that women offered their children to be boiled for food. Things descended into utter chaos, sheer insanity (see 2 Kings 6).

Four lepers who were starving outside the city walls finally said to themselves, "Why are we sitting here until we die? . . . Now, therefore, come, let us surrender to the army of the Syrians. If they keep us alive, we shall live; and if they kill us, we shall only die" (7:3–4). So they set out for the Syrian camp.

When they arrived, everything was deathly still. Not a soul was in sight. They searched every tent looking for someone, but everybody was gone. Scripture explains:

"For the Lord had caused the army of the Syrians to hear the noise of chariots and the noise of horses—the noise of a great army; so they said one to another, 'Look, the king of Israel has hired against us the kings of the Hittites and the kings of the Egyptians to attack us!' Therefore they arose and fled at twilight, and left the camp intact—their tents, their horses, and their donkeys—and they fled for their lives" (verses 6–7).

When the lepers realized this, they went throughout the camp eating and drinking their fill. Then they went back to the city and called out, "Come with us! You absolutely will not believe it, but the Syrians have fled their camp" (see verse 10).

The Lord had taken a desperate, seemingly hopeless situation and turned it completely around by His power. He took the spoils of warfare and used them to restore and refresh His people, maintaining His cause on earth.

Just when it looks like it is all over, God comes through for His children. He will for you. God is faithful!

Rev. David Wilkerson was perhaps best known for his early days of ministry to young drug addicts and gang members in New York City. His story is told in *The Cross and the Switchblade*, a book he coauthored in 1962 that has been read by over fifteen million people in some thirty languages. The story was made into a Hollywood motion picture in 1970.

Rev. Wilkerson served as pastor in small churches in Pennsylvania until 1958, when he saw a photograph in *Life* magazine of several New York City teenagers charged with murder. Moved with compassion, he was drawn to the city and began a street ministry to what one writer called "desperate, bewildered, addicted, often violent youth." A year later, Rev. Wilkerson founded Teen Challenge in Brooklyn, a ministry which today reaches youth and adults with life-controlling problems through more than 1,000 centers in 82 countries.

Working under his global ministry, World Challenge, Inc., Rev. Wilkerson conducted evangelistic crusades and pastors' conferences, produced films, authored over thirty books and instituted feeding programs—which continue to this day—in some of the world's poorest areas.

In 1987, he founded Times Square Church in New York City. Today, the mission-focused congregation includes almost eight thousand people representing over one hundred nationalities.

On April 27, 2011, Rev. Wilkerson posted on his daily devotional blog, "To those going through the valley and shadow of death, hear this word: Weeping will last through some dark, awful nights, and in that darkness you will soon hear the Father whisper, 'I am with you. I cannot tell you why right now, but one day it will make sense. You will see it was all part of my plan. It was no accident.'" That afternoon, Rev. Wilkerson was killed in a car accident. His wife, Gwen, resides in Texas and is surrounded by their four children and their spouses, ten grandchildren and two great-grandchildren.

To learn more about David Wilkerson's ongoing ministry, go to http://www.worldchallenge.org.

To read more of David Wilkerson's daily devotions, you may go to http://davidwilkersontoday.blogspot.com/.

More From

David Wilkerson!

With over 15 million copies sold, this is the riveting true story of how God used David Wilkerson, a simple country pastor, to reach one of the most notorious gangs in New York. You won't want to miss this amazing story of how God used an unlikely man to found Teen Challenge and leave a legacy of His faithfulness that has touched millions of lives the world over.

The Cross and the Switchblade

Here is a stirring, passionate call to a deep walk of daily discipleship. Wilkerson reminds us that Jesus wants to give the abundant life we long for. But first we must seek to know God's heart and cry out against the sins that break it. This is a book of hope and inspiration for those who hunger to know Christ as they never have.

Hungry for More of Jesus

What happens when grief and depression seem so overwhelming that we feel like giving up? In this hopeful and encouraging book, Wilkerson examines the universal problem of discouragement. He shows you how to let God heal your wounds, restore your faith, and give you genuine, lasting peace.

Have You Felt Like Giving Up Lately?

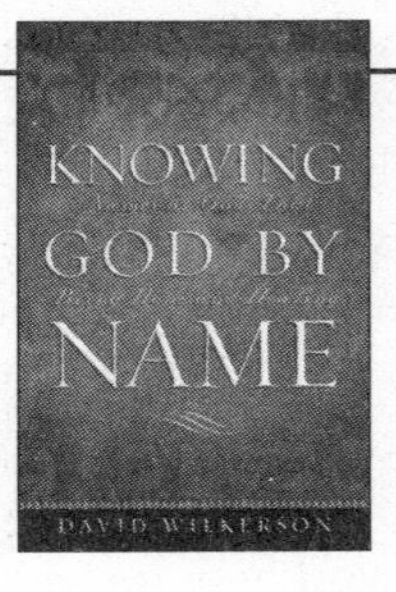

The Lord has pledged to keep you, teach you, put His fear in you, cause you to walk in His ways, give you His Holy Spirit and blot out all your sins and replace them with His lovingkindness. All of this awaits you from the One who longs for you to know Him by name. Weaving biblical teaching and personal anecdotes, Wilkerson will help you get to know your heavenly Father on a heart-to-heart level.

Knowing God by Name